The Need for
a Sacred Science

SUNY Series in Religious Studies
Harold Coward, editor

The Need for
a Sacred Science

Seyyed Hossein Nasr

State University of New York Press

Published by
State University of New York Press, Albany

© 1993 State University of New York

For information, address the State University of New York Press,
90 State Street, Suite 700, Albany, NY 12207

Production by Christine M. Lynch
Marketing by Lynne Lekakis

Library of Congress Cataloging-in-Publication Data

Nasr, Seyyed Hossein.
    The Need for a Sacred Science / Seyyed Hossein Nasr.
       p.   cm. — (SUNY series in religious studies)
    Includes bibliographical references.
    ISBN 0-7914-1517-1 (cloth : acid-free). — ISBN 0-7914-1518-X
    (pbk. : acid-free)
    1. Holy, The.   2. Religion-Philosophy.   3. Religion and
    science—1946-   I. Title. II. Series.
BL50.N29 1993
200' .15—dc20   92-26202
                                                          CIP

10 9 8 7 6 5 4 3 2

Contents

Introduction   1

Part One — The World of the Spirit — A Metaphysical Context for the Cultivation of Sacred Science

1. God is Reality   7

2. Self-awareness and Ultimate Selfhood   15

3. Time — The Moving Image of Eternity   25

Part Two — The Unity of the Divine Stratosphere — The Diversity of the Human Atmosphere

4. One is the Spirit and Many its Human Reflections — Thoughts on the Human Condition Today   45

5. The *Philosophia Perennis* and the Study of Religion   53

Part Three — Science: Traditional and Modern

6. Western Science and Asian Cultures   71

7. The Traditional Sciences   95

8. The Spiritual Significance of Nature   119

Part Four — Tradition, Sacred Science and the Modern Predicament

9. Sacred Science and the Environmental Crisis — An Islamic Perspective   129

10. The Concept of Human Progress through Material Evolution: A Traditional Critique   149

11. Reflections on the Theological Modernism of Hans Küng   159

Postscript — *The Need for a Sacred Science*   173

Index   177

Bismi'Llāh al-Raḥmān al-Raḥīm

Introduction

Our Lord! Thou Embracest all things in mercy and knowledge!
(Quran XL.7)

The very term 'sacred science' may appear contradictory to those for whom 'science' is identified with that particular mode of knowledge which has come to monopolize almost completely the term science since the seventeenth century in the West. Science, thus understood, has by definition nothing to do with the sacred, a term which is meaningless in its worldview, while what is called sacred, to the extent that this category still possesses meaning in the contemporary world, seems to have little to do with science. Even if the term sacred science is used from time to time, it is in relation to ancient civilizations and bygone days. It appears, therefore, even more strange that one should speak of the need for a sacred science in a world where not everyone understands what is meant by sacred science and fewer still are aware of its absence and therefore have a conscious sense of need for such a science. And yet there does in reality exist a profound need for a sacred science in a world which, having lost such a science, is groping in the dark for many false substitutes and also suffers grievously from the lack of such a science even if it remains unaware of the causes for this suffering.

We have had occasion to deal extensively with the relation between knowledge and the sacred in several of our other writings[1] and do not wish to repeat here the metaphysical principles which relate knowing and being as well as knowing and the sacred which is the direct manifestation of Being in becoming, of the Eternal in the temporal. What we wish to do here is to discuss what we mean by sacred science before delving into the various aspects and branches of sacred science in itself and in its relation to modern thought.

There is first of all the Supreme Science or metaphysics, as understood traditionally, which deals with the Divine Principle and Its manifestations in the light of that Principle. It is what one might call *scientia sacra* in the highest meaning of the term. It is the science which lies at the very center of man's being as well as at the heart of all orthodox and authentic religions and which is attainable by the intellect, that supernaturally natural faculty with which

1

normal human beings of an intellectual bent, whose inner faculties have not become atrophied by the deformations caused by the modern world, are endowed.[2] This principial knowledge is by nature rooted in the sacred, for it issues from that Reality which constitutes the Sacred as such. It is a knowledge which is also being, a unitive knowledge which transcends ultimately the dichotomy between the object and the subject in that Unity which is the source of all that is sacred and to which the experience of the sacred leads those who are able to reach the abode of that Unity. The term sacred science is of course nothing other than the English translation of the Latin *scientia sacra*; yet it is used in this and certain other works not as metaphysical knowledge itself but as the application of metaphysical principles to the macrocosm as well as the microcosm, to the natural as well as the human worlds. Sacred science is science as the term is used today to the extent that it too deals with various domains of nature in addition to the psyche of man, his art and thought and human society. But it differs drastically from science as currently understood in that it has its roots and principles in metaphysics or *scientia sacra* and never leaves the world of the sacred in contrast to modern science whose very premises, immersed in empiricism and rationalism, have their nexus severed from any knowledge of a higher order, despite the fact that the findings of modern science, to the extent that they correspond to an aspect of reality, cannot but possess a meaning beyond the phenomenal. But those meanings cannot themselves be understood and interpreted save in the light of metaphysical principles and the sacred sciences, including the science of symbolism, which derive from the Supreme Science.

For all intents and purposes the sacred sciences are none other than the traditional sciences cultivated in traditional civilizations,[3] if these sciences are understood in the light of their cosmological and metaphysical significance and not as either crude and elementary background for the rise of the modern quantitative sciences or as superstitious old wives' tales to be relegated to the domain of historical relics or occultism. Today, precisely because of the thirst for other modes of knowledge and in the light of the fact that only one science of nature is officially recognized in the mainstream of Western modern thought, many of the traditional sciences are avidly cultivated in a truncated and often mutilated fashion which makes them veritable superstitions. And yet the very proliferation of the remnants of the traditional or sacred sciences, ranging from various schools of medicine to geomancy, usually without regard for their cosmological principles and the sacred worldview to which they belong and within which they alone possess meaning, is itself proof of the present need for a veritable sacred science.

The essays which follow seek to present certain aspects of sacred science, or one might say some but not all of the different sacred sciences in the context of not one but many spiritual and intellectual traditions and with references to civilizations as far apart as the Chinese and the Western. In part one we return to first principles to begin with two essays concerned with the nature of God and the Spirit, essays which technically belong to *scientia sacra* as defined above. These essays are followed by a study on Eternity and time, a subject which again belongs to the domain of metaphysics but also concerns any science dealing with the domain of contingency and change.

These studies are followed in part two by two essays which consider the basic question of the multiplicity of sacred forms and religious universes. This consideration is necessary both because the traditional religious boundaries have lost their old meaning to a considerable degree and have gained another significance today as a result of the advent of modernism, and also because one of the important branches of the sacred sciences in the contemporary context is precisely the science of forms and symbols as understood in a global and multireligious context. Comparative religious studies can succeed in avoiding the pitfalls of relativism and secularism and the danger of destroying the sacred through the very process of studying it only if comparative religion is itself practiced as a sacred science, rooted in metaphysical principles and aware of that Divine Empyrean where alone the revealed forms and symbols of various religions can be seen in a harmony which cannot be observed and experienced in the purely human atmosphere.

Part three turns to the discussion of traditional or sacred sciences especially as these sciences have been cultivated and preserved in non-Western civilizations, which have naturally not suffered as greatly from the effects of secularism and a purely secular science as has the West, where modernism was first born and where it had its period of incubation and growth before spreading to other continents. Here the tension between Western science and Asian cultures where the sacred sciences are still alive to some extent is brought out, as is the spiritual message of nature which the traditional cosmological sciences bear and in fact convey to those able to understand their full import.

Finally, three chapters are devoted to the confrontation between the traditional worldview and the modern predicament, the first dealing with the very timely and crucial issue of the environmental crisis, which is viewed here from the point of view of the sacred study of nature within the more specific context of the Islamic tradition. This discussion is followed by a traditional critique of the idea of progress through material evolution so avidly supported by most of the exponents of modern science if not proven by the findings of modern science itself. This part concludes with an essay on theological modernism, which represents the penetration of secular science into the very realm of the sacred, into the domain of theology, which was considered the "queen of the sciences" in traditional Christian civilization. Our study concludes with a return to the theme of sacred science itself and the need for its cultivation and understanding in the contemporary context.

Our goal in this book has not been to simply criticize modern science, which is legitimate if kept within the boundaries defined by the limitations of its own philosophical premises concerning the nature of physical reality as well as its epistemologies and methodologies. Our aim has been to present at least some elementary notions concerning the sacred sciences and the meaning of such sciences in the contemporary world. But this endeavor itself requires opening a space for such a science in the present-day intellectual climate and hence criticizing the totalitarian claims of modern science or at least that scientism and positivism which claim a monopoly upon knowledge.

Many of the essays presented in this volume were printed earlier in various times and climes, some in the West and others in the East. In most cases they have been thoroughly revised and in many cases rewritten, while certain of the essays appear in print for the first time here. We hope that their presentation in this volume and as an organic whole will make them more readily accessible and that the work will be a humble contribution to a better understanding of the traditional and sacred sciences so much needed by the modern world, lost in the maze caused by its forgetfulness of the traditional and perennial wisdom of which these very sciences are applications and depositories. But ultimately God knows best. *wa'Llāh*^{u} *a'lam.*

> Seyyed Hossein Nasr
> Bethesda, Maryland
> June 1991

Notes

1. See especially our *Knowledge and the Sacred* (Albany, N.Y., 1989).

2. All human beings, by virtue of being human, possess the intellectual faculty but in most cases this faculty is in a virtual state and most often eclipsed by veils of passion which present it from functioning wholly and fully.

3. Throughout this work we use the term tradition and traditional as referring to principles of Divine Origin along with their transmission and applications within a particular world, which for that very reason is called traditional. See our *Knowledge and the Sacred*, chapter two, "What is Tradition?", pp. 65ff.

PART ONE

The World of the Spirit — A Metaphysical Context for the Cultivation of Sacred Science

CHAPTER ONE

God Is Reality

The sensualist and empirical epistemology, which has dominated the horizon of Western man in the modern period, has succeeded in reducing reality to the world experienced by the external senses, hence limiting the meaning of reality and removing the concept of 'reality' as a category pertaining to God. The consequence of this change in the very meaning of reality has been nothing less than catastrophic, reducing God and in fact all spiritual realms of being to the category of the abstract and finally to the unreal. At the base of the loss of the sense of the reality of God by modern man in his daily life lies the philosophical error of reducing the meaning of reality to the externally experienced world, of altering the meaning of realist in its early medieval sense to the connotation it has gained in various schools of philosophy since the rise of nominalism at the end of the Middle Ages. Cut off from the twin sources of metaphysical knowledge, namely revelation and intellection,[1] and also deprived of that inner spiritual experience which makes possible the concrete realization of higher levels of being, modern man has been confined to such a truncated and limited aspect of reality that of necessity he has lost sight of God as Reality. Also, even if he continues to have faith in the Divinity, the conception of the Divinity as Reality does not at all accord with that empirically determined worldview[2] within which he lives and whose premises he accepts unwittingly or often unconsciously.

It is possible for man to gain knowledge of God and to come to know Him as Reality because of the very nature of human intelligence, which was made to know the Absolute as such. But to gain this knowledge, it is necessary to have access to those twin sources of metaphysical knowledge and certitude, namely revelation and intellection. Moreover, the second is accessible to man in his present state only by virtue of the first, while the fruit of wisdom which it bears lies at the heart of revelation and it also resides at the center of man's own being. To reach the inner man or the heart which is the seat of the intellect with the aid of the grace issuing from revelation, and to reach the heart of revelation by means of the penetrating rays of this sanctified intellect, enables man to gain an adequate metaphysical knowledge of God as Ultimate Reality and in the light of this knowledge an awareness of relativity as relativity or more precisely as veil.

It can be said that not only does modern man not possess an adequate doctrine of God as Reality in its absolute sense, but also that because of this lack of knowledge he is deprived of an adequate understanding of relativity as veil. To conceive the Absolute in relative terms is also to absolutize the relative in some sense. To remove from God the attribute of reality is also to fail to see the world as only partial reality, as a veil which at once hides and manifests, the veil which as al-ḥijāb in Islam or māyā in Hinduism plays such a basic role in Oriental metaphysics.

Moreover, it is necessary to mention that whereas an adequate metaphysical doctrine pertaining to God as Reality can be found in traditional Christian metaphysics as seen in the works of such masters as Erigena, St.Bonaventure and St.Thomas, the doctrine of the veil is more implicit and less clearly stated even in traditional schools in the West than it is in either Islam or Hinduism, although there are certainly allusions to it in the works of such sages as Meister Eckhart. The reformulation of an adequate metaphysical doctrine concerning the nature of God in a contemporary language requires, therefore, not only a doctrine concerning God as Ultimate Reality or the absolutely Real but also the doctrine of cosmic illusion, the veil, or that creative power which at once manifests the Divine Principle as relativity and veils the Principle through that very manifestation which is none other than the veil— so that a Sufi could address God as "O Thou who hidest Thyself by that which is none other than Thee."

God as Ultimate Reality is not only the Supreme Person but also the source of all that is, hence at once Supra-Being and Being, God as Person and the Godhead or Infinite Essence of which Being is the first determination. Both He or She and It and yet beyond all pronominal categories, God as Ultimate Reality is the Essence which is the origin of all forms, the Substance compared to which all else is accident, the One who alone is and who stands even above the category of being as usually understood.

God as Reality is at once absolute, infinite and, good or perfect. In Himself He is the Absolute which partakes of no relativity in Itself or in Its Essence. The Divine Essence cannot but be absolute and one. All other considerations must belong to the order of relativity, to a level below that of the Essence. To assert that God is one is to assert His absoluteness and to envisage Him in Himself, as such. The Divine Order partakes of relativity in the sense that there is a Divine Relativity or Multiplicity which is included in the Divine Order, but this relativity does not reach the abode of the Divine Essence. God in His Essence cannot but be one, cannot but be the Absolute. To speak of God as Reality is to speak of God as the Absolute.[3]

God as Reality is also infinite, *the* Infinite, as this term is to be understood metaphysically and not what it means mathematically. Ultimate Reality contains the source of all cosmic possibilities and in fact all possibilities as such even the metacosmic. God is infinite not only in the sense that no limit can be set upon Him, but also in the sense that, as Ultimate Reality, He contains all possibilities. Metaphysically, He is the All-Possibility.[4] When the Bible states that with God all things are possible or the Quran asserts that God has power over all things, these scriptural statements must not be understood only in the usual theological sense of alluding to God's infinite power. They also refer to God's nature as the All-Possibility and confirm in other language the Quranic verse, "In His hands is to be found the dominion (malakūt) of all things" (XXXVI.83), that is, the essential reality of all things is to be found in the Divine Nature. It is useful to recall here that the words possibility, puissance and potentiality are from the same root. To say that God is the All-Powerful, the All-Potent, is also to say that He is the All-Possibility.

The understanding of the Divine Infinity is so essential to an adequate doctrine of the nature of God, that its neglect has been the main cause for the philosophical objections to the religious idea of God as goodness and perfection, the source of all that is good and at the same time creator of an imperfect world. No problem has been as troublesome to Western man's understanding of God as presented in the mainstream of Christian theology and philosophy as the famous problem of theodicy, that is, the question of the creation of a world in which there is evil by a Creator who is good. The lack of a complete metaphysical doctrine in the modern West has brought about the eclipse of the doctrine of Divine Infinity and the grades of manifestation or levels of being with the help of which it is possible to understand perfectly well why a world in which there is evil has its origin in God who is pure goodness.[5]

Here it is necessary to add that there would in fact be no agnostics around if only it were possible to teach metaphysics to everyone. One cannot expect every person to comprehend metaphysics any more than one could expect everyone to understand physics or mathematics. But strangely enough, whereas modern man accepts the discoveries of physics on faith and is willing to undergo the necessary training to master the subject if he wishes to understand physics himself, unlike traditional man he does not extend this faith to the fruits of metaphysical knowledge. Without willing to undergo the necessary discipline and training, which in traditional metaphysics, and in contrast to modern science, includes also moral and spiritual considerations, modern man expects to understand metaphysics immediately and without any intellectual or spiritual preparation. If he fails to comprehend the subject, then he rejects the very possibility of that knowledge which alone can solve the antinomies and apparent contradictions of the problem of theodicy and evil. In fact many people in the modern world do not even accept the revealed truths on the basis of faith, as was the case of traditional man, who usually possessed a greater awareness of his own limitations than does his modern counterpart.

In any case, the doctrine of the Divine Infinity makes it possible to understand why there is a world which is limited and imperfect. The Divine contains all possibilities, including the possibility of its own negation, without which it would not be infinite. But this possibility implies a projection toward nothingness which, however, is never reached. This projection constitutes the world, or rather the many worlds standing below their Divine Origin. Since only God is good, this projection means, of necessary, separation from the source of goodness and hence the appearance of evil, which is a kind of "crystallization of nothingness," real on its own level of existence but an illusion before God, who alone is Reality as such. The root of the world resides in the infinity of the Divine Nature.

The metaphysical doctrine of God as absolute and infinite is contained in an explicit fashion in the Quranic chapter called Unity or Sincerity, al-Tawḥīd, or al-Ikhlāṣ (CXIII), which according to Muslims summarizes the Islamic doctrine of God:[6]

> In the Name of God—Most Merciful, Most Compassionate
> Say: He is God, the One (al-Aḥad)!
> God, the eternal cause of all beings (al-Ṣamad)!
> He begetteth not nor was He begotten.
> And there is none like unto Him.

The "Say" (qul) already refers to the source of manifestation in the Divine Principle, to the Logos which is at once the Divine Instrument of Manifestation and the source of manifestation in the Divine Order. He (huwa) is the Divine Essence, God in Himself, God as such or in His suchness. Al-Aḥad attests not only to God's oneness but also to His absoluteness. God is one because He is absolute and absolute because He is one, al-aḥadiyyah or quality of oneness implying both meanings in Arabic. Al-Ṣamad, a most difficult term to render in English, implies eternal fullness or richness which is the source of everything; it refers to the Divine Infinity, to God being the All-Possibility. The last two verses emphasize the truth that God in His Essence is both above all relations and all comparisons. The chapter as a whole is therefore the revealed and scriptural counterpart of the metaphysical doctrine of the Divine Nature as absolute and infinite, this knowledge also being "revealed" in the sense that it issues from that inner revelation which is the intellect.[7]

There is, however, one more statement in this Quranic chapter with which in fact the other chapters of the Quran also open and which is related to the third aspect of the Divine Nature referred to above, namely goodness. God is not only absolute and infinite, but also goodness and perfection. To use the Quranic terminology, He is al-Raḥmah, mercy in Himself, and being mercy and goodness cannot but manifest Himself. The expansive or creative power of the Divinity, which "breathing upon the Divine Possibilities" manifests the world, issues from this fundamental aspect of the Divine Nature as goodness or mercy. That is why the Sufis consider the very substance of the universe to be nothing other than the "Breath of the Compassionate" (*nafas al-raḥmān*).[8] If God is both absolute and infinite, goodness or mercy also reside in His very nature for as Ibn 'Arabī has said, "Mercy pertains to the essence of the Absolute because the latter is by essence 'Bounteous'."[9] To reinstate the integral metaphysical doctrine of the Divine Nature in the contemporary world, it is necessary to go beyond the relativity of various prevalent formulations to gain access to the total and complete doctrine of God as that Reality which is absolute, infinite, and good, perfect, and merciful.

Such a doctrine of the Divine requires not only an adequate knowledge of the Principle as absolute but also an adequate grasp of the meaning of relativity, of levels and the hierarchy of existence, of the relatively real and even of the 'relatively absolute,' an elliptical term which far from being contradictory contains an indispensable key to the understanding of the science of God. To use the two mutually exclusive categories of Creator and created, as is done theologically, is to fall into certain dichotomies which can only be bridged over by an act of faith, in the absence of which there is usually skepticism concerning the very tenets of revealed religion. To begin with the world considered as reality, as is done by most modern philosophy, is to reach an even more dangerous impasse. This of necessity leads to nihilism and skepticism by reducing God to an abstraction, to the 'unreal,' and philosophy itself to the discussion of more or less secondary questions or to providing clever answers to ill-posed problems.

To avoid such impasses, it is essential to revive the doctrine of the veil already alluded to above and to rediscover the traditional teaching about the gradations of reality or of being. To understand God as Reality, it is necessary to understand that there are levels of reality and that reality is not only an empirically definable psychophysical continuum "out there." The world is real to the extent that it reveals God who alone is Real. But the world is also unreal to the extent that it hides and veils God as Reality. Only the saint who sees God everywhere can claim that what is seen and experienced "everywhere" is real.

Moreover, a particular object cannot be said to be real or unreal in only one sense of these terms, but it partakes of levels of reality, or one might say unreality, from being an opaque object, an "it" or "fact" as understood in modern science which is its face as *māyā* in the sense of illusion, to its being a transparent symbol, a theophany, a reflection of the Divine Presence and a witness to the Divine *māyā* which is none other than the Divine Creativity.[10]

To understand God as Reality is also to grasp the world as unreality, not nothingness pure and simple but as relative reality. It is to be saved from that central error of false attribution which issues from our ignorance and which causes us to attribute reality to the illusory and, as a consequence, the character of illusion to that which is Reality as such and which ultimately is alone Real.

To reinstate the doctrine of God as Reality is, needless to say, impossible without a change in the way we envisage the question and possibility of knowledge. As long as the prevalent empiricism or its complementary rationalism continue to reign or are replaced by that irrationalism which erupted in the nineteenth-century Europe from below, there is no possibility to grasp the validity of that traditional wisdom, or that *sophia perennis*, which has always seen God as Reality and the world as a dream from which the sage awakens through realization and remembrance and the ordinary man through death. To grasp this doctrine, the traditional sapiential perspective based on the possibility of principial knowledge from the twin sources of the intellect and revelation must be reinstated along with the metaphysics which is the fruit of this way of knowing.[11]

In light of this fact, the role of traditional wisdom or what the Quran calls *al-ḥikmah* in the contemporary discussion on the nature of God becomes clear. This wisdom resides at the heart of all traditions and can be discovered in those traditions which have preserved their sapiental dimension to this day. It can be found in one of its purest forms in the Vedānta, and one can see an alternative formulation of it in Buddhism.[12] It can likewise be found in the Kabbala[13] and in traditional Christian metaphysics as found in the works as Christian sages such as Eckhart and Erigena. It is also expressed with great clarity in traditional Islamic metaphysics. Furthermore, Islam is a religion which is based completely on the doctrine of the oneness of God, and is a religion in which God is seen as both Reality and Truth, the Arabic term *al-ḥaqīqah* meaning both. In fact the word *al-Ḥaqq* (The Truth), which is related to *ḥaqīqah*, is a Name of God. Therefore, Islamic wisdom can play an important role in enabling modern man to rediscover that plenary doctrine of the nature of God as Reality, a doctrine whose loss has led to the unprecedented skepticism and relativism which characterize the modern world. Islam is able to help in the achievement of this goal not only because of the nature of the Quranic revelation, based as it is in an uncompromising manner upon the doctrine of Divine Unity, but also because it has preserved intact to this day its sapiental tradition. This tradition guards the absoluteness of God and His transcendence in its formal teachings meant for everyone. But it also allows those who possess the qualifications necessary to attain wisdom to gain full access to the metaphysical doctrine of God as at once absolute, infinite and perfect good, and makes it possible for those who have realized this wisdom to hear in the song of the bird and smell in the perfume of the rose the sound and breath of the Beloved, and to contemplate in the very veil of creaturely existence the Face of God. According to Islam's own teachings, this doctrine is not unique to Islam but lies at the heart of all revelations. But as the last echo of the primordial Word upon the stage of human history during this present cycle of terrestrial existence, Islam still reverberates in a particularly vivid manner to that eternal melody of Divine Oneness, recalling man to his perennial vocation as witness on earth to that Reality which is at once absoluteness, infinitude, and boundless goodness and mercy.

Notes

1. Throughout this book, as in our other writings, the intellect is distinguished rigorously from reason, which is its mental reflection. See Nasr, *Knowledge and the Sacred*, chapters 4 and 5.

   For a synthesis of the traditional doctrine of the intellect as it pertains to epistemology, see F.Schuon, *From the Divine to the Human*, trans. G. Polit and D. Lambert (Bloomington, Ind., 1981), pp. 5–35.

2. Although modern rationalism is in many ways opposed to empiricism, it is as far as the present discussion is concerned, nothing more than a complement of empiricism because it, too, has to rely finally for its premises upon the evidence of the senses and the use of reason as limitated by the mental plane as a result of its denial of both intellection and revelation. See F. Schuon, *Logic and Transcendence*, trans. P. Townsend (New York, 1975), pp. 7–55.

3. It is not only possible for man to know God as the Absolute, but it is only the Absolute that man can know absolutely. Human intelligence was made to know the Absolute as such and no amount of "anti-metaphysical cleansing of language" by various types of positivists can remove from intelligence this power to know God as Reality and this Reality as the Absolute. If the use of human language to express such metaphysical assertions has become meaningless to many modern philosophers, it is not because of the shortcoming of such a language or the impossibility to make metaphysical assertions, but because such assertions become meaningless the moment human intelligence is cut from its own roots and made subservient to the dictates of a purely sensualist and empirical epistemology.

4. This doctrine has been expounded in an incomparable manner in the metaphysical works of F. Schuon, who has brought the metaphysical term *"Toute-possibilité"* into current usuage. See especially his "The Problem of Possibility," in *From the Divine to the Human*, pp. 43–56, in which the difficult and at the same time cardinal metaphysical concept of possibility is discussed.

For a general introduction to the works of this very important but often neglected figure, see S. H. Nasr, *The Essential Writings of Frithjof Schuon* (New York, 1983).

5. To understand this doctrine, it is necessary to distinguish between God as Beyond—Being which manifests all possibilities, including the possibility of its negation and separation from the Source which is the origin of what appears on the human plane as evil—and God as Being or the Person, who wishes the good. This doctrine has been explained fully in several of Schuon's works, for example, *Survey of Metaphysics and Esoterism*, trans. G. Polit (Bloomington, Ind., 1986), especially pp. 65-76; and *Esoterism as Principle and as Way*, trans. W. Stoddart (Pates Manor (U.K.), 1981).

6. On the Islamic doctrine of God, see S. H. Nasr, "God," in Nasr (ed.), *Islamic Spirituality—Foundations* (New York, 1987), pp. 311-23.

7. This inner revelation cannot, however, become operative except by virtue of that external revelation which provides an objective cadre for it and enables it to be spiritually efficacious. If there are exceptions, it is because the "wind bloweth where it listeth."

8. This doctrine has found its classical formulation in the *Wisdom of the Prophets* or the *Bezel of Wisdom* (*Fuṣūṣ al-ḥikam*) of Muḥyī al-Dīn ibn 'Arabī. See the translation of R.W.J. Austin (New York, 1980). See also T. Izutsu, *A Comparative Study of the Key Philosophical Concepts in Sufism and Taoism*, part one, (Tokyo, 1966), chapter IX; H. Corbin, *Creative Imagination in the Sufism of Ibn 'Arabī*, trans. R. Mannheim (Princeton, 1969), part one; T. Burckhardt, *Introduction to Sufi Doctrine*, trans. D.M. Matheson (London, 1976), p. 58ff.; W. Chittick, *The Sufi Path of Knowledge* (Albany, N.Y., 1989), p. 19; and S.H. Nasr, *Science and Civilization in Islam* (New York, 1992), p. 344ff.

9. From the *Fuṣūṣ*, quoted in Izutsu, *A Comparative Study*, p. 110.

10. A.K. Coomaraswamy in fact translated *māyā* as "Divine Creativity," while Schuon has rendered it as "Divine Play." On *māyā* and veil, see Schuon, "The Mystery of the Veil," in his *Esoterism as Principle and as Way*, pp. 47-64; and "Māyā," in his *Light on the Ancient Worlds*, trans. Lord Northbourne (London, 1965), pp. 89-98.

11. See Nasr, *Knowledge and the Sacred*, chapters 2 to 4.

12. In Buddhism one does not speak of God or the Self, but one finds in this tradition other ways of expressing the truths of traditional metaphysics and ontology and not a negation of these truths themselves. See A.K. Coomaraswamy, *Hinduism and Buddhism* (New York, 1943).

13. On the metaphysical doctrines of the Kabbala, see L. Schaya, *The Universal Meaning of the Kabbalah*, trans. N.Pearson (London, 1971).

CHAPTER TWO

Self-Awareness and Ultimate Selfhood: The Role of the Sacred Science of the Soul

The fruit of several centuries of rationalistic thought in the West has been to reduce both the objective and the subjective poles of knowledge to a single level. In the same way that the *cogito* of Descartes is based on reducing the knowing subject to a single mode of awareness, the external world which this knowing self perceives is reduced to a spatio-temporal complex limited to a single level of reality—no matter how far this complex is extended beyond the galaxies or into aeons of time, past and future. As mentioned in the previous chapter, the traditional view as expressed in the metaphysical teachings of both the Eastern and Western traditions is based, on the contrary, upon a hierarchic vision of reality, not only of reality's objective aspect but also of its subjective one. Not only are there many levels of reality or existence stretching from the material plane to the Absolute and Infinite Reality which is God, but there are also many levels of subjective reality or consciousness, many envelopes of the self, leading to the Ultimate Self, which is Infinite and Eternal and which is none other than the Transcendent and Immanent Reality both beyond and within.[1] Moreover, the relation between the subjective and the objective is not bound to a single mode. There is not just one form of perception or awareness. There are modes and degrees of awareness leading from the so-called "normal" perception by man of both his own ego and the external world to awareness of Ultimate Selfhood, in which the subject and object of knowledge become unified in a single reality beyond all separation and distinction.

Self-awareness, from the point of view of traditional metaphysics, is not simply a biological fact of life common to all human beings. There is more than one level of meaning to 'self' and more than one degree of awareness. Man is aware of his self or ego, but one also speaks of self-control, and therefore implies even in daily life the presence of another self which controls the lower self, for as asserted by so many Christian authorities *duo sunt in homine*. Tradition, therefore, speaks clearly of the distinction between the self and the Self, or the self and the Spirit which is the first reflection of the Ultimate Self; hence the primary distinction between *anima* and *spiritus* or *al-nafs* and *al-rūḥ* of Islamic thought and the emphasis upon the fact that there is within every man both an outer and an inner man, a lower self and a higher one. That is why also tradition speaks of the self as being totally distinct from the Ultimate Self, from Ātman or ousia, and yet as a reflection of it and as the solar gate through which man must pass to reach the Self. Traditional metaphysics is in fact primarily an autology, to quote A.K. Coomaraswamy,[2] for to know is ultimately to know the Self. The ḥadīth, "He who knoweth himself knoweth his Lord," attests on the highest level to this basic truth.

There are, moreover, many stages which separate the self and the Self. In its descent towards manifestation, the Self becomes shrouded by many bodies, many sheaths, which must be shed in returning to the One. That is why the Buddhist and Hindu traditions speak of the various subtle bodies of man, and certain Sufis such as 'Alā' al-Dawlah Simnānī analyze the "physiology" of the inner man or the man of light in terms of the laṭā'if or subtle bodies which man "carries" within himself and which he must "traverse" and also cast aside in order to reach the Self.[3]

In order to reach the Ultimate Self through the expansion of awareness of the center of consciousness, man must reverse the cosmogonic process which has crystallized both the variations and reverberations of the Self within what appears through the cosmic veil (al-ḥijāb) as separate and objective existence. And this reversal must of necessity begin with the negation of the lower self, with the performance of sacrifice, which is an echo here below of the primordial sacrifice, the sacrifice which has brought the cosmos into existence. The doctrine of the creation of the cosmos, whether expounded metaphysically or mythically in various traditions, is based upon the manifestation of the Principle, which is at the same time the sacrifice (the yājña of Hinduism) of the luminous pole of existence, of the Universal Man (al-insān al-kāmil), of Puruṣa, of the Divine Logos which is also light, of the Spirit (al-rūḥ) which resides within the proximity of the Ultimate Self and at the center of the cosmos. The Ultimate Self in its inner infinitude is beyond all determination and cosmic polarization, but the Spirit or Intellect which is both created and uncreated, is already its first determination in the direction of manifestation. It is māyā in Ātman and the center of all the numerous levels of cosmic and universal existence.[4] Through its 'sacrifice' the lower levels of the cosmic order in their objective as well as subjective aspects become manifest. The human self, as usually experienced by men who have become separated from their archetypal reality, is itself a faint echo upon the cosmic plane of the Spirit and ultimately of the Self, and exists only by virtue of the original sacrifice of its celestial Principle. Hence, it is through the denial of itself or of sacrifice that the self can again become it-Self and regain the luminous empyrean from which it has descended to the corporeal realm.

Self-awareness can only reach the Ultimate Self provided it is helped by that message from the Divine Intellect which is none other than revelation in its universal sense. The gates through which the Spirit has descended to the level of the human self are hermetically sealed and protected by dragons which cannot be subdued save with the help of angelic forces. Self-awareness in the sense of experimenting with the boundaries of the psyche, with new experiences, with the heights and depths of the psychological world, does not result in any way in moving closer to the proximity of the Self. The attempted expansion of awareness in this sense, which is so common in modern man, who is anxious to break the boundaries of the prison of the materialistic world he has created for himself, results only in a horizontal expansion, but not in a vertical one. Its result is a never-ending wandering in the labyrinth of the psychic world and not the end of all wandering in the presence of the Sun which alone is. Only the sacred can enable the awareness of the self to expand in the direction of the Self. The Divine reveals to man His Sacred Name as a holy vessel which carries man from the limited world of his self to the shores of the World of the Spirit where alone man is his Real Self. That is why the famous Sufi, Manṣūr al-Ḥallāj, through whom the Self uttered "I am the Truth," (*ana'l-Ḥaqq*) prays in this famous verse to the Self to remove the veil which separates man's illusory I from the Self who alone is I in the absolute sense.

Between me and thee,
It is my "I-ness" which is in contention:
Through Thy "it is I"
Remove my "I-ness" from between us.[5]

With the help of the message and also the grace issuing from the Self, the lower self or soul is able to become wed to the Spirit in that alchemical marriage between gold and silver, the king and the queen, the heavenly bridegroom and the earthly bride, which is the goal of all initiatic work. And since love is also death (*amor est mors*) and marriage is death as well as union,[6] the perfection of the self implies first of all the negation of itself, a death which is also a rebirth, for only he who has realized that he is nothing is able to enter unto the Divine Presence. The only thing man can offer in sacrifice to God is his self, and in performing this sacrifice through spiritual practice he returns the self to the Self and gains awareness of the real 'I' within, who alone has the right to claim "I am." As Rūmī has said in these celebrated and often quoted verses concerning the real 'I'[7]

I died as mineral and became a plant,
I died as plant and rose to animal,

I died as animal and I was Man.
Why should I fear? When was I less by dying?
Yet once more I shall die as Man, to soar
With angels blest; but even from angelhood
I must pass on: all except God doth perish.
When I have sacrificed my angel-soul,
I shall become what no mind e'er conceived.
Oh, let me not exist! for Non-existence
Proclaims in organ tones: "To him we shall return."

One of the factors which most sharply distinguishes traditional metaphysics from that part of postmedieval Western philosophy which is called metaphysics today is that traditional metaphysics is not mere speculation about the nature of Reality but a doctrine concerning the nature of the Real, combined with methods revealed by the Origin or Absolute Reality to enable the self or the soul, as usually understood, to return to the abode of the Self. The Ultimate Self cannot be approached by the efforts of the self alone, and no amount of human knowledge of the psyche can increase the awareness or the consciousness of the self which will finally lead to the Ultimate Self.

The contemplative disciplines of all traditions of both East and West insist in fact on the primacy of the awareness of the self and its nature. As the great thirteenth-century Japanese Zen master Dogen has said, "To study Buddhism means nothing other than inquiring into the true nature of the ego (or the self)."[8] The famous dictum of Christ that the Kingdom of God is within you is likewise a confirmation of the primacy of the inward journey towards the Ultimate Self as the final goal of religion.

Traditional psychology or rather pneumatology, which however must not be confused in any way with modern psychological studies, is closely wed to traditional metaphysics, for it contains the means whereby the soul can understand its own structure and with the help of appropriate spiritual disciplines transform itself so as to finally realize it-Self. This is as much true of the Yogācāra school of Mahāyāna Buddhism as of various forms of Yoga in Hinduism or of the contemplative schools within Judaism, Christianity and Islam. In the latter tradition for example, a whole science of the soul has been developed based on the progressive perfection and transformation of the self towards the Self.[9] In Arabic the word *nafs* means at once soul, self and ego. As ordinarily understood, the *nafs* is the source of limitation, passion and gravity, the source of all that makes man selfish and self-centered. This *nafs* which is called the *al-nafs al-ammārah* (the soul which inspires evil), following the terminology of the Quran, must be transfigured through death and purgation. It must be controlled by the higher self. With the help of the Spirit the *nafs al-ammārah* becomes transformed into the *nafs al-lawwāmah* (the blaming soul), gaining greater awareness of its own nature, an awareness that is made possible through the transmutation of its substance. In the further stage of inner alchemical transmutation, the *nafs al-lawwāmah* becomes transformed into the *nafs al-muṭma'innah* (the soul at peace), attaining a state in which it can gain knowledge with certainty and repose in peace because it has discovered its own center, which is the Self. Finally according to certain Sufis, the *nafs al-muṭma'innah* becomes transmuted into the *nafs al-rāḍiyah* (the satisfied soul), which has attained such perfection that it has now become worthy of being the perfect bride of the Spirit, thus returning to its Lord, as the Quran asserts, and finally realizing the Self through its own annihilation (*fanā'*) and subsequent subsistence (*baqā'*) in God.[10]

The traditional science of the soul, along with the methods for the realization of the Self, a science which is to be found in every integral tradition, is the means whereby self-awareness expands to reach the empyrean of the Ultimate Self. This traditional science is the result of both intellectual penetration and experiment with and experience of the self by those who have been able to navigate over its vast expanses with the aid of a spiritual guide. It is a science not bound by the phenomena or accidents which appear in the psyche or which the self of ordinary human beings display. Rather, it is determined by the noumenal world, by the Substance to which all accidents ultimately return, for essentially *samsāra* and *nirvāṇa* are the same.

Traditional cosmology is also seen, from the practical point of view of the perfection of the soul and the journey of the self to Self, as a form of the sacred science of the soul, as a form of autology. The cosmos may be studied as an external reality whose laws are examined by various cosmological sciences. But it may also be studied with the view of increasing self-awareness and as an aid in the journey towards the Ultimate Self. In this way the cosmos becomes not an external object but a crypt through which the seeker of Truth journeys and which becomes interiorized within the being of the traveller to the degree that by "travelling" through it he is able to increase his self-awareness and attain higher levels of consciousness.[11] Again to quote Rūmī:

The stars of heaven are ever re-filled by the star-like souls of the pure.
The outer shell of heaven, the Zodiac, may control us; but our inner essence rules the sky.
In form you are microcosm, in reality the macrocosm:
Though it seems the branch is the origin of the fruit, in truth the branch only exists for the fruit.
If there were no hope, no desire for this fruit, why should the gardener have planted the tree?

So the tree was born of the fruit, even though it seems the other way
round.
Thus Muḥammad said "Adam and the other prophets follow under my
banner."
Thus that master of all knowledge has declared in allegory "We are the
last and the foremost."
For if I seem to be born of Adam, in fact I am the ancestor of all ancestors.
Adam was born of me, and gained the Seventh Heaven on my account.[12]

The process through which man becomes him-Self and attains his true
nature does not possess only a cosmic aspect. It is also of the greatest social
import. In a society in which the lower self is allowed to fall by its own weight,
in which the Ultimate Self and means to attain it are forgotten, in which there
is no principle higher than the individual self, there cannot but be the highest
degree of conflict between limited egos which would claim for themselves
absolute rights, usually in conflict with the the claims of other egos—rights
which belong to the Self alone. In such a situation, even the spiritual virtue
of charity becomes sheer sentimentality. The traditional science of the soul,
however, sees only one Self, which shines, no matter how dimly, at the center
of oneself and every self. It is based on the love of one-Self which however
does not imply selfishness but on the contrary necessitates the love of others,
who in the profoundest sense are also one-self. For as Meister Eckhart has
said, "Loving thy Self, thou lovest all men as thy Self."[13]

The sheer presence in human society of those who have attained the
Ultimate Self has an invisible effect upon all of society far beyond what an
external study of their relation with the social order would reveal. Such men
and women are not only a channel of grace for the whole of society but the
living embodiment of the truth that self-awareness can lead to the Ultimate Self
only through man's sacrificing his self and realizing his own limitations and
that the only way of being really charitable in an ultimate and final sense is
to see the Self in all selves and hence to act towards my neighbor not as if
he were myself, but because he is at the center of his being my-Self. The love
of other selves is metaphysically meaningful only as a function of the awareness
not of our limited self but of the Ultimate Self. That is why the injunction of
the Gospels is to first love God and then one's neighbor. Knowledge of the
self in its relation to the Self reveals this basic truth that the inner life of man
leaves its deepest imprint upon the social order even if one were to do nothing,
and that harmony on the social level can only be attained when the members
of a society are able to control the self with the help of the means which only
the Ultimate Self can provide for them. To quote Dogen again,

To be disciplined in the Way of the Buddha means getting disciplined in dealing properly with your own I. To get disciplined in dealing with your I means nothing other than forgetting your I. To forget your I means that you become illumined by the things. To be illumined by the things means that you obliterate the distinction between your (so-called) ego and the (so-called) ego of other things.[14]

The traditional sciences of the soul deal extensively with all the questions relating to sense perception, inner experiences, contact and communication with other conscious beings and the like. But their central concern is above all with the question of the nature of the Self, of the center of consciousness, of the subject which says "I". In fact, one of the chief means to reach the Ultimate Self is to examine thoroughly the nature of the I, with the help of the spiritual methods provided within the matrix of various traditions, as was done by the great contemporary Hindu saint Śri Rāmana Maharshi.[15] As awareness of the self expands and deepens, the consciousness of the reality of the only I which is begins to appear, replacing the ordinary consciousness which sees nothing but the multiple echoes of the I on the plane of cosmic manifestation. The consciousness of the only I, which is the source of all consciousness, lead the person who has realized this truth to sing with 'Aṭṭār that,

All you have been, and seen, and thought,
Not you, but I, have seen and been and wrought.[16]

The realization of the Ultimate Self, of the I who alone has the right to say "I am", is the goal of all awareness. Through it man realizes that although at the beginning of the path the Self is completely other than the self, ultimately the self is the Self, as Hindu masters have been especially adamant in emphasizing. But this identity is essential, not phenomenal and external. The self is on the one hand like the foam of the ocean wave, insubstantial, transient and illusory, and on the other hand a spark of the Light of the Self, a ray which in essence is none other than the supernal Sun. It is with respect to this spark within the self of every human being that it has been said that "there is in every man an incorruptible star, a substance called upon to become crystallized in immortality: it is eternally prefigured in the luminous proximity of the Self. Man disengages this star from its temporal entanglements in truth, in prayer and in virtue, and in them alone."[17]

Notes

1. Traditional metaphysics speaks of Ultimate Reality either as the absolutely Transcendent or the absolutely Immanent, which however are one, *Brahman* being the same as *Ātman*.

Hindu metaphysics, however, emphasizes more the language of immanence, and Islamic metaphysics that of transcendence without one language excluding the other.

See F. Schuon, *Spiritual Perspectives and Human Facts*, trans. by P. Townsend (London, 1987), p. 90ff. See also Schuon, *Language of the Self*, trans. by M. Pallis and D.M. Matheson (Madras, 1959), especially chapter XI, "*Gnosis. Language of the Self.*"

2. See A.K. Coomaraswamy, *Hinduism and Buddhism*, p. 10ff.

3. See H. Corbin, *The Man of Light in Iranian Sufism*, trans. N. Pearson (London, 1978). In diverse traditions, the return of the self to the Self has been compared to the shedding of outward skin by a snake, which by virtue of this unsheathing gains a new skin and a new life.

4. See F. Schuon, "*Ātmā-Māyā*", in his *In the Face of the Absolute* (Bloomington, Ind., 1989), pp. 53–64.

5. L. Massignon (ed.), *Le Dîwân d'al-Hallâj* (Paris, 1955), p. 90.

6. It is of interest to recall that in Greek *teleo* (τελέω) means at once to gain perfection, to become married and to die.

7. R.A. Nicholson, *Rumi—Poet and Mystic* (London, 1950), p. 103.

8. Quoted in T. Izutsu, "Two Dimensions of Ego Consciousness in Zen", *Sophia Perennis*(Tehran), vol. II, no. 1 (1976), p. 20.

9. See M. Ajmal, "Sufi Science of the Soul," in S.H. Nasr (ed.), *Islamic Spirituality—Foundations*, pp. 294–307.

10. On these stages of the soul and its purification, see Mir Valiuddin, *Contemplative Disciplines in Sufism* (London, 1980); also Ajmal, "Sufi Science."

11. See S.H. Nasr, *An Introduction to Cosmological Doctrines* (Albany, 1993), chapter 15.

12. Rūmī, *Mathnawī*, ed. by R.A. Nicholson, trans. by P. Wilson (London, 1930), IV, Book IV, vv. 519–28.

13. F. Pheiffer, *Meister Eckhart*, trans. by C. de B. Evans, London, 1924, 1.139. Quoted in Coomaraswamy, *Hinduism and Buddhism*, p. 13.

14. Izutsu, p. 33.

15. Śri Rāmana Maharshi in fact based the whole of his teachings upon a method which asked "Who am I?" His most famous work, a collection of answers given to one of his disciples, Sivaprakasam Pillai, who arranged and amplified them, is called *Who am I?* (Tiruvannamalai, 1955). See A. Osborne, *Ramana Maharshi and the Path of Self Knowledge* (Bombay, 1957).

16. From the *Manṭiq al-ṭayr*, trans. by F.S. Fitzgerald, in A.J. Arberry, *Classical Persian Literature* (London, 1958), p. 131.

17. F. Schuon, *Light on the Ancient World*, p. 117.

CHAPTER THREE

Time—The Moving Image of Eternity

*The Time (that has parts) cooks (pacati, matures) all things, in the Great
Self, indeed; but the Comprehensor of That (Time without parts) in which
time itself is cooked, he knows the Vedas!*
> —Hindu sacred text, trans. A.K. Coomaraswamy,
> Time and Eternity [Ascona, 1947], p. 16

*[Zeus] designed to make out of Eternity a something moving; and so, when
He was ordering the whole Heaven (Universe), He made out of that Eternity
that ever abides in its own unity a sempiternal image, moving according
to number, even that which we have called "time".*
> —Plato, Timaeus, trans. A.K. Coomaraswamy

*From this shore of existence to the other stands the army of oppression,
But, opportunity for the dervishes stretches from pre-Eternity to
post-Eternity.*
> —Ḥāfiẓ

Man lives in the world of change and becoming wherein he experiences time,
which marks his earthly life and which finally conquers him as it leads him
ineluctably to his death. Yet he is in turn able to conquer time because he has
issued forth from the Eternal Order. Man has an innate awareness of Eternity
whose idea is deeply imprinted upon his mind and its experience still echoes
in the depth of his soul where something remains of the lost paradise which
he inhabited before joining the caravan of terrestrial life. The traditional universe
is dominated by the two basic realities of Origin and Center, both of which
belong to the realm of the Eternal. Man lives a life removed from the Origin
on a circumference distanced from the Center. And it is precisely this removal
and distancing which constitute for him the experience of time. He is, therefore,
a being suspended between time and Eternity, neither a purely temporal creature
nor a being of the Eternal Realm, at least in his ordinary earthly state. That
is why all religions focus their teachings upon the question of the relation
between time and Eternity, as do all traditional philosophies. To understand
the nature of man is to become aware of his existential situation as a being
belonging to the Eternal Order but living in time, which itself cannot but be
related to Eternity since all orders of reality are of necessity interrelated.

The question thus revolves around the meaning of Eternity and of time, whose understanding has been so central to both the metaphysical and religious concerns of humanity over the ages. The comments which follow seek to elucidate but a few strands in the vast tapestry of traditional doctrines concerning time and Eternity[1] and to contrast them when necessary with certain prevalent modern concepts which have succeeded in veiling the traditional teachings in those sectors of the contemporary world which are called modern and now increasingly postmodern.

The notion of Eternity evokes at once the idea of changelessness, immutability and perfection. It is related to the Divine Order, to the Divine Principle itself as well as the world of the Spirit residing in the Divine Proximity, hence the usage of the term 'eternal life'.[2] It is known by man through the tenets of revelation as well as through intellection[3] and can be experienced even in this life through spiritual realization and the "eye of the heart" or the frontal eye of Śiva whose gaze is ever fixed upon the Eternal Order. In any case there is in principle no need of the world of becoming in order for man to know the Eternal, except that as the subject of this knowledge man is himself situated in the world of becoming. Even there, however, he is able to know and experience Eternity directly as a being who belongs ultimately to the Eternal Order, though not simply as a creature who is the product of the world of change and becoming for only the like can know the like.

As for time, man has an immediate awareness of it and lives in this world as if he knew perfectly what time is. But a further analysis of the meaning of time reveals it to be the most elusive of the parameters of cosmic existence, unlike space, form, matter and number, which are easier both to define and to measure.[4] That is why philosophers have often found time to be one of the most difficult of problems to treat and why, especially since the rise of modern science and its adoption of the purely quantitative notion of time, those concerned with the traditional understanding of the subject have had to emphasize the distinction between time and duration, qualitative and quantitative time or even levels of meaning of time itself.[5] Paradoxically, while time seems to be so much easier to grasp and experience than Eternity, it is not possible to know or measure it as it is usually understood without the world of becoming which surrounds man. While there is a direct nexus between man and Eternity independent of this world, the relation of man to time always involves this world, for there is no time without becoming.

In order to experience time in the ordinary sense of the word, there is need of the manifested or created order in its changing aspect, hence the world of becoming. There is also need of the polarity between the subject and the object. It is human subjectivity with its particular hierarchic structure which is able to know time and duration, and because it is the human subject it is able to experience time while being aware of its termination for the particular subject who is experiencing time, hence the awareness of death. The yearning for transcendence which characterizes normal man means that he is not only able to experience time but also to have an awareness of its limitation and termination and of his own existence as an immortal being beyond time. To understand time in itself and in relation to Eternity, it is therefore necessary to turn to the ontological status of the world of becoming and the universal hierarchy of existence which makes it possible to understand the meaning of time and also its relation to Eternity, of which it is the "moving image."

The Divine Principle is at once the Absolute, the Infinite and the Supreme Good, which cannot but manifest Itself as the myriad of worlds that become ever farther removed from It as a result of their separation from their ontological origin. The Divine Infinitude, by virtue of its infinity, must contain the possibility of manifestation or creation, a possibility which must of necessity be realized as it is in the nature of the Good to give of itself and to radiate. This radiation, however, implies projection, hence separation from the Divine Principle which remains unaffected by Its manifestations as *Ātman* remains unaffected by the cosmic veils of *māyā*, to use the language of Hinduism. The very infinitude of the Divine Principle implies the necessity of the existence of the world or many worlds, hence ontologically speaking the world of becoming as distinct from Being.[6]

Metaphysically, one can distinquish between the Supreme Principle or Beyond Being, Its self-determination or Being, and cosmic existence, which can be identified, except for its summit, with the world of becoming. The Beyond-Being and Being of course do not become or change, although the phases of what Hinduism calls the days and night of Brahma contain the principle of the cosmic cycles and hence the rhythms according to which the world of becoming is manifested. In the highest sense, the quality of Eternity belongs to the Beyond-Being and Being, although that which participates in the world of the Spirit, that lies at the center of the cosmos and in the proximity of the Divine Reality Itself, can also be said to be eternal, hence the eternal life of the blessed spoken of in various religious traditions as distinct from the perpetual or unending state which characterizes the infernal states.[7]

As for the world of becoming, it is already removed from Eternity by the very fact that it is becoming. The origin of time resides in this very separation of the world of becoming from its ontological principle and origin. To become is to change or to move as this verb is understood in traditional natural philosophy such as that of Aristotle. Moreover, in the same way that becoming has its roots in Being and the cosmos derives its existence from Being without which it would be literally nothing, time which characterizes the state of becoming must be related to and have its root in the Eternal Order; hence the famous Platonic saying that time is the moving image of Eternity. This metaphysical assertion summarizes the relation of time to Eternity. It asserts first of all that Eternity has an "image," that is, the Eternal Principle manifests Itself. Secondly, since this manifestation is in the mode of becoming and in fact constitutes the world of becoming, it is a moving image. And time is none other than this moving image. If there were to be no moving image there would be no time, and if there were no Eternity or the Eternal Reality which is at once the Absolute, the Infinite and the Perfect Good, there would be no moving image.

The very fact that the Absolute alone is absolute while the world is contingency necessitates the distinction between Eternity and time. Those who deny the Eternal Order are also those who fail to distinguish between the Absolute and the contingent and hence bestow upon the world the quality of absoluteness which belongs to the Divine Principle alone.[8] Moreover, Eternity characterizes the Divine Infinitude and also the transcendent aspect of the Divine Principle with its quality of majesty and rigor, while the Divine Omnipresence which complements Eternity is related to Immanence with its quality of beauty and mercy. One is the principle of time and the other of space, one of change, transformation, death and rebirth and the other of preservation and permanence which in the world of becoming must of course be understood in a relative manner.[9]

Moreover, the very principle of manifestation implies hierarchy. In the same way that there are vast universes of light or angelic realities separating Being from the material part of the cosmos in which man resides, Eternity is separated from time as ordinarily understood by intermediate stages and levels. That is why various traditions speak of *aeons*, *zurvān*, *dahr*, etc. which belong to intermediate ontological levels between the Supreme Principle or the Eternal as such and the world of time.

In the Islamic tradition for example, a distinction is made between *sarmad* (Eternity or the purely changeless), *dahr* (the relation of the changeless to that which changes) and *zamān* (time which concerns the relation between the changing and the changing). It is furthermore said that *dahr* is the principle or spirit (*rūḥ*) of *zamān* while *sarmad* is the principle or spirit of *dahr*.

Traditional doctrines also distinguish between the ordinary experience of time and the experience of other modalities of time belonging to higher levels of reality and consciousness, without those modalities being simply the consequence of individual subjective experience lacking correspondence with an objective realm.[10] The more a person rises in the hierarchy of existence and levels of consciousness from the world of outward experience toward the Divine Emperean which is the Eternal, the more does he experience higher modes of what one could still call "time" which are penetrated to an ever greater degree by Eternity until he leaves the domain of becoming altogether. It is not accidental that the Quran asserts, "A day with Thy Lord is as a thousand years" (XXII. 47), that in Hinduism a single day in the life of Brahma corresponds to a vast number of years according to man's earthly reckoning and that the Psalmist sings, "From everlasting to everlasting, thou art God. . . . A thousand years in Thy sight are but as yesterday" (Psalm XC.2,4).

Turning to the experience of the phenomenal world itself, it can be said that the content of this world is constituted of matter (whose dynamic dimension is energy), form (as this term has been understood traditionally) and number. As for the container of this content, it is constituted of time and space.[11] If there were to be no phenomenal world, there would be no becoming and hence no time or space as these terms are usually understood. In man's experience of the world, however, it seems that time and space stand there as objective realities within which material objects possessing form function and move. Both of these views have been reflected in traditional schools of philosophy, although it is only since Descartes that the purely quantitative conception of time and space, as defined mathematically by the x,y,z Cartesian coordinates to which t (time) is added, has come to replace the earlier teachings in which time was never reduced to pure quantity. For the nexus between the phenomenal world and higher levels of existence was never forgotten and the parameters of cosmic existence were never reduced to mathematical abstractions of a purely quantitative nature.

As a matter of fact, all the parameters mentioned above have their principle in higher levels of being. There is a matter of the intermediate psychic and higher celestial worlds as there are forms belonging to these worlds. There are symbolic meanings to numbers and higher worlds have their own "space" as well as their own "time" as already mentioned. That is why in certain traditions such as Hinduism which combine the metaphysical and the mythical, the functions of the gods and various divinities acting in different worlds above the terrestrial are related to the cosmic significance of the principles of those realities which appear to man on earth as matter, form, number, space and time.

Coming back to time as experienced in the phenomenal world, it must be added that this existential condition has an objective and a subjective mode. There is what one can call objective time and what can be called subjective time, to which certain authors have given other names. Also the basic distinction between the Principle and its manifestation is reflected also on the level of phenomenal existence in what is usually called "abstract" and "concrete," the former being beyond human experience and notional and the second the subject of possible human experience. There is therefore an *abstract* time and a *concrete* time.

As far as concrete time is concerned, it is the most immediate and most easily understood type of time. It is the time which we associate with changing phenomena within the sea of becoming in which we are immersed. In the same way that a person thrown in the sea experiences immediately the wetness of water, being immersed in the sea of becoming ennables us to experience immediately the changing character of phenomena which constitute concrete time. As for abstract time, it is the duration which is measurable as a result of this change. This is the time to which Aristotle referred when he said that time is the measure of motion. Without motion which in Aristotelian physics means change, there would be no time in the sense of abstract time, which most human beings divide into hours and minutes with little awareness of its relation to Eternity and impervious to the fact that with the passage of every one of those very hours and minutes man draws a step closer to the meeting with that Reality which is none other than the Eternal.

As far as objective time is concerned, it consists of the spiroidal flow of cosmic becoming and is comprised of four basic phases. These phases can be seen first of all in the doctrine of the four cosmic cycles developed more elaborately in Hinduism than in any other tradition.[12] They are also to be seen in the time which surrounds man directly in his life such as the four seasons, the four periods of the day and the four stages of humand life consisting of childhood, youth, maturity and old age.[13] Objective time is cyclic rather than linear, being related to the universal cycles of manifestation which then determine cycles on lower levels of existence. Objective time is measured by the movement of the earth around its axis or the heavens around the earth depending on which reference point is used for the measurement of motion and then the motion of the heavens, all of which are circular, or almost circular. Moreover, these motions correspond to cosmic rhythms which are cyclic or more exactly spiroidal in the sense that a cycle never returns exactly to the same point as before for there cannot be an exact repetition in manifestation. That is why what is called the "myth of eternal return," although a powerful way of speaking of cosmic cycles, is not cosmologically exact since there is never an exact return to the previous point of origin of a cycle in the same way that the new spring season is never exactly the previous spring but nevertheless it is a return to spring.[14]

In any case the traditional understanding of objective time based upon cycles is totally different from the linear conception of the flow of time which has developed in the West especially in modern times. The secularization of the Christian conception of the march of historical time, marked by the three central events of the fall of Adam, the first coming of Christ and his second coming, has led to a quantitative and linear conception of history that is totally alien to the cyclic conception seen in Hinduism, the ancient Greek religion and even Islam if one take into consideration the meaning of the cycles of prophecy (*dā'irat al-nubuwwah*) which mark Islamic sacred history. To reduce objective time, whether it be cosmic or historical, to a quantitatively conceived linear time to which the idea of indefinite progress in the eighteenth and nineteenth century European thought is usually added, is to lose sight of the nature of time as the moving image of Eternity. It is to bestow a kind of absoluteness to time itself by forgetting its relation to the cosmic cycles of manifestation which reach, in an ever-ascending order, the Supreme Principle of all manifestation or the Eternal as such.

While speaking of linear time, which came to the fore in Western philosophy and science as a result of a complex set of factors related to the secularization of the Christian doctrine of the incarnation as well as certain other philosophical and scientific ideas, it is important to distinguish between qualitative and quantitative objective time. Mainstream modern Western thought, especially its more scientific vein, not only rejects the idea of Eternity and other categories of time mentioned above, but it also reduces time to pure quantity, emptying it of all qualitative aspects. It either speaks of an empty quantitative time stretching for "billions of years" within which cosmic events take place or relates time to matter and energy as in the theory of relativity but once again in a purely quantitative manner. That is why in modern science and all philosophies derived from it, there is a uniformitarianism which governs the history of the cosmos and its laws. Such a perspective cannot conceive of the crystallization of higher forms of being in the spatio-temporal complex at certain moments of cosmic history and not at others. Hence its need to posit the logically absurd theory of evolution as practically a dogma not allowed to be even questioned by serious scientists. Nor can such a perspective even imagine the possibility of the integration of the physical part of the cosmos into higher orders of reality at other moments of cosmic history corresponding to what various religions have described as eschatological events of various orders leading finally to the Apocatastasis, *al-qiyāmat al-kubrā* or *mahāpralaya*.

Then there is subjective time, which is experienced directly by the consciousness of the human subject without any external measurement. Nor is in fact any quantitative measurement of this 'inner time' possible. The individual subject can experience subjective time in many ways, in a state of contraction or expansion, in pain or in joy, in separation from God or in His proximity. The very duration of this experienced time differs according to these inner conditions. When the soul is in a state of spiritual deprivation or suffering, subjective time expands and an hour measured objectively is experienced as a much longer time. On the contrary, when the soul is in a state of spiritual contemplation or ecstasy, a contraction of time itself takes place. Many hours appear as if they were a moment. In this case, because of the rise of the experiencing subject in the levels of being, subjective time approaches Eternity or that 'eternal present' which is the direct reflection of Eternity in time, the moment when according to Dante, "every *where* and every *when* is focussed" (Paradiso, XXIX.12).

Subjective time is also experienced as past, present and future. The past is experienced precisely as the past of a particular subject experiencing time, as are the present and the future. This tripartite division of time, although illusory from the point of view of the "Eternal Now" which alone is ultimately real, is nevertheless of metaphysical and spiritual significance. The past represents not only what has already disappeared from life and is therefore no longer accessible, but also the Origin from which man hails and hence the Divine Alpha. The future is not only indefinite moments of earthly life in which the imagination continues its dream of worldly forgetfulness, but also the direction toward paradise for which the soul prepares itself through its actions on earth and for which it has deep nostalgia as its homeland of origin. For as the poet Ḥāfiẓ has said,

I was an angel and the exalted paradise was my abode,
It was Adam who brought me into this half replenished, half ruined convent.

Finally there is the present which not only corresponds to the point through which man can assert his passionate impulses, immersing himself in immediate gratification of the senses impervious to his origin and his end as an immortal being, but also constitutes the only moment which connects man to the Eternal. It is in the present moment that man can assert his faith, can perform correct action and above all can remember and recollect (the *dhikr* of Sufism) who he is and what is Reality. The present moment is the only gateway in this life to the abode of Eternity because this moment stands already outside of time and "is" in principle already in the Eternal Realm. The present moment is already beyond time like the moment of death when serial time comes to an end. That is why in the Catholic rosary the faithful pray to the Virgin Mary for mercy "now" and at the moment of death.[15]

One can carry out endless discourse about time and Eternity while the flow of time itself draws human life ever closer to the moment of truth when subjective time as experienced on earth comes to an end. But that discourse itself will not lead to the Eternal, which is the goal of human life. What is needed is to seize the present moment, to live in it and to pierce, with the help of the "eye of the heart" the cosmic veils of *māyā* and hence to know and experience that reality which is Eternity. All the traditional doctrines which speak of the present moment as the "point whereto all times are present"[16] do so in order to guide the soul to seize the present moment as the unique point of contact with the eternal Reality rather than to daydream about a past over which man can no longer wield any power or a future which has not yet come and in which again man cannot act. Man can be, know and act only now. Even the poems of the Persian sage Khayyām, long considered as a hedonist in the West, refer in reality to the metaphysical and initiatic significance of the Eternal Now. When Khayyām sings,

> Ah, fill the Cup: — what boots it to repeat
> How Time is slipping underneath our Feet:
> Unborn, Tomorrow, and dead yesterday,
> Why fret about them if To-day be sweet![17]

he is not encouraging hedonism and Epicurean pleasure-seeking, which is the opposite of the attitude of the sage, but rather wishes to underline the significance of the present moment, of today, of the only moment when we can *be* and become what we are in reality in the Eternal Order. That is why the Sufi is called the son of the moment (*ibn al-waqt*), for he lives in the Eternal Moment, already dead to the illusory life of forgetfulness. He who lives in the present is in fact already dead in the traditional sense in which the spiritual man is referred to as a walking dead man and in which the Prophet of Islam advised his followers to die before dying. To die to the corrosive flow of a time spent in the forgetfulness of God is to live already in Eternity while being still outwardly alive in this world. It is in fact to possess real life compared to which the life of the world is a petrified imitation, a death parading as life.

But while man possesses potentially this most precious treasure of the present moment, it is difficult for him to make it actually his own by virtue of living in it rather than in the past or the future. The fallen nature of the humanity of this present phase in the cosmic cycle is such that the mind is too dispersed and the imagination too entangled in worldly forms to enable the vast majority of men to simply live in the eternal present by their own will. There is need of help from the Eternal Itself to make this attachment to the Eternal possible. Hence, the necessity of revelation and sacred forms which, issuing from the Eternal, enable man to live in the Eternal Now.

At the heart of these sacred and revealed forms and teachings which constitute religion stands prayer, which links man who lives in time to God and the Eternal Order. Through prayer man transcends the accidentality of time and space and regains his direct contact with the Eternal. The temporal and the Eternal are miraculously united in prayer as in the realization of the Truth through sapiential knowledge. The subject who prays to the Eternal and the subject who knows that only the Supreme Reality is I, has already journeyed

beyond the realm of temporality to reside in the Eternal Order. He has ceased
to become and having passed through the solar gate can only be said to be.
For him time has ceased to manifest itself as the moving image of Eternity.
It has become a constellation of eternal moments or rather a single moment
of the Eternal Now whose reverberations through the levels of cosmic
manifestation make it appear as many moments.

The sacred itself is the manifestation of the Eternal in the temporal order,
as are miracles. That is why the means which make possible the realization
of the Eternal for a humanity living in historic time is contained in sacred
tradition. Through sacred rites, objects and forms in time are brough back to
the bosom of Eternity. Time itself is sacralized through celebrations of rites
and recollection of theophanic realities. A distinction is thereby made between
secular time, which is the time associated with what has come to be known
as ordinary life, and sacred time, which redeems life by inundating the soul
in the river of the eternal spring of the Spirit.

Likewise, miracles mark an irruption of the Eternal Order in the temporal.
And since the Eternal Order is real, this irruption takes place no matter how
much the downward flow of time, which characterizes cosmic and historical
cycles, makes the temporal world appear to be independent of the Eternal. In
the occurence of miracles, not only are the ordinary laws of physical existence
penetrated by laws belonging to higher orders of reality, but the ordinary rapport
between time and Eternity is drastically changed. The particular time-span in
which the miracle takes place partakes of the Eternal and hence the trace of
such a 'time' impringes itself in a permanent manner upon the souls of the
individuals who have experienced the miraculous event. This is true for miracles
of a limited nature surrounding a particular saint or sage as well as the major
miracles surrounding the life of the founder of a new religion or an *avatāra*.
In the latter case, the perfume of the Eternal subsistsd permanently for a whole
human collectivity, who therefore celebrate such events annually or in other
cyclic periods of times on occasions which transcend history and bring the life
of the humanity concerned back again and again to that moment when Heaven
and earth touched each other and when the Eternal transformed a particular
span of cosmic and historical time.[18]

One cannot speak of the penetration of the Eternal into the temporal order
without mentioning sacred art, which lies at the heart of traditional art and
is most directly concerned with the central rites, myths and symbols of the
religion that has given rise to the tradition in question.[19] Since the sacred is
the "presence" of the Eternal in the temporal, of the Center in the periphery,
sacred art marks also the "presence" of the Eternal in the human order. Of
course, by sacred art is not meant only an art that has a religious theme but

one which is executed according to norms of traditional art and reflects symbols and forms of an ultimately Divine Origin, forms which are earthly reflections of the celestial archetypes which Plato called the *paradigma*. Therefore, postmedieval European religious art is not sacred but only religious art, as is much of the popular religious art of Asia which has been created during the past two centuries as a result of the influence of both European naturalistic and humanistic art and a certain weakening of the spiritual forces within Asian civilizations and the decadence into which tradidtional civilizations have fallen in modern times.[20]

Truly sacred art, whether it be architecture or painting, poetry or music, pierces through the veils of temporal existence to confront the beholder with a reality which shines from the other shore of existence, from the Eternal Order. When one stands before the Himpi Temple near Madras, in the interior of the Jāmiʿ Mosque of Isfahan or before the portals of the Chartres cathedral, one is not standing only in India, Persia or France but at the "center" of the cosmos joined by the forms of the sacred art in question to that Center which is beyond time and which is none other than the Eternal. Likewise, a Japanese Buddhist statue of the eleventh or twelfth century, a traditional Tibetan *t'hanka*, a Sung landscape painting, an icon of the Eastern Christian Church or an illuminated Mamlūk Quran, all of which play a role in the total economy of the religious and ritual life of the religions in question, mark the presence of a reality which is not of this world of change, becoming and death. They belong to the Eternal while residing miraculously in the world of time and space which surrounds man in his earthly journey.

The same holds true for poetry and music. The verses of a Dante or a Rūmī, of Kalidasa or a Li T'ai Po, or the melodies of an Indian *raga* or a Gregorian chant are not tainted in their impact upon the beholder by the limitations of temporality but seem to have issued from a timeless source. That is why they speak to us so eloquently and are so much more 'timely' than productions of much more recent origin which, belonging only to 'their times' and impervious to the reality of the Eternal, have already become outmoded and 'timed.' In fact now more than ever before, in a world which has lost its moorings and can no longer envisage time as the moving image of Eternity, there is nothing more timely than the 'timeless' whether it be in art or thought.

The truly timeless is none other than the Eternal. The symbols, forms and inspiration of sacred art issue not from the domain of contingency wherein a particular artist resides, but from the Eternal, to which the traditional masters who have produced the models and also supreme examples of sacred art have had access thanks to the methods of spiritual realization and a grace (or what in Arabic is called *barakah*) made possible by tradition. Sacred art opens a door, whether it be through stone or ink, words or melodies, to the Beyond, to the reality which does not become but is. Through sacred art man is able to transcend his temporal accidentality and regain that paradisal state whose beatitude is reflected here below for those who are able to receive the message of such art, in the joy of the experience of sacred art.

The reflection of the Eternal in the temporal order through the forms of sacred art is directly related to the beauty which such forms of art emanate. Beauty is a Divine Quality as stated in the Islamic context in the famous saying of the Prophet, "God is beautiful and He loves beauty." As "the splendor of the Truth," to quote the famous saying of Plato, beauty belongs to the Divine and hence the Eternal Order, despite its ambivalence for souls caught in the throes of human passion. For the contemplative, beauty is the gateway to the Eternal as well as the bark that carries man to the abode of Eternity.

On a deeper level, it might be said that beauty *is* itself the "presence" of the Eternal in time. That is why the experience of great beauty transforms the very meaning of time even in ordinary human experience, while its experience on the highest level is synonymous with the direct experience of the Eternal Order. One needs only recall the case of Ramakrishna who would go into a state of *samādhi* on beholding a thing of beauty or of numerous Sufi saints who would experience the ecstasy of Divine Union in hearing a beautiful melody or poem. If time is the moving image of Eternity, it is also a condition for a form of existence, namely the physical and terrestrial, in which through sacred art and the beauty it reflects the image stands still and the Eternal itself shines forth as if there were no time. In those instances in human life when man is permitted to experience great beauty, or for that matter great love which is inseparable from beauty, he is transported beyond the realm of temporality. He is allowed to savor something of the Eternal Order and share, albeit for a moment, in the never ending-ecstasy of the eternal life, which the saints and sages whose gaze is fixed upon Eternity enjoy inwardly even here below.

It might appear as paradoxal, but virgin nature, that grand work of sacred art created by the Supreme Artisan, also manifests the beauty of the Eternal Realm through its forms and rhythms, through the grace that flows from her and the subtle metaphysical message imprinted upon the pages of cosmic reality. One usually thinks of nature only as the abode of change bound in the clutches of time, and indeed that is what it is if viewed scientifically and from the point of view of natural philosophy, the word *natura* itself being the Latin equivalent to the Greek *physis*, which means that which is born and enters into the domain of change. But there is not only nature as *natura naturata* but also as *natura naturans*, to use the medieval Scholastic distinction between "created" and "creating" nature.[21] An eternal reality shines through the very forms and processes of change which we identify with nature, a reality to which modern science is totally impervious. This reality was, however, the very foundation of the traditional cosmologies and sciences of nature.It also remained and still remains the vivid background for the daily experience of nature by traditional man, who perceives, thanks to tradition, the permanent forms reflected upon the surface of that flowing river of time in which man cannot ever put his finger in the same water twice.

Despite the ravages brought upon nature by modern civilization and the destruction of so many of the natural life-patterns on earth, the face of nature as reflecting the Eternal has not by any means disappeared. Not only the vast vault of the heavens and the dark starry night remind us of the immensity of the Beyond and the 'coldness' of Eternity, but the ever renewed life of the animals and plants recalls the joys of paradisal life beyond the transient character of the temporal order. Every blooming flower is a message from the Eternal Order and its withering a reminder that time is not Eternity and that, although we live in time, we are born for a destiny beyond the world which dies and perishes. We are destined for other worlds into which we enter upon leaving this earthly life in a condition that is determined by our mode of living in time and by whether we have been able to experience time as the moving image of Eternity or have absolutized the temporal order as if it were the only reality.

To be human is to experience a mode of existence in which every moment of time is related vertically to Eternity and in which the mode of one's being and action determines one's final end beyond the temporal order, for as is so often emphasized in Hinduism the chain of one's *karma* affects one's posthumous state and as Islam insists, "this world is the sowing field for the Beyond." Time as experienced by man opens itself unto Eternity, for man by nature belongs to a reality beyond time while living in time. It is remarkable that even those who confine their perspective to a purely quantitative and profane science, can still write of "the history of time" and the origin of cosmic time with the big bang, which means that they can conceive of the origin of time and hence go beyond time. If they were to meditate more deeply upon what they assert even from a purely scientific point of view, they would realize that they must accept that there exists something in man, be it called consciousness or intelligence, whose reality belongs to an order beyond time and which can envisage not only time but also its origin and end. This alone would be proof enough that man is not simply the product of a temporal process. To be human is to be able to envisage the alpha and omega of time because to be human is to be able to relate every moment of time to the Eternal Order to which both the alpha and omega of the temporal process belong. The glory of the human state "so hard to attain" resides precisely in standing on the vertical axis between Eternity and time. If man remains faithful to his vocation and realizes the plenitude of the human state, he can in fact turn every moment of time into a direct echo of Eternity.

Man can realize and experience Eternity while residing in the temporal world through the realization of the Truth, through love and through correct action based upon goodness,[22] these three modes corresponding to the three *margas* of Hinduism, namely, *jñāna*, *bhakti* and *karma* and the *ma'rifah*, *maḥabbah* and *makhāfah* of Islam. Man can transform the time which accompanies the beating of his heart and the rhythm of his terrestrial life and which leads him ineluctably to the end of his earthly existence into a constellation of eternal moments in which he lives already in Eternity while walking and living among men. He can do so by knowing the Truth through that total mode of knowing which illuminates and transforms the being of the knower, and which already belongs to the Eternal Now, where the duality of knower and known is transcended. He can also transcend time through that love which breaks the boundaries of his individualistic ego and allows the grace and mercy which issues from the Beyond to inundate his being, enabling him to experience a reality beyond time. Likewise, selfless action based upon goodness opens the human microcosm to contact with the source of all goodness, which is none other than the Supreme Good or the Eternal Itself. Selfless action based upon goodness frees the soul, albeit for a moment, from the experience of time as confinement and opens it to the universal order which stands above and beyond the temporal.

The alchemy which transforms the flow of time to a constellation of eternal moments and finally the single Moment—which appears multiple only because of its reflection in the mirrors of the manifold cosmic order—is accomplished most of all through prayer and with the aid of the beauty that emanates from sacred art and virgin nature. In praying man already transcends time, while in the prayer of the heart, that quintessential prayer in which the Divine Spark at the center of man's being returns to its Source, the moment of time itself becomes Eternity, and the truth that *māyā* is *Ātman* becomes realized. He whose heart resides in the Eternal Order has gone beyond the illusion of according to *māyā* the status of reality or even of having understood the distinction between *Ātman* and *māyā*. He has realized that ultimately *māyā* is *Ātman*, that time is none other than Eternity projected through the cosmogonic process unto the realm of becoming.

Man stands between the Eternity from which he issues forth and which is the alpha of his existence, which could also be called pre-Eternity (*al-azal* in Arabic), and the Eternity to which he ultimately returns which is the omega of his existence and which may be called post-Eternity (*al-abad* in Arabic). He is a being suspended in time between this alpha and omega. The alpha or *azal* determines his cosmogonic history and his reality up to the present point of the trajectory of his existence. The omega or *abad* marks his final encounter with the Absolute and the Eternal, the last syllable of his book of existence. How he lives in time and what attitude he displays vis-à-vis the Eternal determine the mode of this journey of return.

The spiritual man is already aware, while living in time, of the alpha from which he has issued and the omega to which he returns. He has in fact already returned inwardly to that omega which is also his origin or alpha. He has already transmuted the time which is 'his time' into the Eternal Now which belongs to the Eternal Order. For such a person, in the word of Shams al-Dīn Maghribī,

> Pre-Eternity has become post-Eternity in his mansion,
> While in our world post-Eternity has become pre-Eternity.

How fortunate is he who has realized the unity of the present moment with the alpha and omega of existence. Such a person has realized the fullness of human existence, for to be truly human is to transcend time, to realize the timeless in the temporal order and to bear witness to the Eternal in the world of time in which destiny has placed us. To be veritably human is to fix one's gaze upon Eternity while journeying in time, to travel with the caravan of earthly life while harkening to the call of the Beyond. He who lives in time while fully aware of the Eternal Order has already transcended time and its withering effect. Such a person has not lived in vain. Rather, he has realized what it means to be truly human, to be a being plunged into the river of time but made for immortality.

Notes

1. Some of the most salient quotations from traditional sources concerning time and Eternity have been collected in the masterly study of A.K. Coomaraswamy, *Time and Eternity* (Delhi, 1988).

2. This term is also used in a theological and religious context in a manner that is problematic and that has caused endless theological and philosophical disputes, namely in the phrase "eternal damnation", concerning which mainstream Christian and Islamic theology have different attitudes. It is important to note that in referring to suffering in hell, the Quran uses the term *khālid*, which means everlasting or perpetual, rather a term such as *abad* or *sarmad*, which mean Eternity. For a profound analysis of the idea of Eternity as it concerns man's posthumous states see F. Schuon, *In the Face of the Absolute* (Bloomington, Ind. 1989), pp. 43–52.

3. We use the term intellection as being related to intellect (*intellectus, al-'aql, buddhi*) which, as mentioned earlier, is the *principle* of reason and is distinct from reason in as much as the latter is identified with the analytical functions of the mind.

4. Concerning these basic conditions of the phenomenal world, see F. Schuon, *From the Divine to the Human*, p. 57ff.

5. This point has been discussed by W. Smith in his *Cosmos and Transcendence: Breaking through the Barrier of Scientific Belief* (La Salle, Ill., 1984)

6. This theme has been treated in a magisterial manner by F. Schuon in several of his writings, especially *From the Divine to the Human, In the Face of the Absolute* and *Esoterism as Principle and as Way*. See also S.H. Nasr, *Knowledge and the Sacred*, p. 130ff.

7. In Christian theology this distinction is often glossed over and the term eternal is used in reference to both the paradisal and infernal states, although there are views to the contrary. In Islamic theology the distinction is clearer, although still disputed among exoteric religious authorities. From a metaphysical point of view, however, it can be said without reservation that Eternity in the ultimate sense belongs only to the pole of Being and not becoming and therefore only that which is can be said to be truly eternal in contrast to perpetual or perennial.

8. It was to safeguard the majority of believers who are not metaphysicians that Muslim, Christian and Jewish theologians attacked so vehemently the idea of the eternity of the world as one sees in the treatises of John Philopponos and al-Ghazzālī, while philosophers such as Ibn Sīnā who defended the *qidam* or literally 'oldness' of the world, a term which is also usually translated as eternity, insisted upon the world's contingency (*imkān*). Although opposed to each other, both the philosophers and theologians were trying in their own way to preserve the basic distinction between the Absolute and the contingent.

9. The rapport of these functions to those of Śiva and Viṣṇu in Hinduism is obvious. See F. Schuon, *In the Face of the Absolute*, p. 51. Concerning the spiritual significance of Eternity and Omnipresence, both of which derive from the Divine Infinitude, Schuon writes,

> "the Divine Omnipresence, while constituting a threat to the proud and the evil-doers—and there is no 'mortal sin' without pride—has on the contrary something reassuring and consoling for the good, who in any case represent the norm; the Omnipresent is the refuge that is everywhere accessible; those who love God are nowhere separated from Him. In its turn, however, the Divine Eternity, while nourishing the hope of the man who knows he is in exile here below and who aspires to the heavenly homeland, has about it something cold and terrifying from the point of view of earthly dreams; for the Eternal is He who is enthroned immutably above the evanescent things of this world below; He seems to look upon them with the implacability of the stars. Moreover, the name 'Eternal' is

synonymous with Majesty; whereas the Omnipresent is near, the Eternal is remote. The two aspects meet and merge in their common Infinitude, thus in Divinity as such." Ibid., pp. 51–52.

10. There are numerous myths and accounts in sacred history which can only be understood by having recourse to the doctrine of levels of time and experience of time beyond the measurable movements of the astronomical heavens, for example, the story of the Seven Sleepers of the Cave (ahl al-kahf) in the Quran (XVIII.8ff) and the story of the parade of the ants in Hinduism. For the former see the many studies of L. Massignon on the subject such as "Les sept dormants d'Ephèse (Ahl al-Kahf) en Islam et Chrétienté . . . ," *Revue des Etudes Islamique*, vol.26, (1958), pp. 1–9 and vol. 27 (1959), pp. 1–8. As for Hindu story, see H. Zimmer, *Myths and Symbols in Indian Art and Civilization*, ed. J. Campbell, (Princeton, 1974), pp. 3–10.

11. A brilliant analysis of these conditions of existence is given by Schuon in his *From the Divine to the Human*, p. 57ff. What follows in our discussion of phenomenal time is based on his exposition.

12. It must be emphasized that the cyclic idea of time differs from the linear in not only its "circularity" as against linearity, but also against its non-uniformity as against the uniformity of linear time. In this connection one must remember the contraction of time as the cycle flows from the *Krita* to the *Kali Yuga*. On the Hindu doctrine of cyclic time, see H. Zimmer, *Myths and Symbols*, pp. 11–19; and R. Guénon, *Formes traditionnelles et cycles cosmiques*, (Paris, 1970).

13. See Schuon, *From the Divine to the Human*, pp. 60–63.

14. This myth has been studied in depth and contrasted with the linear conception of time by M. Eliade in his *The Myth of the Eternal Return*, trans.W. Trask (Princeton, 1974).

15. See S.H. Nasr, *Knowledge and the Sacred*, chapter seven, "Eternity and the Temporal Order."

16. Dante (Paradiso, XVII.17). See W.N. Perry, *A Treasury of Traditional Wisdom* (New York, 1986), p. 838ff., where under the title of "The Eternal Now" the author has assembled this and numerous other texts drawn from diverse traditional sources to point to the unanimity of traditional teachings concerning the significance of the present moment as the nexus between man and Eternity. See also Coomaraswamy, *Time and Eternity*, most of which deals with the theme of the "Eternal Now."

It needs to be added that the fact that according to the theory of relativity there is no 'now' which is 'now' throughout the physical universe does not at all negate the significance of the Eternal Now from the metaphysical and also initiatic points of view.

17. Quoted by Perry, *A Treasury*, p. 840.

18. Examples of such realities abound in all religions, for example, the resurrection of Christ in Christianity or the martyrdom of Ḥusayn in Islam made permanent through

their annual celebration, which lifts these events above and beyond a specific historical time.

19. On traditional and sacred art, see the many writings of A.K. Coomaraswamy, F. Schuon and T. Burckhardt especially Coomaraswamy's *The Transformation of Nature in Art* (New York, 1956); and Burckhardt's *Sacred Art—East and West*, trans. Lord Northbourne (London, 1967).

20. On the distinction between sacred and religious art, see S.H. Nasr, *Islamic Art and Spirituality* (London, 1987), p. 64ff.

21. This distinction was drawn by John Scotus Erigena in the ninth century in his *Periphyseon* and became well known in later medieval European philosophy. See M.Cappuyns, *Jean Scot Erigène* (Brussels, 1969); and I.P. Sheldon-Williams (ed.) *Iohannis Scotti Eriugenae Periphyseon*, 3 vols. (Dublin, 1968-1981).

22. Beauty is present in all these modes of realization in different forms and degrees.

PART TWO

The Unity of the Divine Stratosphere—
The Diversity of the Human Atmosphere

One Is the Spirit and Many Its Human Reflections— Thoughts on the Human Condition Today

To speak of sacred science or the traditional metaphysics which provides the necessary and essential background for the cultivation of sacred science, necessitates discussing the question of the multiplicity of sacred forms as well as the denial of these forms by secularized man. While truth is one, its expressions are many, especially for modern man who lives in a world in which the homogeneity of the traditional ambience is destroyed and in which there is on the one hand the acceptance and in fact "absolutization" of secular man and the humanism based upon man conceived in such a manner, and on the other hand the presence of diverse sacred traditions whose reality can no longer be neglected. Consequently, if one is to address the human condition today, one must not only assert the unity of the truth and the oneness of the Spirit, but also the multiple reflections of the world of the Spirit in the human ambience. Furthermore, this task must be carried out with full awareness and critical appraisal of that process of secularization which has sought to destroy the reality of the world of the Spirit while praising the human spirit with all the ambiquities and deficiencies which the latter entails and replacing the traditional concept of man with one which divorces him from his Divine Archetype of which he is the earthly embodiment.

For several centuries, and in fact since the Renaissance, Western man has extolled the human spirit while de-sacralizing the whole of the cosmos in the name of the supremacy of man, only to end now in a situation which for the first time in history threatens man with truly infrahuman conditions on a scale never dreamt of before. Clearly the classical humanism which claimed to speak for man has failed,[1] and if there is to be a future for man, there must be a profound change in the very concept of what man is and a thorough re-examination of the secular humanism of the past few centuries in the light of the vast universal and perennial spiritual traditions of mankind which this humanism has brushed aside with the claim of giving man freedom. Today people speak with passion of the human family and the unity of mankind, but if there is to be a human family, its members must first of all be human themselves.

One cannot cry with compassion for the human family while dehumanizing human beings in the name of purely earthly well-being. In fact, the experience of the recent past has shown that even on the level of preserving the quality of even a purely earth-bound human life, modern civilization is facing grave problems to say the least and, far from freeing man, has enslaved him as never before. Man must be rendered his humanity again if there is going to be even hope for the continued existence of humanity, and this can only be achieved through the rebirth of the traditional conception of man which the Promethean revolt of the modern world has placed in oblivion,[2] and an understanding of other human beings whose life and culture reveal other reflections of the one Spirit which resides at the center of the being of all men and women whether they be of the East or the West.

The current concept of man as a self-centered creature not responsible to any authority beyond himself and wielding infinite power over the natural environment cannot but end in the aggression of man against himself and the world of nature on a scale which now threatens his own existence. The type of Promethean man who conceives himself as being in revolt against God, complete master of his own and others' destinies and possessing unbounded energy and power over the earth, which is used to an ever greater degree to quench his insatiable passions, cannot but reach a state of disequilibrium and chaos which is exactly what modern man faces at every juncture of his life today. This disequilibrium leads occasionally to war, which is its most obvious and threatening symptom. At this point an attempt is being made to overcome this symptom and to establish some kind of peace. But this is carried out not with the hope of correcting this disequilibrium and of turning the chaos into order but of allowing the innately unstable state of things to continue somewhat longer without excessive disturbance. Few even ask if modern man deserves to live in peace while he is at war inwardly with the inner man, who despite everything continues to live within him, and outwardly with the cosmic order and the metacosmic Reality, which continue to be present and will have the final word whether man heeds the call of the Real or not.

To prop up the disequilibrium which he carries within himself, modern man has sacrificed everything at his disposal. He has accepted to forgo the certitude of metaphysical and religious doctrine and even accept that two and two makes three in order to compromise with someone who has insisted that it makes two. He has raped nature with unparalleled ferocity in order to fulfill ever increasing "needs" which in turn enable him to forget himself, his end and the purpose of life as much as possible.[3] He has turned the urban environment into a veritable hell on the way to establishing heaven on earth.

Nothing has escaped being sacrificed to sustain the disequilibrium contained innately in the modern concept of man, nothing—from religion to virgin nature, and finally to the sacrosanct character of the human person itself. But all this is of no avail because the disequilibrium continues and threatens at every moment to cause the destruction of the world of those who have so glibly and so persistently defended the concept of man as the lord of the earth, possessed of unlimited power to do what he wills, and even with pretentions of eradicating every form of evil from human life, as if anything other than the absolute Good could be absolutely good and anything other than Perfection Itself could be devoid of the mark of imperfection.

To speak of the possibility of a happy future or simply a future for mankind without a fundmental change in the currently held conception of what man is, is no more than a sentimental and fleeting dream. Men want to live together and they must literally live together more than ever before thanks to the destruction of the ecological equilibrium and the population explosion which are the fruits of modern man's own doings and which cannot be blamed upon traditional civilizations, in which man was seen as the theomorphic being that he is. And in order to live together, men speak of the one human spirit, a single human family or the global village. But they are forced to remain content with only speaking about such ideals. The one spirit somehow evades modern man, leaving in its wake a multitude of contending egos, of feuding families and of general social disintegration. Nevertheless people continue to speak in these terms, seeing the necessity of living together on a planet whose resources cannot bear any longer any major aggressions against either other nations or the natural order.

The oneness which people of good intention seek cannot, however, be achieved save through contact with the Spirit, which is one in itself and many in its earthly reflections. The noble Quran mentions concerning the Spirit that it is "from the command of my Lord" (*qul al-rūḥ min amrⁱ rabbī*) (XVII.85). No contact with the Spirit is possible save through the dimension of transcendence, which stands always before man and which connects him with the Ultimate Reality whether It be called the Lord or Brahman or *śūnyata*. To forget the Spirit and settle for its earthly reflections alone is to be doomed to the world of multiplicity, to separation, division and finally aggression and war. No amount of extolling the human spirit can fill the vacuum created by the forgetting of the Spirit which kindles the human soul but is not itself human. It is necessary to realize the unity of the Spirit behind the multiplicity of religious forms in order to reach the peace that human beings seek. The human spirit as understood in the humanist sense is not sufficient unto itself to serve as basis for the unity of humanity and human understanding across cultural and religious frontiers. What is essential is that sacred science of religious forms and symbols which transforms opaque facts into transparent symbols and apparent obstacles into bridges to another world of discourse.

In Islamic thought, and following the language of the Quran, the spiritual dimension of man is identified with the "face of God" (*wajh Allāh*), which is also the aspect of the Divinity turned towards the world. To speak of the human spirit without consideration of the Spirit in its transhuman reality is to speak essentially of a faceless humanity which is then reduced by force to animality and the tedious uniformity which stands at the very antipode of Unity.[4]

The problems faced by modern man all point to the same cause, namely to man's living below his own possibilities and to the forgetfulness of who he is. Today those who have pondered over the human condition and the future of man with any degree of depth assert in unison that certain new and at the same time old qualities must be cultivated by man if he is to survive, qualities such as self-restraint, humility, charity towards one's neighbor including the world of nature, magnanimity, justice, etc. But to allow a heavy stone to fall and then extol the way it accelerates is one thing, and to move against gravity quite another. What is going to induce men and women, whom all the external forces of human society have been pushing to an ever greater degree of outwardness, of self-aggrandizement, and the like in recent centuries, to suddenly turn towards the inner pole and to become transmuted from the state of a falling stone to that of a soaring eagle? What force is able to turn the interest of men from purely quantitative growth to the qualitative which so many students of the ecological crisis suggest as the only hope for averting a major catastrophe? If some think that sentimental assertions or political resolutions will achieve such ends, they are mistaken, for they neglect completely the power of the human passions, of the dragon within, which only a St. George can slay.

The reversal of all the tendencies which are now threatening the whole of life on earth and are making the very existence of a future for man doubtful amidst all his futurology, cannot come save through the reversal of the pole of attraction. Only contact with the Spirit can provide a pull from on high and reverse the powerful gravitation which drags men ever more rapidly downwards away from the Unity which characterizes the Spirit. To speak of one human family without recourse to this celestial pole is no more than to dream, with no guarantee that this dream will not turn into a nightmare.

Men speak with great confidence about creating the future and draw plans which appear perfectly logical on the level of blueprints, but which soon become tainted by all kinds of imperfections not envisaged at the planning stage. The reason is that the human beings who are thought to be agents for the execution of these plans are not seen to be what they really are, namely creatures with imperfections and with a lack of the necessary knowledge of the nature of things.

They are permeated with an imperfection which touches everything they do and which becomes more dangerous to the extent that its existence is denied. It is forgotten that no condition can be any better than the imperfect state of those who act in bringing it about.

The modern vision of remaking the world to bring about peace and harmony in the "human family" is again based upon a fallacy related to the false conception of man which has grown within modern civilization since the Renaissance, a concept which posits a perfection for man in his present state, a supposed perfection which is simply not there. The result of this falsification of the real nature of man, who lives below his possibilities yet does not recognize his own evils, is that reform in the modern world is carried out in every domain except in that which concerns man himself. Even the Divine Norms which can alone judge man and guide him towards perfection are deformed to fit his ever changing state. No one takes it seriously enough upon himself to ask whether modern man should not begin remaking the future by reforming himself and by seeing himself as he really is, namely God's vicegerent on earth, endowed with exceptional powers but also with great responsibility towards all creatures, a responsibility which he cannot shun at any price except through his own destruction.

The great role of religions today should be not to placate the weaknesses of modern man by reducing themselves to one more 'ism' or ideology to compete with the many existing ideologies which man has spun around himself over the past few centuries. Rather, their task is to hold before men the norm and the model of perfection of which they are capable and to provide the channels for that contact with the Spirit which alone can show the myriad colors and hues of the human spirit to be not sheer multiplicity and division but so many reflections of Unity. Their task is also to present to the contemporary world the sacred science and wisdom which they have guarded in their bosom and within their inward dimension over the millennia. The human spirit is One only at the summit of the human soul. Therefore, means must be found for men to climb to this summit of their own being. Otherwise on the level of external forms, of the earthly aspect of the human soul, there reigns but multiplicity leading to division and strife, and now, thanks to new means of destruction there is the possibility of total annihilation.

The incomparable Persian Sufi poet Jalāl al-Dīn Rūmī sang already seven centuries ago that:

The difference between creatures comes from outward form:
When the meaning (literally the Spirit) is reached there is peace.

Man can only live in harmony if he lives on the level of the full possibilities of the human state, which means centrality and authority on the terrestrial plane combined with responsibility, but which is also inseparable from receptivity toward Heaven and of submission to the Divine Norm which determines man from on high whether he wills it or not. Man can speak of one human spirit provided he envisages the human spirit as an extension and reflection of the Divine Spirit and searches for his oneness at the summit where the terrestrial mountain touches the infinite expanses of the sky, where man leaves the human atmosphere to enter into the Divine Stratosphere where alone harmony among various forms and manifestations of the Spirit resides.

One can speak of a single humanity provided the sacrosanct character of man is preserved as well as the hierarchy which resides in the nature of things. It is possible to speak of a human family provided the sacred origin of the family is understood. In nearly all religions there has always been a holy or sacred family which has served as the prototype of family life itself. For example, the family of the Prophet of Islam has served not only a purely religious function but also has been the model for every Muslim family from the social point of view. Over the millennia, therefore, as long as religion remained strong, men were not faced with any problems in preserving the institution of the family. But one cannot break the norm and cause an eclipse of the archetype and yet hope to preserve its earthly reflection. How can one speak of one human family for a generation in which the male and female elements within the primary family unit are in constant strife rather than harmony and equilibrium, where all sense of authority which is based on the hierarchy that is in the nature of things is forgotten and where the nuclear family is the target of bombardment from every direction leading to its splitting with the same success that man has been able to split the atom? If by the family is meant the painful chaos which so many of the young have come to experience in urban centers throughout the world during the past few decades, then it is better not to have one human family at all.

To live within the human family in the positive sense of family, to speak of the human spirit, to hope for peace and harmony means first and foremost that man should awaken to his own condition, that he should submit himself to a thorough criticism and reestablish peace and equilibrium within himself and vis-à-vis the Divine Norm. There is no hope for a peaceful future for a creature who is usurping his position and who is living in such a way as to be in total disequilibrium with regard to both the natural environment and members of those cultures which are still anchored in the teachings which have descended from the world of the Spirit. There is no hope for man to preserve his humanity unless he reaches for the transcendent beyond himself. To seek to be merely human is ultimately to fall into the infrahuman state, as nearly five centuries of Western history have demonstrated amply for the whole world.

The condition of the world should cause us to pause and consider not only what we should do in the future but most of all what we should be, for only he who is what he should be according to the profoundest demands of the human state can also act rightly and according to the norms which of necessity govern all things. Only such a person can live at peace with himself, with other human beings and with the natural environment. Only such a person can come to possess that sacred science of forms which alone can enable men to understand the diversity of sacred religious forms and the unity which is veiled and revealed by this diversity and also to comprehend the significance of the cosmos and man's position in it. And ultimately it is upon the knowledge, words, acts and most of all presence of such persons, more than any form of socio-economic planning, that the possibility of the realization of the Oneness of the Spirit and of harmony among human beings living amidst diversity and the multiplicity of forms, depends. To be concerned with mankind in depth cannot but lead to the wish and prayer for the continuing and ever increasing presence, in all human societies, of persons in harmony with the Real and in possession of that sacred science which has been nearly completely eclipsed from the intellectual sky of modern man since the advent of modernism.

Notes

1. We have in mind here humanism as usually understood and associated with the secularizing tendencies of the Renaissance and not what some authors have called Christian, Jewish or Islamic humanism. Humanism as used in the current context means ultimately substituting the "Kingdom of Man" for the "Kingdom of God" and making terrestrial man the ultimate and final arbitrator and judge of truth and himself the reality which is of the highest value. See T. Lindbom, *The Tares and the Good Grain*, trans. A. Moore, (Macon, GA, 1988); and F. Schuon, *Light on the Ancient World*.

Even during the Renaissance itself, there were certain strands of thought which sought to cling to the traditional concept of man as a theomorphic being. This was true especially in the case of those who were interested in 'sacred science'. But this type of thought lost out to the type of thought which emphasized the notion of *virtù* and a rationalistic concept of man. See J.F. Maillard, "Science sacré et science profane dans la tradition ésotérique de la renaissance," *Cahiers de l'Université Saint Jean de Jerusalem*, vol.I (1974), pp. 111-26.

2. See Nasr, *Knowledge and the Sacred*, chapter five, "Man Pontifical and Promethean," p. 161ff. On the traditional concept of man, see also G. Eaton, *King of the Castle* (Cambridge, 1991), chapter 5; and G. Durand, *Science de l'homme et la tradition* (Paris, 1979). F. Schuon has also written many works on the traditional concept of man; see for example his *From the Divine to the Human*, part three p. 75ff. and S.H. Nasr (ed.), *The Essential Writings of Frithjof Schuon* (Rockport, Mass., 1991), p. 385ff.

3. See Nasr, *Man and Nature—The Spiritual Crisis of Modern Man* (London, 1989); and Ph. Sherrard, *The Rape of Man and Nature* (Ipswich, Suffolk, 1987).

4. See H. Corbin, *Face de Dieu, face de l'homme* (Paris, 1983), especially pp. 237–310, where he speaks of this theme in the context of Shi'ite esoterism.

CHAPTER FIVE

The Philosophia Perennis *and the Study of Religion*

In the absence of adequate metaphysical knowledge, the very diversity of religious and sacred forms poses a major challenge to the reformulation of a sacred science in a world so much in need of such a science. There is a great deal of study of diverse religions being carried out in both academic and more popular circles in the West, but there is little understanding of religious realities as religion and sacred forms as sacred realities. What is missing in most scholarly and academic circles is that science which can do justice to the study of religion by drawing from that perennial wisdom which lies at the heart of all religious traditions.

In fact one of the most remarkable characteristics of the current academic study of religion as such and religions in their relation with each other is that, despite the enormous theological difficulties encountered by Western scholars of comparative religious studies who are also interested in religion itself, so little attention has been paid in academic and religious circles to the approach of the traditionalist school which is none other than that of the perennial wisdom or *philosophia perennis*. One would imagine that at least in cases where one's current conceptual framework does not do justice to the subject at hand, one would be willing to consider seriously another point of view which has dealt in such a universal and comprehensive fashion with the study of religion both in itself and in the multiplicity of forms in which it has manifested itself in human history.

It is first of all necessary to clarify what is meant in this essay by *philosophia perennis*, which could also be called, from the point of view adopted here, *sophia perennis*, although the two terms are not completely identical, one emphasizing more the intellectual and the other the realized aspect of the same truth.[1] Since 'perennial philosophy,' the English equivalent of the Latin term, has been used widely by groups ranging from contemporary neo-Thomists to Aldous Huxley, whose celebrated book bearing this name[2] made the term famous for many nonspecialized students of religion and philosophy, it is necessary to clarify its meaning in the context of this study. By *philosophia perennis*—to which should be added the adjective *universalis*, as insisted upon so often by A.K. Coomaraswamy—is meant a knowledge which has always been and will always be and which is of universal character both in the sense of existing among peoples of different climes and epochs and of dealing with universal principles. This knowledge which is available to the intellect[3] is, moreover, contained at the heart of all religions or traditions,[4] and its realization and attainment is possible only through those traditions and by means of methods, rites, symbols, images and other means sanctified by the message from Heaven or the Divine which gives birth to each tradition. Although theoretically it is possible for man to gain this knowledge, at least on a more outward level, by himself because of the nature of the intellect, that "supernaturally natural" faculty which is ingrained in the very substance of man, the norm is such that the attainment of this knowledge depends upon the grace and the framework which tradition alone provides. If there are exceptions, they are there to prove the rule and bear witness to the well-known dictum that "the Spirit bloweth where it listeth."

The *philosophis perennis* possesses branches and ramifications pertaining to cosmology, anthropology, art and other disciplines, but at its heart lies pure metaphysics, if this latter term is understood, as already mentioned, as the science of Ultimate Reality, as a *scientia sacra*[5] not to be confused with the subject bearing the name metaphysics in postmedival Western philosophy. Metaphysics understood in the perspective of the *philosophia perennis* is a veritable "divine science" and not a purely mental construct which would change with every alteration in the cultural fashions of the day or with new discoveries of a science of the material world. This traditional metaphysics, which in reality should be used in the singular as metaphysic, is a knowledge which sanctifies and illuminates; it is gnosis if this term is shorn of its sectarian connotations going back to early Christian centuries. It is a knowledge which lies at the heart of religion, which illuminates the meaning of religious rites, doctrines and symbols and which also provides the key to the understanding of both the necessity of the plurality of religions and the way to penetrate into other religious universes without either reducing their religious significance or diminishing our own commitment to the religious universe to which we who wish to study other religions belong.

The approach of the *philosophia perennis* to the study of religion, as understood in this essay, is none other than the traditional approach as the term tradition has been understood and explained by masters and expositors of the teachings of what one can call the traditional school,[6] that is, such men as R. Guénon, A.K. Coomaraswamy, M. Pallis, T. Burckhart, M. Lings, Lord Northbourne, L. Schaya, W.N. Perry, H. Smith and especially F. Schuon. The point of view of this school should not be identified with either that sentimentalism that sees all religions as being the same or that neo-Vedantism which spread in America after the Second World War and which, despite the passing interest of some of its leading figures in the *philosophia perennis* and tradition, should not be confused with the traditional perspective. If there is one principle which all the traditional authors in question repeat incessantly, it is orthodoxy which they, however, do not limit to the exoteric level but also apply to the esoteric. They are orthodox and the great champions of universal orthodoxy. This point alone should clarify their radical difference from the neo-Vedantists and similar groups with whom they are often identified by opponents who have taken little care to examine in depth what the traditionalists have been saying.[7]

Those who have spoken from the perspective of the *philosophia perennis* have concerned themselves with every aspect of religion, with God and man, revelation and sacred art, symbols and images, rites and religious law, mysticism and social ethics, metaphysics, cosmology and theology. This school is concerned with religion in its transhistorical reality, refusing to accept the historicism of the academic approach to *Religionwissenschaft* developed in Europe in the nineteenth century. Yet, in contrast to the later school of phenomenology, it is not impervious to the historical unfolding of a particular tradition or the significance and the value of a particular religious 'phenomenon' in the cadre of a tradition which has its own distinct history. It can be seen even from the outside that the traditional school in fact encompasses more of the field of religion and allows a meaningful understanding of a greater portion of the very complicated reality of religion than any other available approach.[8] As for those who speak from within this perspective, they believe that only this school is able to provide the key to the understanding of the full length and breadth of both religion and religions, of the complexities and enigmas of a single religion and the significance of the plurality of religions and their interrelationship.

It is not possible to deal in detail here with the teachings of this school concerning all these issues. It would in fact require a separate book simply to summarize what the traditional authors have written on the different aspects of religion.[9] What we wish to deal with somewhat more fully is the approach of this school to the study of *religions*, and the multiplicity of sacred forms, that is, the field which has come to be known as comparative religion or the history of religion.

To understand the approach of the traditional school or the *philosophia perennis*, as here understood, to the study of religions, as well as religion as such, it is necessary to point out certain fundamental features of the vision of reality or the metaphysics which underlies all the teachings of this school.[10] According to the *philosophia perennis*, reality is not exhausted by the psychophysical world in which human beings usually function, nor is consciousness limited to the everyday level of awareness of the men and women of present-day humanity. Ultimate Reality, as pointed out already in the opening chapter of this book, is beyond all determination and limitation. It is the Absolute and Infinite from which issues goodness like the rays of the sun which of necessity emanate from it. Whether the Principle is envisaged as Fullness or Emptiness depends upon the point of departure of the particular metaphysical interpretation in question.[11] If a critic asserts, as in fact has been done, that according to this or that Oriental sage *māyā* is *Ātman* or *samsāra* is *nirvāna*, one can answer that such an assertion is only possible if one first realizes that *māyā* is *māyā* and *samsāra* is *samsāra*. The Principle can be envisaged as the Pure Object but also as the Pure Subject or the Supreme 'I', in which case ordinary consciousness is then seen as an outward envelope of the Supreme Self rather than the descent of the Supreme Reality into lower realms of the universal hierarchy. But in either case, whether seen as the Transcendent or the Immanent, the Principle gives rise to a universe which is hierarchical, possessing many levels of existence and of states of consciousness from the Supreme Principle to earthly man and his terrestrial ambience.

It is in this hierarchic universe that man's life takes place and possesses meaning. Religion is not only the key to the understanding of this universe, but also the central means whereby man is able to journey through the lower stages of existence to the Divine Presence, this journey being nothing other than human life itself as it is understood traditionally. The doctrines, symbols and rites of a religion possess therefore a meaning which is not confined to the spatio-temporal realm. In contrast to most modern theologians and philosophers and scholars of religion who have either consciously or unconsciously adopted the scientistic view which reduces Reality as such to physical or historical reality, the traditionalists refuse to reduce the existence of religion to only the terrestrial and temporal realm. Religion for them is not *only* the faith and practices of a particular human collectivity which happens to be the recipient of a particular religious message. Religion is not *only* the faith of the men and women who possess religious faith. It is a reality of Divine Origin. It has its archetype in the Divine Intellect and possesses levels of meaning and reality like the cosmos itself. If a religion were to cease to exist on earth, that does not mean that it would cease to possess any reality whatsoever. In this case its life cycle on earth would have simply come to an end, while the religion itself as an 'Idea' in the Platonic sense would subsist in the Divine Intellect in its transhistorical reality. The efficacy of its rites here on earth would cease, but the archetypal reality which the religion represents would persist.

The traditional school does not neglect the social or psychological aspects of religion, but it refuses to reduce religion to its social or psychological manifestations. Religion in its earthly manifestation comes from the wedding between a Divine Norm and a human collectivity destined providentially to receive the imprint of that Norm. From this wedding is born religion as seen in this world among different peoples and cultures. The differences in the recipient are certainly important and constitute one of the causes for the multiplicity of religious forms and phenomena, but religion itself cannot be reduced to its terrestrial embodiment. If a day would come when not a single Muslim or Christian were to be left on the surface of the earth, Islam or Christianity would not cease to exist nor lose their reality in the ultimate sense.

The radical difference between the traditionalists and most other schools of thought concerned with the study of religions comes precisely from this vast difference in the views they hold concerning the nature of reality. The traditionalists refuse to accept as valid that truncated vision of reality currently held in the Western world and arising originally from the postmedieval rationalism and empiricism that became prevalent in Europe and came to constitute the background for most of religious studies especially in academic circles. It must be remembered, however, that the perspective held by the traditionalists is the same as the worldview within which the religions themselves were born and were cultivated over the millennia until the advent of the modern world. That is why the traditional studies of religion are able to penetrate into the heart of the subject in such a fashion and also why these studies, in contrast to those of most modern scholars of religion, are so deeply appreciated by the traditional authorities of different religions outside the modern Western world and its cultural extensions into other parts of the globe.

The school of the *philosophia perennis* speaks of tradition and traditions. It believes that there is a Primordial Tradition which constituted original or archetypal man's primal spiritual and intellectual heritage received through direct revelation when Heaven and earth were still 'united.' This Primordial Tradition is reflected in all later traditions, but the later traditions are not simply its historical and horizontal continuation. Each tradition is marked by a fresh vertical descent from the Origin, a revelation which bestows upon each religion lying at the center of the tradition in question its spiritual genius, fresh vitality, uniqueness and the "grace" which make its rites and practices operative, not to speak of the paradisal vision which constitutes the origin of its sacred art or of the sapience which lies at the heart of its message. But because the Origin is One and also because of the profound unity of the human recipient despite important existing racial, ethnic and cultural differences, the fact that there is both the Primordial Tradition and traditions does not destroy the perennity and universality of the *philosophia perennis*. The anonymous tradition reflects a remarkable unanimity of views concerning the meaning of human life and the fundamental dimensions of human thought in worlds as far apart as those of the Eskimos and the Australian Aborigines, the Taoists and the Muslims.

The conception of religion in the school of the *philosophia perennis* is vast enough to embrace the primal and the historical, the Semitic and the Indian, the mythic and the 'abstract' types of religions. Tradition, as understood by such masters of this school as Schuon, embraces within its fold all the different modes and types of Divine Manifestation. The doctrine of tradition thus conceived makes it possible to develop a veritable theology of comparative religion—which in reality should be called a metaphysics of comparative religion—able to do theological justice to the tenets of each religion while enabling the student of religion, who is at once interested objectively in the existence of religions other than his own and is at the same time of a religious nature himself, to cross frontiers as difficult to traverse as that which separates the world of Abraham from that of Krishna and Rama or the universe of the American Indians from that of traditional Christianity.

In the same way that the rejection of the reality of hierarchy in its metaphysical sense by so many modern scholars has affected their worldview and methodology in every field and domain, the acceptance of this principle constitutes an essential feature of the traditionalist school in its study of religion in its different aspects. Religion itself is hierarchically constituted and is not exhausted by its external and formal reality. Just as the phenomenal world necessitates the noumenal—the very word phenomenon implying a reality of which the phenomenon is the phenomenon—the formal aspect of religion necessitates the essential and the supra-formal. Religion possesses at once an external, outward or exoteric dimension concerned with the external and formal aspect of human life, but, because it is religion, it is in itself sufficient to enable man who follows its tenets and has faith in its truths to lead a fully human life and to gain salvation. But religion also possesses an inner or esoteric dimension concerned with the formless and the essential with means to enable man to reach the Supernal Essence here and now. Moreover, within the context of this most general division, there are further levels within both the exoteric and the esoteric, so that altogether there exists within every integral religion a hierarchy of levels from the most outward to the most inward which is the Supreme Center.

There is also in religion a hierarchy of approaches to the Ultimate Reality which can again be summarized in a schematic fashion as the ways of work, love and knowledge, the already cited and famous *karma marga, bhakti marga* and *jñāna marga* of Hinduism or *al-makhāfah, al-maḥabbah,* and *al-ma'rifah* of Islam. Likewise, there is a hierarchy among followers of religion or human types seen from the religious perspective corresponding to these modes of approach to the Ultimate Reality. It is to these types that the sapiential tradition of the ancient Greeks referred as the *hylikoi, psychoi* and *pneumatikoi.* Islam also distinguishes between the *muslim,* the *mu'min* as well as the possessor of spiritual virtue or *iḥsān*, who is referred to in the Quran as *muḥsin*, although this latter term is not as common in later religious literature as the first two.[12]

The hierarchy of ways to God or of human types in their religious quest is innate to the paths or ways in question, the higher comprehending the lower in the sense of both understanding and encompassing it, but the lower not able to comprehend what stands beyond and above it. Hence the inner tension between various religious schools and paths even in traditional settings. These traditional oppositions, however, are very different in nature from the modern attack against the whole hierarchic perspective of the traditionalist school on the charges that it is "elitist" or something of the sort. If by this charge is meant that the traditional school accepts the saying of Christ that "many are called but few are chosen," then yes, it is elitist. This school asserts that not everyone is able to know everything, but it also affirms strongly that all levels of religion are precious and from Heaven, that all human beings can be saved if only they follow religion according to their own nature and vocation. It also asserts that with respect to the possibility of being able to call upon God and ultimately to reach the Divine, all human beings are equal by virtue of being human without this equality destroying the hierarchy mentioned or obliterating the obvious distinctions between human types, their aptitudes and capabilities. Being based on the primacy of knowledge, the *philosophia perennis* is elitist in the sense that it distinguishes between those who know and those who do not, according to the famous Quranic verse, "Are they equal, those who know and those who know not?" (XXXIX.9), which the Quran answers with a strong nay. What is difficult to understand is why this charge of elitism is even made by certain scholars, unless it be to keep up with current fads, but in that case one wonders why modern physics is not called elitist since some people are able to understand it and others are not able to master its tenets.

The *philosophia perennis* sees a unity which underlies the diversity of religious forms and practices, a unity which resides within that quintessential truth at the heart of religions that is none other than the *philosophia perennis* itself. But this unity is not to be found at the level of external forms. All religions do not simply say the same thing despite the remarkable unanimity of principles and doctrines and the profound similarity of applications of these principles.[13] The traditionalist school is opposed to the sentimental ecumenism which sees all religions as being the same at the expense of reducing them to a common denominator or of putting aside some of their basic teachings. On the contrary, the traditionalists respect the minutiae of each sacred tradition as coming ultimately from Heaven and to be treated with reverence, as every manifestation of the sacred should be. They are fully aware of the particular spiritual genius of each religion and its uniqueness and insist that these features are precise proof of the transcendent origin of each religion and the reality of its archetype in the Divine Intellect. These characteristics also demonstrate the falsehood of the view which would reduce a religion to simply historical borrowing from an earlier religion.

The unity to which the traditionalists refer is, properly speaking, a transcendental unity above and beyond forms and external manifestations.[14] The followers of this school would accept the current criticism of academic scholars against that levelling "unity of religions" movement that emanated mostly out of India during the last decades of the nineteenth and early decades of the twentieth century. Wherein they differ from most academic scholars of religion is that the traditionalists breathe within the traditional universe in which the reality of a thing, most of all, religious forms, rites and symbols, is not exhausted by its spatio-temporal aspect. Each form possesses an essence, each phenomenon is related to a noumenon, each accident issues from a substance. Using the language of traditional Western philosophy hallowed by its employment by the representatives of the *philosophia perennis* in the Latin Middle Ages, the traditionalists distinguish between the external form and the essence which that form manifests, or form and substance, so the external forms of a religion are seen as "accidents" which issue forth from and return to a substance that remains independent of all its accidents.[15] It is only on the level of the Supreme Essence even beyond the Logos or on the level of the Supreme Substance, standing above all the cosmic sectors from the angelic to the physical within which a particular religion is operative, that the ultimate unity of religions is to be sought. If as the Sufis say "the doctrine of Unity is unique" (*al-tawḥīd^u wāḥid*), one can also say that the transcendent unity underlying the diversity of religions cannot be but the Unique or the One Itself. Below that level, each religion possesses distinct qualities and characteristics not to be either neglected or explained away.

Within the particular genius and structure of each religion, however, one can discern certain features which are again universal. There is at the heart of every religion what Schuon calls the *religio perennis*,[16] consisting ultimately of a doctrine concerning the nature of reality and a method for being able to attain what is Real. The doctrinal language varies from one religion to another and can embrace concepts as different as those of *śūnyatā* and Yahweh. The method can also vary in numerous ways ranging from Vedic sacrifices to Muslim daily prayers. But the essence and goal of the doctrine and method remain universal within every religion.

The traditionalist school does not, moreover, simply place all religions alongside each other in the manner of a certain type of phenomenological approach which would collect religious phenomena without any normative judgment as if one were collecting molluscs. Basing itself on the knowledge provided by the *philosophia perennis*, the traditional school judges between grades of Divine manifestation, various degrees and levels of prophecy, major and minor dispensations from Heaven, and lesser and greater paths even within a single religion. It possesses a normative dimension and studies religions in the light of a truth which for it is truth and not something else, but it does so without falling into subjectivism. On the contrary, this truth alone permits the individual scholar to escape from the prison of subjectivism and the passing fads of a particular period within which the scholar in question happens to live, for this truth is supra-individual in nature, being a *sophia* that is at once perennial and universal.

It is in the light of this truth embodied in the *philosophia perennis* that the traditionalist school can also speak about truth and falsehood in this or that religious school as well as greater and lesser truth. The presence of this truth is also the reason why this school is able to be judgmental about a particular religious phenomenon and speak about authentic and pseudo-religion without falling into a narrow dogmatism on the one hand or simply indifference to truth on the other, two alternatives which dominate much of the religious scene in the modern world.

Based on the vision of the truth as such, as contained in the *philosophia perennis*, this school not only distinguishes between religion and pseudo-religion and different types of manifestations of the Divine Principle, but it also penetrates into each religious universe to bring out the meaning of its teachings in comparison with other religions and in the light of the perennial *sophia* without ending up in the relativization of religious truth. Today one of the major problems for man, in a world in which traditional boundaries and borders of both a physical and religious nature are removed, is how to study other religions sympathetically without losing the sense of absoluteness in one's own religion which is a *sine qua non* of the religious life and which reflects the fact that religion does come from the Absolute.

The traditional school insists on the study of religion religiously and opposes all the relativization that characterizes much of the modern academic study of religions, while also opposing that parochial conception of the truth which sees a particular manifestation of the Truth as the Truth as such. This school insists upon the principle which as a tautology should be obvious but is often forgotten, the principle being that only the Absolute is absolute. All else is relative. There is also a key concept, again developed most of all by Schuon, of an apparently contradictory nature but metaphysically meaningful, the concept of the 'relatively absolute.' Within our solar system our sun is *the* sun, while seen in the perspective of galactic space, it is one among many suns. The awareness of other suns made possible by means as abnormal to the natural and normal human state as the 'existential' awareness of several religious universes, does not make our own sun cease to be *our* sun, the center of *our* solar system, the giver of life to *our* world and the direct symbol of the Divine Intellect for *us* who are revivified by its heat and illuminated by its light.

In the same way, within each religious universe there is the logos, prophet, sacred book, avatāra or some other direct manifestation of the Divinity or messenger of His Word and a particular message which, along with its 'human container,' whether that be the Arabic language of the Quran or the body of Christ, are 'absolute' for the religious universe brought into being by the revelation in question. Yet only the Absolute is absolute. These manifestations are 'relatively absolute.'[17] Within each religious universe the laws revealed, the symbols sanctified, the doctrines hallowed by traditional authorities, the grace which vivifies the religion in question are absolute within the religious world for which they were meant without being absolute as such. At the heart of every religion is to be found the echo of God exclaiming "I". There is only one Supreme Self who can utter "I," but there are many cosmic and even metacosmic reverberations of the Word which is at once one and many and which each religion identifies with its founder. As Jalāl al-Dīn Rūmī, speaking as a Muslim saint, says:

When the number hundred has arrived, ninety is also present.
The name of Aḥmad (the Prophet of Islam) is the name of all prophets.

The traditional school studies the ethics, theology, mysticism or art of each religion in the light of the absoluteness of its Divine Origin, without either negating the other manifestations of the Absolute or the possibilities of change and transformation which all things that exist in time must of necessity undergo. This school does not, however, identify the reality of religion only with its historical unfolding. Each religion possesses certain principial possibilities contained in its celestial archetype. These possibilities are realized or become unfolded in the historical period and within the humanity providentially determined to be the temporal and human containers of the religion in question. Each religious phenomenon is both a phenomenon of religious character in itself not to be reduced to any other category, and a phenomenon which reveals its full meaning only in the light of the archetypal reality of the tradition in question along with its historical unfolding. Not all religions, therefore, have at their disposal all of their possibilities in a state of actuality at a given moment of human history. Religions decay and even die in the sense that their earthly career terminates. They can also become revived as long as the nexus between their earthly manifestation and their celestial origin remains intact. For the traditionalist school it is not a question of which religion is "better" since all authentic religions come from the same Origin, but there does exist the question from the operative and practical point of view of what possibilities are available at a particular juncture of history, of what one can in practice follow and what is no longer in fact available at a given historic moment within a particular religion.[18]

The range of subjects within the field of religion treated by the followers of the *philosophia perennis* is very wide and their treatment is always in depth and in relation to what is essential. Studies emanating from this school have ranged from those concerning the most subtle aspects of Christianity to Jodo-Shin Buddhism, from the ancient Egyptian religion to contemporary Islam. Such major subjects in religious studies as Tibetan Buddhism and the Sufism of the school of Ibn 'Arabī were first dealt with in their fullness in the modern West by the traditionalists.[19] The meaning of the sacred art of the Orient in general and Hindu and Buddhist art in particular was first brought to the attention of the West by A.K. Coomaraswamy, one of the foremost figures of the traditionalist school, while the rapport between Islamic and Christian spirituality in its multifarious dimensions has never been treated with such amplitude and depth as in the works of Schuon. The religious subjects dealt with by this school range from metaphysics and cosmology to sacred art with which they are especially concerned, and from traditional psychology and anthropology to ethics and social structure, for only through the sacred form can one reach the Formless.[20]

The followers of this school emphasize the importance of scholarship and some like Coomaraswamy have been among the greatest scholars who have ever lived. They pay much attention to philological considerations and historical facts, but they are neither philologists nor slaves to some form of historicism. They distinguish between historiality and historicism and do not follow the implicitly accepted guideline of many a modern scholar for whom what one does not observe in physical or archaelogical and historical records simply does not exist. The approach of the traditionalists is, rather, metaphysical. They go from principles to their applications, but their religious studies are no less scholarly, scientifically accurate or logical than that of those academic scholars who work with other conceptual frameworks and methods of research. It could in fact be said that from the point of view of logical rigor, few academic works can match those of the traditionalist school whose major figures are all at once metaphysicians, theologians, logicians and scholars.

Nowhere is the combination of those qualities more clearly observable than in the works of Schuon, who is certainly the greatest figure of this school in the field of religion. In his work is to be found a remarkable combination of metaphysical penetration and 'theological concern' in the sense of traditional Christian theology, poetic sensitivity and trenchant logic, objective concern for the truth and love and compassion for that immortal being who is the subject of all religious injunctions and the recipient of the Divine Message.[21] Among the traditional authors it is especially he who has given the most extensive and comprehensive exposition of religion from the point of view of the *philosophia perennis*, including a large number of studies devoted to the spiritual significance of the *anthrōpos* and the role of what he calls "the human margin" in certain aspects of religious life and thought which cannot be understood or explained except by means of the comprehension of the nature of the human recipient and the ambiguities of the human soul.[22]

Since the traditionalist school encompasses so much and has dealt with so many aspects of religion in depth and in such a unique fashion, it might be asked why it is not better known in academic circles. Why is it that in France where the books of Guénon are still reprinted regularly fifty or sixty years after their appearance, he is passed over nearly completely in silence in university circles, and why in other countries where there is not the same planned conspiracy of silence the situation is not much better? The reason must be sought in the nature of the *philosophia perennis* itself. To accept to follow it demands not only the dedication of the mind of the scholar but his whole being. It needs a total *engagement* which is more than many scholars are willing to give except those who speak as committed Christians, Jews, Muslims, etc. from the vantage point of their own particular religion. In the academic world of religious studies, however, such a total *engagement* does not come easily. For the traditionalist school the study of religion and religions is itself a religious activity and of religious significance. In this point, they share the lifelong concern of a small number of academic scholars of religion such as W.C. Smith and H. Corbin. For the traditionalists, as for this small circle of academic scholars, the study of religion can only be meaningful if it is itself of religious significance. And their studies are indeed religiously significant and often "disturbing" for those with ultimate concerns. There are therefore fewer scholars attracted to the traditionalist school, which demands so much of its adherents.

Nevertheless, as other contemporary maps of the high seas of theology and religion lead ships into the whirlwind of debilitating and mortally dangerous storms and fashionable "isms" remain incapable of either explaining major features of religion or of providing serious orientation even of a purely theoretical nature in the field of comparative religious studies, more and more the teachings of the followers of the *philosophia perennis* gain the attraction of scholars in the academic world, especially in America and Great Britain, where there is greater openness academically in the field of religious studies than elsewhere. During the past years not only have some well-known scholars of religion adopted the traditional perspective as their own,[23] but to an ever greater degree other notable scholars have become attracted to this school as at least one of the schools of religious studies to be considered seriously.[24]

Interest in this school is also bound to grow as the need for ecumenism is felt to an increasing degree, while most current ecumenism leads to a lessening of religious fervor and the diluting of the Divine Message, making worldly peace the goal of religion rather than the Divine Peace which surpasseth all understanding. The followers of the *philosophia perennis* chart a course that makes possible an authentic ecumenism, which can in fact only be esoteric, for religious harmony can only be achieved in the "Divine Stratosphere," to quote Schuon, and not in the human atmosphere where so many seek it today at the expense of reducing the Divine Stratosphere to the human atmosphere.

The traditional school, far from being a modern innovation drawn from some neo-Vedantic strand of modern Hinduism, bases itself upon that ancient and venerable wisdom—which in fact was sometimes called in the West *philosophia priscorium*—the *sanātana dharma* of Hinduism or the *al-ḥikmat al-khālidah* of the Islamic traditional known also under its Persian name *jāwīdānkhirad*. The *philosophia perennis* has always been present. What the expositors of this school have done is to forge certain keys from its enduring substance in order to open the doors which block the way of modern man today. The solutions they propose for the questions which arise from the study of both religion in the context of the modern secular world and religions in relation with each other, deserve to be considered seriously by all who are interested in the religious significance of religious studies today. Their views are significant for all concerned with the multiple reflection of the Spirit in the multiplicity of the human world and with the nature and destiny of men and women as beings whose very substance is molded from those realities with which religion has been concerned perennially, realities which are and will continue to be present as long as human beings live and breathe in this earthly abode.

Notes

1. On these terms and the history of the usage of *philosophia perennis*, see S.H. Nasr, *Knowledge and the Sacred*, p. 68ff; and C. Schmitt, "Perennial Philosophy: Steuco to Leibnitz," *Journal of the History of Ideas*, vol. 27 (1966), pp. 505–32.

2. See A. Huxley, *The Perennial Philosophy* (New York, 1945) and many later editions.

3. One of the most basic doctrines of the *philosophia perennis* is that *intellectus* is not to be confused with *ratio*. Reason as currently understood is the reflection upon the plane of the mind of the Intellect, which is able to know God directly and which is at once divine and of access to human beings provided they are aware of who they really are. On the distinction between intellect and reason as understood in the perspective in question, see F. Schuon, *The Transcendent Unity of Religions*, trans. P. Townsend (New York, 1975), pp. xxviii and 52; also F. Schuon, *Stations of Wisdom*, trans. G.E.H. Palmer (London, 1978), chapter I.

4. Tradition emphasizes more the aspect of continuity and transmission and religion revelation and the reception of a message of Divine Origin. Otherwise, the two constitute

basically the same reality. It needs to be added that throughout this book the term tradition is used, not as custom or habit, but as a truth and reality of transcendent Origin with its manifestations in history not only as religion, which lies at its heart, but also as art, philosophy, science, etc.

> It will already be apparent to the reader that by tradition more is meant than just custom long established. . . . All that can usefully be said of it at the moment is that wherever a complete tradition exists this will entail the presence of four things, namely a source of inspiration or, to use a more concrete term, of Revelation; a current of influence or Grace issuing forth from that source and transmitted without interruption through a variety of channels; a way of 'verification' which, when faithfully followed, will lead the human subject to successive positions where he is able to 'actualize' the truths that Revelation communicates; finally there is the formal embodiment of tradition in the doctrines, arts, sciences and other elements that together go to determine the character of a normal civilization. (M. Pallis, *The Way and the Mountain* [London, 1991], pp. 93–10).

See also Nasr, *Knowledge and the Sacred*, chapter two, "What is Tradition?"

5. See Nasr, *Knowledge and the Sacred*, chapter four.

6. In reality the traditional perspective cannot be considered from its own point of view as simply one school among others. But in the context of the contemporary world with numerous 'schools,' methodologies and philosophies for the study of practically any subject save science which insists upon the monopoly of its approach to the study of nature, it is legitimate to speak of the "traditional school" identified with the names mentioned above as well as others who cannot be cited here because of limitation of space. On the traditional school and its representatives, see Nasr, *Knowledge and the Sacred*, p. 100ff.

7. A case in point is the criticism of the late R.C. Zaehner against the writings of F. Schuon in his *The Comparison of Religions* (Boston, 1958), p. 169. Zaehner's uneasiness with Schuon's theses and in fact with gnosis or sapiential wisdom in general, a concern which is found also in Zaehner's study of Sufism, reflects more than anything else his own religious life and the inner fear he had of losing his faith in exoteric religion through the attraction of the esoteric, to which he was drawn by an inner sympathy and which he nevertheless sought to avoid because of the history of his own inner religious struggles and the fear of recurring skepticism.

8. It is interesting to note that one of the foremost American scholars of religion, Huston Smith, who has adopted the point of view of the *philosophia perennis*, has written that one of the factors which first drew him to this school and especially the works of F. Schuon was that the perspective of this school makes it possible to include so much of the religious universe within its all-inclusive embrace. This quality does not of course imply the indifference of the traditional point of view to pseudo-religion or falsehood,

theologically speaking. On the contrary, no school in the contemporary world has insited as much as this school on the necessity to emphasize the question of truth and therefore falsehood, without any sentimentality or rationalistic relativizing.

9. For the works of traditional authors on religion in its more exclusive sense and also the comparative study of religion, see R. Guénon, *Introduction to the Study of Hindu Doctrines*, trans. R. Nicholson (London, 1945); and his *Man and His Becoming According to the Vedanta*, trans. R. Nicholson (London, 1945); A.K. Coomaraswamy, *The Bugbear of Literacy* (Bedfont, 1979); and his *Hinduism and Buddhism*; M. Pallis, *The Way and the Mountain*; Lord Northbourne, *Religion in the Modern World* (London, 1963); and W.N. Perry, *A Treasury of Traditional Wisdom* (Bedfont, U.K. 1979).

As for the writings of F. Schuon, all of them are related to the domain of religion, but those which are most directly concerned with religion and wherein is to be found the most universal and penetrating study of diverse religions from the perspective of the *philosophia perennis* include *The Transcendent Unity of Religions*; *Formes et substances dans les religions* (Paris, 1975); *Esoterism as Principle and as Way*; *Christianity/Islam: Essays on Esoteric Ecumenism* (Bloomington, Ind., 1985); and *In the Face of the Absolute*; see also S.H. Nasr (ed.), *The Essential Writings of Frithjof Schuon*.

10. For a synopsis of this metaphysics, see F. Schuon, *From the Divine to the Human*; Schuon, *Survey of Metaphysics and Esoterism*; also R. Guénon, "Oriental Metaphysics" in J. Needleman (ed.), *The Sword of Gnosis* (Baltimore, 1974). For a more facile approach to these metaphysical doctrines as far as the general American public is concerned, see H. Smith, *Forgotten Truth* (San Francisco, 1992); and E.F. Schumacher, *A Guide for the Perplexed* (New York, 1977).

11. For the traditional school the Buddhist or Taoist vision of the Void does not at all negate the universality of the metaphysics enshrined in the *philosophia perennis*; in fact it provides a most powerful expression of this metaphysics in a language which is complementary but not contradictory to that of, let us say, Hinduism and Islam.

12. The Quran distinguishes between *islām*, *īmān* and *iḥsān*, literally "surrender," "faith" and "virtue." These terms in the traditional context refer definitely to a hierarchy. All Muslims, that is, those who accept the Quranic revelation, are *muslim*, but only a smaller number who possess great piety and intensity of faith are *mu'mins*, and even a smaller number, identified later with the Sufis, possess *iḥsān* and are *muḥsins*. See F. Schuon, *L'Oeil du coeur* (Paris, 1974), pp. 91–94; also S.H. Nasr, *Ideals and Realities of Islam* (London, 1989), pp. 133–34.

13. *The Treasury of Traditional Wisdom* of W.N. Perry is a monumental testament to this truth.

14. That is why perhaps the most important work of this school on the relation between religions, namely *The Transcendent Unity of Religions* of Schuon, was in fact entitled *De l'unité transcendante des religions* in its original French and not simply "de l'unité des religions."

15. See F. Schuon, *Formes et substances dans les religions.*

16. One of his more recent books in fact is entitled *Sur les traces de la religion pérenne* (trans. in his *Survey of Metaphysics and Esoterism*); see also his *"Religio Perennis"* in *Light on the Ancient Worlds*, trans. Lord Northbourne (London 1965), pp. 136–44.

17. On the highest metaphysical level it can be said that the Beyond-Being or Supra-Being is the Absolute and Being Itself the 'relatively absolute.'

18. As far as the crucial question of the practice of religion is concerned, which is beyond the scope of this essay, it must be emphasized that for the traditionalist school the goal of the study of religion is the participation in a tradition and the practice of religion. Otherwise religious studies would be as fruitless as studying musical notes without ever having the music performed, without ever hearing the actual music. As far as practice is concerned, the followers of the *philosophia perennis* insist first of all that one can practice only one religion and stand opposed to all forms of eclecticism and syncreticism of religious rites. Secondly, they repeat that while the intellectual study of other religions has become a necessity today, the practice of one integral religion is both necessary and sufficient, for as Schuon has stated, to have lived one religion fully is to have lived all religions.

19. We have in mind the *Peaks and Lamas* of M. Pallis, and *La Sagesses de prophètes* (*Fuṣūṣ al-ḥikam*) of Ibn 'Arabī, annotated and translated by T. Burckhardt.

20. Some of the most luminous pages on sacred art are to be found in the works of Coomaraswamy and Schuon, while those of T.Burckhardt are the first to make the spiritual significance of Islamic art fully known to the West.

21. On his writings and their significance, see the introduction of H. Smith to Schuon, *The Transcendent Unity of Religions*; and Nasr's introduction to *The Essential Writings of Frithjof Schuon*. The complete bibliography of Schuon is to be found in S.H. Nasr and W. Stoddart (eds.), *Religion of the Heart—Essays presented to Frithjof Schuon on His Eightieth Birthday* (Washington, D.C., 1991).

22. For a synthesis of Schuon's spiritual anthropology, see his *From the Divine to the Human*, p. 75ff. As for the question of the 'human margin,' see "La marge humaine" in Schuon's *Forme et substance dans les religions*, p. 185ff.; reprinted also in *In the Fact of the Absolute*, pp. 65–105; and *Esoterism as Principle and as Way*, part II.

23. We have in mind such scholars as J.E. Brown, V. Danner, H. Smith and J. Cutsinger in America and P. Moore and F. Whaling in Great Britain.

24. For example, in a recent work, the Canadian theologian and scholar of religion P.J. Cahill writes: "Perhaps the most provocative theory to explain and maintain the unity and diversity of religion . . . is that of Frithjof Schuon . . . If we accept Schuon's hypothesis, and it makes more sense than any other with which I am acquainted, then what is at work in diverse religions are symbolic forms that are more or less adequate to express some religious intentionality to point to transcendence." *Mended Speech* (New York, 1982), pp. 88 and 93.

PART THREE

Science: Traditional and Modern

CHAPTER SIX

Western Science and Asian Cultures

*He who knows the Self more and more clearly is more and more fully
manifested. In whatever plants and trees and animals there are, he knows
the Self more and more fully manifested. For in plants and trees only the
plasm is seen, but in animals intelligence. In them the Self becomes more
and more evident. In man the Self is yet more and more evident; for he
is the most endowed with providence, he says what he has known, he sees
what he has known, he knows the morrow, he knows what is and is not
mundane, by the mortal he seeks the immortal. But as for the others,
animals, hunger and thirst are the degree of their discrimination.*
—Aitareya Āraṇyaka 2.3.2

The traditional sciences were cultivated in all the traditional civilizations known
to man raning from the Egyptian to the Aztec and Mayan, but since the more
elaborate formulations of the traditional sciences which have survived at least
to some extent to this day are to be found mostly among Oriental civilizations
such as the Indian and Islamic, it is appropriate to turn to these worlds to examine
their relation to Western science. If there is to be a resuscitation of sacred science
in contrast to the secular science which claims for itself global domination and
has in fact nearly gained such a domination, it is necessary to examine the
relation between Western science and the Oriental cultures which have been
the main repositories of the traditional and the sacred to this day. It is also
necessary to deal more fully with the nature of Western science, which nearly
all Asian and other non-Western countries seek to emulate with varying degrees
of success but in almost all cases impervious to the consequences of the blind
adoption and application of these sciences for their own traditional cultures
and for the sacred sciences which they have developed and nurtured over the
millennia within their intellectual and spiritual citadels.

Today more and more people are becoming aware that the applications
of modern science, a science which until a few decades ago was completely
Western and which has now spread to other continents, have caused directly
or indirectly unprecedented environmental disasters, bringing about the real
possibility of the total collapse of the natural order. And also many realize that
it is necessary to investigate once again the relation of Western science with
the Oriental cultures, now busy in adopting this science and the technology

71

based upon it.[1] It will of course be said by many people that Western science is not solely Western and that it drew heavily from Islamic as well as Greek and Indian sciences. It will also undoubtedly be asserted that there is not a complete enough harmony of either form or content among Oriental traditions to classify them together in one group or to consider them as representing a single point of view.

Within the scope of the present discussion the answer to these objections can be formulated simply in these terms: Western science is of course inextricably linked to the Islamic and before it Graeco-Alexandrian, Indian, ancient Iranian as well as Mesopotamian and Egyptian sciences. But what occurred during the Renaissance and especially in the seventeenth century Scientific Revolution was the imposition of a new and alien "form" or paradigm upon the content of this scientific heritage, a "form" which was derived directly from the anthropomorphic and rationalistic nature of the thought of the age and the secularization of the cosmos to which the whole development of the so-called Renaissance led, often in spite of the attempts of some of its leading intellectual figures to keep alive the vision of the sacred character of the cosmic order.[2] This new "form" resulted in a unilateral and monolithic science that has remained ever since that period bound to a single level of reality and closed to any possibility of access to higher states of being or levels of consciousness, a science which is profoundly terrestrial and "externalized" even when attempting to deal with the farthest reaches of the heavens or depths of the human soul.[3]

We are concerned then with the science whose objective pole does not extend beyond the psycho-physical complex of the natural world surrounding man and whose subjective pole does not transcend human reason, conceived in a purely anthropomorphic manner, and cut off completely from the light of the Intellect. This science, which operates within a universe from which man has been abstracted, although it is still completely bound to the purely human manner of understanding things, is totally different in its perspective and *Weltanschauung* from the sciences of the great Oriental traditions such as the Indian and the Islamic, and therefore needs to be discussed in terms of its full confrontation with Oriental cultures.

As for the differences existing between various Oriental cultures, this is hardly a point to be denied by a serious student of these cultures. But the elements unifying Oriental cultures, especially in their confrontation with Western science and its applications, are such that we can still refer in a profound sense to an Orient which in fact extends beyond the confines of Asia to embrace much of Africa as well. The most important of these elements is of course religion in its widest sense, or tradition as this term has been used by traditional authors in the East and the West such as A.K. Coomaraswamy, R. Guénon and F. Schuon during the past half century. Whether as monotheism found in its most universal form in Islam, or as cosmic dualism in the ancient Iranian religions, or as a polytheism in whose depth is contained the profoundest metaphysics based on the nonduality of the ultimate Principle as in Hinduism, or as a way related to the nonpersonal and nontheistic view of the Divinity as in Buddhism, the Oriental traditions have emphasized the hierarchic nature of reality, the predominance of the spiritual over the material, the sacred character of the cosmos, the inseparability of man's destiny from that of the natural and cosmic environment, and the unity of knowledge and the inter-relatedness of all things. These and many other basic teachings of the various Oriental traditions in fact comprise the metaphysical aspect of Oriental cultures and are the unifying bonds between these cultures.[4] Yet it is precisely such teachings that are openly challenged today even by Orientals themselves as a result of the ever-increasing spread of Western science and its applications in the form of technology in Asian countries.

Of course the debate between modern science and religion or spirituality is hardly new. Voluminous works have been devoted to the "warfare" between theology and science in the West. In the East also for over a century numerous figures from nearly every Oriental tradition have tried to harmonize science and religion usually with a sentimental optimism and lack of intellectual rigour that is far below the dignity of civilizations which have produced their Śaṇkaras, Nāgārjunas, Ibn Sīnās and Menciuses. In fact pseudo-scientific theories such as that of evolution have entered in certain cases into the domain of religion itself, and some have attempted to synthesize such theories with the existing metaphysical and spiritual teachings of the Oriental traditions in question with results that cannot be called anything less than catastrophic.[5]

The encounter between Western science and Oriental cultures and the debate about this problem is to be sure an old one.[6] In fact this encounter has already caused notable changes within these cultures themselves. But certain new factors have appeared upon the stage of history during the past few years which call for a renewal of this apparently time-worn discussion and an awakening of interest on the part of all those in the East who are seriously interested in the future of their cultures in this momentous period of history. The days of facile syntheses between Oriental spirituality and Western science and technology—according to which, with the help of the two, paradise would be achieved on earth overnight—are over. The air of our cities may become so polluted as not to allow us to remain impervious to the destruction of the environment by taking deep-breathing exercises according to Yoga practices, which require at least some amount of fresh air from which the body can draw the necessary energy for its spiritual and physical practices.

A glance at the present-day scene throughout the world shows clearly that indeed the situation has changed in this respect. Just a generation or two ago if one were to survey the intellectual climate of the world, one would discover that in the West only a few lonely visionaries foresaw the profound crisis of the modern world and an impending calamity that would occur unless modern man changed the basic suppositions of his modern culture. When in 1927 R. Guénon criticized the modern world relentlessly in his *The Crisis of the Modern World*,[7] he was attacked for being too severe and excessively pessimistic. Likewise, over half a century ago a poet like T.S. Eliot wrote in his "Love Song of J. Alfred Prufrock" of the abysmal background of modern city life as "a patient etherised upon a table," and in his "The Hollow Men" spoke of secularized, modern man in these terms:

> We are the hollow men
> We are the stuffed men
> Leaning together
> Headpiece filled with straw. Alas!
> Our dried voices, when
> We whisper together
> Are quiet and meaningless
> As wind in dry grass
> Or rats, feet over broken glass
> In our dry cellars,
> Shape without form, shade without color,
> Paralyzed force, gesture without motion.

But his words were also taken mostly not as an expression of the state of things but as the fruit of the mind of an oversensitive poet. The vast majority of Western men remained completely confident that with modern science and its applications they had the key to solve every problem which could possibly present itself.

Today we are witness to a new situation in the West. Many physicists are studying Oriental works of wisdom such as the Tao-Te-Ching and the Upanishads and young students in the best universities are searching everywhere,from books describing the visions of a Mexican *brujo* to those inspiring pages which contain the perennial truths brought to men by the prophets and seers of Asia over the ages. Groups and societies are even founded to bring back to life the Oriental cosmological sciences, not to speak of spreading the spiritual teachings of the Oriental traditions. Moreover, prophets of doom lurk at every corner and predictions of crisis turning into catastrophe, far from being taken as the hallucinations of fools, are seen as sober descriptions of events by the wise. In fact, today the danger in the West is not so much the neglect of the spiritual cultures of Asia but their deformation and profanation in bastard forms in the hands of charlatans who are willing to rape the most sacred treasures of their culture to satiate their thirst for either power or wealth.

Needless to say, not all that is presented as Oriental spirituality in the West is false. Far from it. In fact one of the most significant events of this age is the spread of an authentic metaphysical and spiritual teaching to the West after centuries during which the West ignored and denied those teachings. But the authentic is covered, at least before the eyes of those without true discernment and the necessary perspicacity, by a thick veil of deviated and mutilated pseudo-knowledge which parades as the wisdom of the Orient, polluting the spiritual atmosphere in a manner that fully complements the physical pollution of the air. Today the Oriental cultures do not remain ignored by the majority of the educated Western public to be studied only by a small group of specialists, as was the case with previous generations. They are "well known," but not as they are in themselves; rather they are depicted to the majority of Westerners in that deformed state which makes of them a veritable parody of the spirituality in whose light generations of Orientals have lived and died over the millennia.

Likewise in the East itself we observe a different situation from what existed previously. For some time the Westernized leaders of the various cultures of Asia remained totally impervious to the dangers which the complete adoption of things Western posed for the very cultures whose cause they seemed outwardly at least to be championing and they neglected the significance of their own traditional cultures and most of all the traditional sciences. Faced with immediate social and economic problems many of which were in fact directly or indirectly caused by various forms of Western domination, including for example the role of modern medicine in causing the population explosion, many modernized Asians felt that it was possible to adopt Western science and technology to solve their immediate problems and yet avoid the alien worldview and the negative ethical effects which accompanied this process. The intrusion of the concomitants of Western science and technology upon the very life pattern of these cultures seemed a most unlikely possibility not worthy of serious consideration. Nor did anyone believe that a crisis of worldwide or even cosmic proportions could possibly result from simply adopting the Western pattern of life.[8]

Few Asian cultures in fact took the trouble of providing a strong enough cultural and intellectual background drawn from their own traditions to make it possible for their intellectual elite to master Western science and technology in depth and to try at least to avoid the undesirable factors that accompany their spread. Such a possibility is itself doubtful in the usual manner that the problem is considered.[9] But even if such a possibility did exist, certainly no serious attempt was made to realize it on anything more than the level of exceptional cases which have stood out as islands in a sea of wishy-washy thinking and planning concerning the vital question of educating the young in the light of the problems posed by their encounter with modern Western civilization and its science and technology.

The result has been that among the newer generation of Westernized Orientals one can observe clearly a penetration of Western attitudes into the heart of the province of culture in a manner which was unimaginable to the older generation that championed the adoption of Western science and technology. Even completely negative and destructive tendencies such as alienation, depression, nihilism and the like which mark Western youth today have reached the proportion of a contagious malady among the so-called intelligentsia of many Oriental cultures. The leaders have now become alarmed, having realized how such attitudes can be dangerous for the life of their nation and its culture. Many now understand the importance of what was glossed over earlier, namely the necessity to gather and to apply all the intellectual powers available within each Oriental culture to study the nature of the impact of Western science and its applications upon the culture in question. This awareness is one of the few hopeful signs upon an otherwise dim horizon, for it gives one the hope that finally the real problem will be seen for what it is rather than being veiled over with sentimental and shallow platitudes.

Another factor which necessitates a new study of the relation between modern science and Oriental cultures is the loss of confidence among those who profess this science, not so much in what this science can accomplish within its limited scope, but in its ability to solve many basic problems because of its very nature. The accomplishments of modern science and technology are of course remarkable considered for what they are. But for several centuries a notable segment of Western humanity has transferred the complete and whole-hearted confidence which it had had in the priesthood in the Middle Ages to the scientists and engineers and in fact has had more confidence in their ability to solve the problems of mankind than serious scientists possess concerning themselves. Of course this confidence has not died out completely, but it has certainly weakened. Even within the sciences themselves, there are serious deadlocks which point to the necessity of a complete rethinking of the theorectical structure of some fields. Some even speak of a new scientific revolution comparable to that of the seventeenth century resulting in a science as different from what is called science today as seventeenth century science was from its medieval predecessor.[10] The idea of a continuous progress of science, as understood in its current sense, is now questioned by many notable minds and some even speak of an eclipse of science in the form known since the seventeenth century and the possible return of men to the intense pursuit of other things such as art, philosophy and even theology, a phenomenon which has been seen often in the long history of science.

As for Western technology, it too is shrouded ever more within clouds of doubt emanating from its own success. Men can land on the moon but cannot find the means of enabling human beings in most big cities to see the moon clearly at night. Means are provided to travel faster and faster but in actuality with ever diminishing speed for the vast majority of men who are forced to travel over ever greater distances for their everyday needs. Through medical technology men are kept alive even while seriously ill, longer than was ever possible before, while the deterioration of the natural environment decreases the quality of that elongated life every day and threatens man with new maladies rarely seen before.

These examples could be multiplied indefinitely. Suffice it to say that here as in science there is, despite outwardly remarkable successes, a crisis of confidence which has induced an army of competent and far-sighted people in the West to search for alternative forms of technology such as soft technology and the like. Man has of course always had some form of technology at least since his becoming deprived of the Edenic state. But modern technology, which is the direct application of modern science, is of quite another order. It has sought until quite recently to manipulate nature with the maximum use of energy and total indifference to the qualitative aspects of nature and what is done consequently to the environment, both human and natural. That is why it has caused the profound crisis which has now brought its own future into serious question. Modern technology has reached such a state in its destruction of the environment that for the first time in human history, man, or more precisely modern man, now threatens the harmony of the whole natural order. There are in fact numerous critics of modern technology in the West who doubt very much that human civilization can survive unless a complete end is put to that whole enterprise called the modern world including its science and technology.

Asian cultures are, therefore, not faced any longer with two permanent ways of seeing the universe: their own traditional perspective and that of Western science, perspectives which some earlier tried to harmonize in an apologetic fashion that appears today as anything from hilarious to pathetic. Today, one way, namely the traditional one, remains in its perennial form because it is rooted in immutable principles, whereas the scientific worldview is not only changing within the orbit of its own becoming, as has been the case since the seventeenth century, but is now challenged at its very roots, at least in certain of its basic aspects. There is no longer the compelling force of a 'scientific' view of the universe according to which matter or—from another point of view—quantity dominates, somehow evolving into life and even more mysteriously into consciousness, matter being led on by this same mysterious but scientifically "proven" process to some kind of superman who will save us all in the future.[11] Rather, Asian cultures face a science that is fluid and itself in search of some kind of a philosophy of nature to hang on to, a science whose leading figures such as Planck, Schrödinger, von Weizäcker and Heisenberg have been and are more seriously interested in theology and traditional philosophy than those mesmerized "philosophers" in the West who have turned philosophy itself into a shadow of experimental science and have forfeited the right of intelligence to principial knowledge.[12]

There is another characteristic of science and technology today which makes it incumbent upon all those who are at the stage of adopting them to study them and their effect upon traditional cultures with prudence. Of late one wakes up every morning with a new crisis directly related to the way in which the industrialized world has been dealing with its natural environment. Only a generation or two ago nations took pride in having very big cities which were signs of status and the urbaneness of their culture. Little was anyone aware how rapidly sedentary life, praised throughout history for being the mother of human culture and refinement, would become so deformed as to cause urbaneness to turn into urban crisis and force men into living in abominable conditions in big cities never paralleled before in their seriousness in human history.

Only a few decades ago Western man still prided himself in removing hills and changing the directions of rivers and spoke with humor or condescension of the "animism", "totemism," "spiritism" or "nature worship" of those peoples who still saw in nature the *vestigia Dei*. Most modernized men prided themselves in their attitude and continued with zeal their increasing activity aimed at satisfying their never ending but ever more intense passions and based upon viewing the world as if it contained unlimited possibilities. We recall that only thirty years ago, when preparing the Rockefeller Series lectures at the University of Chicago which finally appeared in book form as *Man and Nature*,[13] we had the greatest difficulty convincing the majority of intelligent college-educated people in America of the imminent ecological crisis. Then suddenly it dawned upon everyone how dangerous the crisis actually is and how little time there is left for industrialized man to change his way of life to gain at least a breathing space in which to think of a new life-style which would allow him to continue his terrestrial existence. It suddenly became clear that the most immediate danger to human survival came not from disease or hunger, which are of course real and with which man has grappled over the ages, but from this blind rape of nature which the industrialized world—fortified by a pseudo-scientific ideology giving it a clear conscience to destroy all other than its immediate surroundings in order to achieve a "higher" civilization— had carried out since its colonization of the world, beginning in the Renaissance and of course on a much more rapid scale since the Industrial Revolution.

The environmental crisis has come upon the scene to remind man that there is something profoundly wrong with the concept of man and his relationship with nature cultivated since the seventeenth century in the West and based on the forgetfulness of the sacred sciences which view man and the cosmos in one grand harmony. Certain Westerners may continue to blame the goats in the Middle East for the deforestation of hills and mountains. But the truth is that what man has been able to achieve in two centuries through denuding forests and polluting land and water in certain regions of the United States, Europe or the former Soviet Union, goats have been nowhere able to match or even approach over a million years. The responsibility for the problem in its acute present form cannot be placed upon the shoulders of all men throughout history equally or even almost equally. It is nearly completely the outcome of the indiscriminate use of a technology tied to lust and passion by a civilization which has given man absolute rights over nature and even over himself without making him aware of the responsibilities which in all traditional cultures precede rights in the same way that ontologically the Principle (Ātman) precedes all of its manifestations (māyā).[14]

To the list of existing crises has now been added the energy crisis, which again began to loom upon the horizon suddenly two decades ago, taking everyone except a few experts by complete surprise. Until just a few years ago nations were classified according to the amount of energy they consumed and those which used less energy were considered as being in the lower scales of human existence. It was incumbent upon all men to rise as fast as possible on this scale. Energy was considered easily available and the sky was the limit.[15] Meanwhile the wealth of certain nations has grown by leaps and bounds at the expense of others which have been duty-bound to provide cheap sources of energy to make the ever rising spiral of energy usage possible. If someone protests that technologies should develop to conserve rather than waste energy, he is usually brushed aside as being anachronistic and against the progress of mankind, which was in fact until recently considered to be directly related to the amount of energy he was able to use or rather squander. If the figures given by geologists are to be accepted, it took nature 400 million years to create the petroleum which modern men, these scavengers of history, will have exhausted in about 400 years if the present trends of consumption continue.

Now it is suddenly dawning upon everyone that the resources of the earth are limited after all, including both its raw materials and easily accessible means of energy. The energy crisis and the rapid degradation of the environment have forced a rethinking of the applications of science to many fields. They have compelled many men to think again in terms of conservation of energy, maximum use of manual labor, a return to simpler means of transportation and the like. Suddenly many in the West have accepted, albeit reluctantly, that the wisdom ingrained in traditional cultures is most urgently needed to induce the peoples of industrialized nations, many of whom have long forgotten what discipline means, to adapt themselves to the new situation caused by the unparalleled environmental crisis which threatens the very continuity of human existence.

Such instances could be easily multiplied. But the few examples given are sufficient to make it clear that the relation between Western science and its applications and Oriental cultures has changed greatly in both dimension and direction of late, and that it is necessary to bring the profoundest insights of traditional cultures to bear upon the crucial problems created by modern civilization not only for the sake of the East but for the whole of mankind. In the East both those who proposed an indiscriminante adoption of Western science and technology and remained certain that their culture would remain intact, and those who wanted even to dispense with their own cultural and spiritual heritage to adopt one of the Western "isms," from positivism to Marxism, as their ideology, have to reconsider their position in the light of the unprecedented crisis at the very heart of the civilization which they wished to emulate. Strangely enough, the environmental crisis may be a blessing in disguise in providing an opportunity for those still able to ponder over the situation at hand before embarking upon a course from which there may be no return.

Let us consider some of the direct effects of the application of modern science and technology upon human culture, mostly in the West but also of late in the East.[16] There is, needless to say, a distinction to be made between science and technology. But inasmuch as in the West they have become ever more closely associated with each other since the beginning of this century, for the sake of the present discussion they can be considered together. One of the most notable effects, especially from the point of view of traditional cultures, is the compartmentalization of knowledge and finally the destruction of the ultimate science of Reality, the *scientia sacra* or gnosis which lies at the heart of every integral tradition, as well as the eclipse of sacred sciences of the cosmic and natural orders.

Traditional cultures have always envisaged the wise man or the sage as a central figure in human society. The sage might also be learned in particular branches of the sciences, but what characterizes him most of all is his knowledge of the Truth in its universal aspect and, inasmuch as this concerns the well-being and ultimate ends of man, his felicity, *sa'ādah*, in both this world and the next, to use the language of Islam. No doubt the separation of the sciences of nature from philosophy and philosophy itself from religion has enabled men to learn a great deal about the material domain, but by the same token it has deprived man of the knowledge of the whole of Reality, both spatial and nonspatial, which surrounds him and which concerns him in a terribly real manner whether he chooses to take it into account or not. It has also destroyed the reality of the sacred sciences which every traditional civilization has possessed in one form or other.

It took several centuries from the beginning of the Scientific Revolution for the most outstanding thinkers of the West to realize what a terrible loss this plunge into sheer multiplicity, and this loss of a knowledge of the principial order, involves for human society as a whole. For now there is almost no one in the modern world to whom one could turn in order to confide in him with one's whole being, a person who would induce certainty in his followers and companions because he not only thinks but also lives and embodies the sapiential doctrines which he expounds.

The wedding between metaphysics and the cosmological sciences so evident in traditional cultures is not only the expression of the truth which lies in the nature of things, but also a practical reality essential to the welfare of human society. In Hinduism all knowledge is contained in principle in the Vedas, and in Islam in the Quran. This does not mean at all a limiting of knowledge in any particular domain of reality, as is proven by the remarkable developments of astronomy and arithmetic in India or medicine, algebra and physics in Islam. It means, rather, that particular knowledge is always related to the whole and that the harmony of the parts vis-à-vis the whole is always preserved, as in nature itself where the functioning of every living organism is based upon the harmony within the world of the manifold as well as between the manifold and the One, the One which is the principle and source of all multiplicity. The vision of the whole was always related to the sense of the holy, of the sacred which nature displays at every turn. To lose the sense of the whole is also to become blind to the sense of the sacred and ultimately to forget the total order.

The destruction of the wholeness of human life so decried today and the ever increasing and greater compartmentalization of the human mind and disintegration of the human psyche, are ultimately related to the loss of principial knowledge, and the subsequent segmentation of what men learn and know. It is related to the loss of sacred science.

For cultures whose central intellectual figures have always been sages who have unified knowledge in its essential aspect within themselves, such a loss cannot be anything less than tragic. Furthermore, this is particularly unfortunate in that it occurs at a moment when the most intelligent Westerners, especially the young, are searching for a way to reunify various domains of knowledge and to reintegrate themselves as intelligent beings. The Oriental cultures possess the necessary intellectual doctrines to achieve such a goal, for real metaphysical knowledge with its concomitant means of realization has not as yet perished among them. But to achieve this goal requires changing the attitude of euphoria or in certain cases hypnosis before modern science and thought in general and instead applying the intellectual criteria of Oriental traditions to the study, criticism and finally integration of the modern science into a higher form of knowledge, with the result of recreating a state of equilibrium in which sacred science will of necessary play a central role.

The loss of the "Center" in Western civilization has implied not only the segmentation of various branches of knowledge but also a divorce between contemplation and action, leading to the nearly total eclipse of the former by the latter. On another level, this loss has led to a divorce between science and ethics from which the modern world is suffering so painfully today. Due to the decadence which set in among traditional cultures during the last few centuries, many leaders of the East in the past were concerned quite rightly with the evil of lethargy and lack of action within their societies and with the fact, to quote Frithjof Schuon, that "the East is sleeping over treasures." From their perspective, the mode of activity of the West appeared to incorporate an ideal harmony between knowledge and action and to provide a model to follow to overcome the ills which they observed and still observe in many quarters around them. Few were aware that this apparent harmony in the West was based upon the application of an incomplete and partial knowledge to the needs of man considered not as a total being with both spiritual and material needs but as an earth-bound creature, or ultimately as an animal with endless passions and a voracious appetite which in the absence of traditional discipline only increased by leaps and bounds from day to day.

The consequences of the course of action followed by the West during the past three or four centuries are now so evident that even the most ardent champions of secularism in the West are openly concerned with the dangerous ethical consequences of the applications of a science which no matter how innocent in itself often leads to results completely beyond the control of those who are its creators and propagators. The issue has now become of paramount importance since the forces which can be manipulated have gained almost cosmic proportions and the issue at hand is ultimately the survival of the whole of mankind or even life itself on earth.

There are two ethical questions to be deal with which, although outwardly quite distinct, are profoundly interrelated: firstly, the ethical implications of the use of some of the sciences and many forms of technology directly for military purposes and indirectly in ever increasing degree for what is called peacetime goals: and secondly, the ethical behavior of men and women in a society whose spiritual foundations have been eroded by the secularism and materialism implied by the "scientistic" worldview.

The first problem has concerned all serious men ever since the horrors of the First World War, in which mechanized warfare caused devastation to become generalized beyond anything experienced until then, and especially since the mushroom clouds over Hiroshima opened the gates of hell for men who until then had been dreaming of establishing paradise on earth through purely material means. In the East, India has been witness to some of the profoundest debates on this question during this century and has given birth to Mahatma Gandhi, a figure who more than anyone in recent times incited men all over the world to ponder once again the questions of war and peace and their implications for human existence as well as pointing out the inhuman character of modern technology. It is not necessary to enter here once again into the question of the ethical implications of war at a time when most of the causes for which men are willing to go to war are devoid of an ultimate or sacred meaning and even of anything more than material interests, and when the means provided by modern technology for warfare are such as to give a completely new dimension and scope to war and its destructive power in both the human and natural domains.[17]

It must be emphasized, however, that this change in the dimensions and proportions of the effects of modern warfare is directly related to the ethical implications of the applications of science and cannot be disregarded as irrelevant to this problem. There are those who claim that such evil effects of the such applications of science as modern military weapons are due only to social problems of human societies and are unrelated to science itself. But this is to forget that, as the Old Persian proverb says, one should never place a sharp sword in the hands of a drunkard. Those who make sharp swords with certain knowledge that sooner or later they will end up in the hands of drunkards can hardly shun the moral responsibility that such an undertaking involves, and this truth holds most of all when they operate at the source or the frontiers of science and technology where new weapons of ever increasing danger are produced, forcing others to follow suit simply to guard their independence. But these are matters for another discussion and another day and lie outside the main concerns of this work. Their brief mention here is necessary, however, since it is such an awesome aspect of the interaction between Western science and Oriental cultures.

The problem that is less known, especially in non-Western cultures which have begun to adopt Western technology and to familiarize themselves with Western science in recent decades, is the ethical implication of what appear as peaceful uses and applications of science and technology: the ecological crisis is caused directly by the excessive and unguided peaceful applications of science and technology in various forms resulting not only in the depletion of resources, the warming of the climate and the like but also in overpopulation, famine and now certain new forms of disease which directly threaten the lives of human beings. Traditional cultures especially those of Asia, have never been anthropocentric in perspective and have never divorced man from either the Divine Order or the rest of the creatures who share the blessings of the earth with him. Ethics in traditional cultures has included not only human society but all the other creatures on earth, animate and even inanimate, if one considers the sacredness of certain mountains, rivers, stones and the like in many Oriental traditions.

In contrast the anthropocentrism of postmedieval Western society created an ethical code embracing only man, and in fact only Western man since another code was used for the inhabitants of other continents. The other creatures were there to provide for man's "needs" without any rights of their own. This plunder of the natural environment has now turned upon man himself, and suddenly within a single generation even "peaceful" applications of science and technology have gained ethical implications never dreamt of before, leading now to the ultimate question of who should have the right to live and who should not in a world which can no longer feed all of its inhabitants and where human survival is often at the cost of the survival of whole ecosystems. It is a fact to ponder upon that while men considered the earth as their mother and Heaven as their father, the earth managed to feed the children it had begotten: and that since men ceased to regard the earth as their mother but rather as a female captured in war to be prostituted and raped, the earth can no longer feed all her progeny. The bounty and grace (*barakah* in Arabic) of the earth seem to shrivel before a humanity which refuses to see anything in nature beyond the means of satisfying man's animal needs.

The ecological crisis is now upon us with its full implications of doom and disaster unless men rethink their whole approach to the use of their environment and rediscover a sacred science of the cosmic order and ultimately the supreme science of the Real which is pure metaphysics. The ethical implications of science in this domain have become as harrowing as in the military field. And indeed it could not but be so since the activity that has led to the ecological crisis has been for the most part camouflaged as an attempt to achieve peace and prosperity. But in reality this activity has been inseparable from other forms of war: economic war with other nations and even within a single society; conflict with other human beings and with other creatures: and confrontation with oneself and ultimately with the Self or *Ātman*. Both in the conditions called war and peace, which are ultimately both forms of war externalizing man's inner war with his true nature, the ethical implications of the applications of Western science and technology for Oriental cultures are of such dimensions that they need to be carefully studied and analyzed before the blind-imitation of the blind continues any further.

The second ethical question, which does not seem to be related to the above outwardly but which is inwardly inseparable from it, is the ethical behavior of Western society itself. A generation of men and women brought up in affluence and made aware of the overt contradictions within the ethical ideals for which the modern West has stood for some time have turned to various sources for new ethical systems in a state of confusion, while for a large number of people, especially in big cities, the general moral standards have decayed in every way. Whether it be the question of sexual relations or theft or murder, a new situation has arisen whose seriousness hardly needs to be emphasized. The partly traditional cultures are still relatively free of such problems, but as recipients of all that flows across their borders into their homelands they cannot remain indifferent to the effects that the recent "moral revolution" in the West will have upon them.

The ethical crisis of the West is also reflected in the loss of discipline among notable strata of society and the expectation on the part of many to become ever more wealthy while working less and less every day. It is a "right" which people expect without pondering over the responsibilities which are inseparable from any form of right. The ever-recurring economic crisis, despite all the attempts made to blame it on the rise in the price of this or that commodity, are due most of all to this crisis within industrialized societies.

This is also evident in the major problem of implementing the recommendations made by a number of authorities to ameliorate the negative effects of the environmental crisis. Many works by environmentalists and even certain scientists have called for men to turn towards qualitative growth, to the so-called "finer things of life" rather than remain bound completely to the quest of purely material objects.[18] But such recommendations overlook what might be called the forgotten dimension of the ecological debate. Men have forgotten that only a spiritual power can control the dragon of the passions and that in the absence of spirituality, no written or oral scientific advice or political recommendation can cause men to turn their attention away from the material plane towards the spiritual and to cause the storms of the mind and the soul, with their concomitant physical aggression against nature, to subside, as has been the aim of Oriental sages over the ages. That is why the environmental crisis cannot be solved without turning to the spiritual dimension of the problem, which many try so hard to overlook. The loss of a sacred science and of discipline and a lowering of ethical standards have indeed turned against Western man at a moment when he is most in need of this science and discipline and of the virtues from which they are inseparable.

This lowering of ethical standards and even bewilderment as to which ethical system is meaningful might seem outwardly to be independent of Western science and its applications, and many in fact have argued in favor of this thesis. But closer scrutiny reveals that the two are inseparable. Norms of ethical behavior are inseparable from the view held by men concerning the Ultimate

Reality, or metaphysics in its universal sense. Western man has in fact been living since the Middle Ages on the ethical heritage of Christianity while gradually separating himself from the Christian doctrine concerning the nature of things. Now the legacy is nearly exhausted and for that very reason the ethical system which appeared obvious until recently, even to men who attacked its metaphysical and theological foundations, is being challenged in its totality.

The modern sciences themselves are of course innocent of any claims about the ultimate nature of Reality and therefore of any possibility of providing the necessary basis for an applicable and meaningful ethics, despite the extravagant claims of agnostic humanists and proponents of scientific ethics whose ineptitude and innate weakness is demonstrated by the negative role their theories are playing in human society in this supposedly most "scientific" period of human history. But the atmostphere created by those who give a totalitarian interpretation to modern science and who want to forge from its limited understanding of the material plane a key to unlock the mysteries of Heaven, cannot but result in an atmosphere of doubt and agnosticism which corrodes the metaphysical and religious doctrines upon which ethics must of necessity rely. The general change in the ethical behavior of industrialized societies, which display more and more disorders and maladies of a serious nature every day, cannot be considered a characteristic of Western society alone but it is to be found wherever modernization and industrialization have spread. It is related to the indirect effects on the mind and soul of human beings of Western science and its applications, not necessarily through the intention of their propagators but by the very nature of modern science and technology. Surely no one who is seriously concerned with the future of Oriental cultures in their contact and confrontation with Western science and its applications can remain oblivious to the factors which press upon the whole value system and pattern of ethical behavior in societies in the midst of adopting Western science and technology.

As a response to the critical appraisal we have made of the present situation, the oft-repeated cry will no doubt be heard again that the hands of the clock cannot be turned back and that all that is occurring in this field is inevitable. If, however, all is inevitable, then why even bother to think or to act? As for the famous hand of the clock, it cannot without doubt be turned back but strangely enough it usually returns to where it was before if one waits long enough, and also occasionally the clock stops working completely. In any case no argument can withstand the statement of the truth and the necessity for man to conform himself to it no matter how bitter the pains of making this decision and acting accordingly.

It would be absurd to deny the validity of the knowledge acquired through modern physics of the structure of the atom, at least as a way of knowing the structure of matter; or of the insight acquired by modern biology into the workings of the cell as a way of knowing something about life, although it might not be life everlasting. Likewise, it would be ridiculous to deny that trains go faster than ox carts or that modern surgery is more efficient in removing brain tumors than the methods used by the ancient Egyptians or Ibn Sīnā. The question is, however, not to doubt the obvious, but to ask whether all men can or should in fact journey by fast trains and cars and whether this should be considered as the goal of human society; or whether the very conditions which make possible remarkable advances in certain aspects of medicine do not cause other forms of malady, no less serious than those for which cures have been found, to appear on the scene.

Both a knowledge of most branches of Western science and the application of this science through various forms of technology have already spread within various Oriental and other non-Western cultures in different degrees. The question is not whether the process can be stopped immediately or not. We must rather question the way in which the process is to continue in the future in the light of the profound crisis which is taking place within the heartland of the civilization that has produced and nurtured Western science and technology during the past centuries. The question is whether these cultures will copy blindly and end up with various degrees of speed at the dead-end now being faced by Western civilization, or whether they will act judiciously and wisely in a manner which will provide enough protection for their own cultures to survive and even to provide the necessary light to guide men all over the world—even beyond their own cultural borders—to lead out of the labyrinth in which they now find themselves.

As we have already stated, both Western science and technology are in a state of flux and rapid change, beset with uncertainties about which direction they will follow in the future. In physics there are signs of the need for a completely new look at basic particles. Some even speak of the psychon as a "psychic" particle to add to the number of existing particles to explain certain phenomena. In astronomy and astrophysics there are new theories propounded every day almost with the rapidity of changes of fashion, and opinions even about whether the universe is finite or infinite oscillate back and forth every few years. There is no real cosmology—which can only come from higher metaphysical principles—in the West today, and despite all the attempts made (such as the pseudo-synthesis of Teilhard de Chardin), no satisfactory general worldview has been established within which to situate all that man knows and observes in the world about him, not to speak of the world within and beyond.[19] The same can be seen in biology, where after a long period of aping physics there are signs of new interest in a worldview in which the morphology of living forms have a meaning in themselves rather than simply in terms of their chemical components. Finally, in psychology and psychoanalysis after several decades of tyrannical rule by those counterfeits and parodies of traditional doctrines which Freudianism and Jungianism represent, there is now an awareness that these modern disciplines have failed utterly to penetrate into the inner nature of the human soul as it is grounded in and related to the Spirit. There are even attempts to benefit from the insights of the traditional sciences of the soul for which the traditions of Asia such as those of Tibet, India and Sufism are justly so famous.[20]

In all of these and many other fields there is a deep thirst for a sacred science, a philosophy of nature and a total worldview which can give a new direction to the modern sciences themselves. And it is precisely at this critical point that the still surviving traditional cultures can play a major role in the transformation of the modern sciences by providing a wider worldview within which they can be seen for what they really are, and in certain cases even by giving a new form of life to the sciences, transforming them into elements within another universe of knowledge and experience. Some Western scientists and thinkers are already seeking to pursue this goal, but for the most part they do not have access to the genuine teachings of the Oriental traditions and so their efforts always face the danger of resulting in that metaphysically absurd and spiritually dangerous type of eclecticism and pseudo-synthesis of so-called Eastern spirituality and Western science which is more insidious than materialism pure and simple and which is at the antipode of what we have in mind. The creative encounter of Oriental cultures with various branches of the Western sciences at their very frontiers, which is our concern, is not based on the uncritical acceptance of Western science as an inviolable deity and docile surrender to its claims. Rather, it is founded upon regaining full confidence in their own traditions on the part of those Oriental and also certain Western thinkers who are in a position to deal with such matters and to face the problems involved in an intellectual endeavor of such dimensions. It means most of all casting away that sense of inferiority vis-à-vis the West which has plagued so many Westernized Orientals during the past two or three generations, paralyzed their minds and prevented them from acting intelligently before the thought patterns and ideologies which have during the past century inundated the intellectual landscape of various Oriental cultures like a tidal wave.

The same situation exists in the domain of technology. Most non-Western societies are now becoming rapidly industrialized due to various seemingly irresistible forces, both external and internal, at the very moment when the whole meaning of the process of industrialization is being called into question. There is no longer a single model for development to follow. Continuous material progress, measured in terms of GNP and similar figures, which both the West and what was the Communist world until recently have envisaged until now as the natural goal of every society is refuted as even a physical possibility on a worldwide scale, as a result of both the ecological and the energy and raw-materials crises. Nor are such ideals as ever greater speed, ever increasing use of energy and the like considered any longer to be obviously beneficient in themselves. Oriental societies are beginning to emulate Western models in the construction of their cities, means of production, transportation and the like at the very moment when many people in the most advanced industrial countries are seeking new technologies to prevent a major catastrophe from falling upon their heads.

There is no question here of non-Western societies, desisting from feeding and clothing their people or to provide for their medical and educational needs. The question is how to avoid the schooling, energy and medical crises outlined so daringly by such critics of Western civilization as Ivan Illich and Theodore Roszak.[21] The works of such men must at least be seriously studied even if one chooses to chart another course than that which they propose, for they speak of very real and not imaginary problems upon the very material place with which modern man is almost solely concerned.

The Oriental cultures are fortunately still very rich in providing alternatives in various forms of technology. Most of the traditional architectures of Asia such as Islamic architecture have been based on the principle of conserving energy, close rapport with the nature environment, maximum use of natural sources of energy, and the creation of an organic link between the spaces in which man works, sleeps, prays and relaxes. These are all ideas which many contemporary Western urbanists, city planners and architects are seeking to realize, even if not all of them understand that this organic unity of traditional architecture is possible only in the presence of a sacred science, an organically unified society and the unifying spiritual principles which lies at the heart of all traditions. It is, therefore, particularly painful when one observes in so many Asian countries urban monstrosities being built which stand not only against the living architectural traditions of the countries in question but are also opposed to all that those who are trying to cure the maladies of urbanism in the West are acclaiming with the loudest voice possible.

The same problem can be seen in medicine and diet. Many people in the West are now discovering the remarkable possibilities within the traditional schools of Oriental medicine to cure certain types of illness before which Western medicine has remained more or less powerless until now. They also realize the economic value of traditional medicine in smaller towns and especially in villages which are deprived of modern medicine because of the exorbitant cost of training modern doctors. While even the material, not to speak of the spiritual, value of traditional medicine is being realized to a greater degree every day even in the West, in many Oriental cultures everyone is trying to bury and forget the remnants of traditional medicine as soon as possible and to expand the use of the products of modern pharmaceutical industries in order to replace the herbs and minerals drawn directly from the bosom of nature.

To cite yet another example, much is being said today of the virtues of labor-intensive industry, of manual work when and where possible and of the disaster of following blindly the policy of replacing men by machines indiscriminately. The teachings of Gandhi about the innate virtue of manual labor and especially of handicrafts, which were soon forgotten by most men even among his admirers, have of late received renewed attention and attracted new interest. Of course men and women cannot be asked to crank a wheel to run a power station, but they can continue to make many things without their being automatically replaced by the machine. And this can be of benefit not only from a spiritual, social and ecological point of view but also in the long run even economically. The young scientists and engineers in the West who are seeking to create what they call "soft technology" are pursuing this very goal.

In the rapid process of industrialization which many Oriental countries are now undergoing, the necessity of using a sense of discernment and of being judicious is more urgent than ever before. It is even imperative at a time when technology in the West itself is undergoing major changes and men are searching for new life-styles. If this discernment is not used, Oriental societies will continue to eat the bread crumbs and the refuse left from the banquet table and possibly the "last supper" of the industrialized world. But if they do use discernment again with full confidence in their own cultures, they can choose intelligent alternatives whenever possible and draw from their own experience many things from architecture to agriculture, providing in this way a meaningful life-style for themselves and even sources of inspiration for others.

To carry out this immense intellectual task of creatively confronting Western science and technology, the intellectual elite of Oriental societies who are called upon to carry out this task must rely upon their own cultures. They must recall first of all that profound truth which is iterated in every Oriental tradition in a particular form, the truth contained in the myth of the sacrifice of Puruṣa mentioned in the Ṛg-Veda and in the metaphysical doctrine of universal man (al-insān al-kāmil) which forms one of the pillars of Islamic metaphysical doctrine. According to this doctrine, the cosmos is brought into being by the sacrifice of that spiritual reality which is also the prototype of man and constitutes his own essence. To destroy the natural environment before the altar of man's passions means therefore also to sacrifice the inner man for the sake of the human animal, which is nothing but the most externalized aspect of the totality of man. It is also to strangle and destroy man himself, for despite all the appearances, the outward man cannot survive save with the aid of the inner man. To kill "the gods" is finally to commit suicide.

At this critical moment of human history, when the traditional cultures of the Orient must do everything possible not only to survive but also to act as beacons of light in a world of shadows, it is essential to recall the truth for which the myth of the sacrifice of Puruṣa, or the reflections of the prototypes of all things in the Universal Man, and similar traditional doctrines, are the most intelligible symbolic expressions. In the encounter with Western science and its applications, the remembrance of this truth, which is itself a basic component of sacred science and which binds man in the most profound sense to the universe surrounding him, is more urgent than ever before.

In the *Secret Rose Garden* (*Gulshan-i rāz*) of Shabistarī, man is ordered to contemplate upon his intimate relation with the universe about him in these immortal verses:

> Meditate upon the structure of the heavens,
> So that thou may praise the "Truth" in its theophanies.
> Behold the world from end to end within thyself,
> Whatever comes at the end, thou may see beforehand.
> The world of Adam appeared last of all,
> Yet the two worlds became dependent upon his essence.
> Thou art the kernel of the world, situated at its centre,
> Know thyself for thou art the soul of the Universe.
> Thou knowest all the Names of God because
> Thou art the face of the reflection of the "Named."
> O first who art identical with the last!
> O inward who are identical with the outward!
> Thou art cogitating about thyself day and night,
> It is better that thou shouldst think no more of self.

And we read in the Muṇḍaka Upanishad that:

The whole universe is a manifestation and product of that universal, formless, causeless Being. The sun, moon and all the quarters, all knowledge, and the souls of all existing beings are parts and manifestations of that single all-immanent Being. All life and all qualities, functions and activities are forms of that single Energy. He is Fire which has lighted the sun and makes it burn, like a log burning in fire. Thereby does the sun give us warmth and light. The rain does not rain, but it is He that rains through the clouds. Beings come together and multiply, but it is He above that multiplies through them.

The survival of Oriental cultures does not depend so much upon their immediate success in the material domain, no matter how important this success may appear at the moment, as upon the degree to which they are able to preserve this vision of Unity binding the various levels of knowledge and of reality, of the spiritual and material into an inseparable whole. This is a vision which is contained in sacred knowledge and which modern man in search of a way to save himself from the devastating effects of his own activity is also seeking, but having lost the direction of the sky he is for the most part searching for the Sun in the bottom of a well. Nothing could be more tragic for the world as a whole than if, at the moment when Western man who had long forgotten this sense of Unity is searching to rediscover it in order to save himself, Oriental cultures should forget and discard this precious vision of Unity and knowledge of the sacred sciences which lie at the heart of their cultures.

Notes

1. By Oriental in this essay and in fact throughout this book we mean primarily the Far Eastern, Indian and Islamic worlds with their many internal divisions and subdivisions.

2. See Nasr, *Man and Nature—The Spiritual Crisis of Modern Man* (London, 1989), especially chapter II, p. 51ff.

3. As stated earlier, there are now signs of the breakdown of this nearly five-century-old paradigm and a number of physicists and philosophers of science speak of a new paradigm shift, but such a major transformation has not as yet come about within the main body of Western science, which still remains bound to the worldview which was gradually born during the Renaissance and which became formulated categorically in the seventeenth century with Descartes, Galileo, Newton and others.

4. The discussions of the previous part of this book provide keys for seeing the unifying principles beyond the diversity of forms within the Oriental traditions under discussion here. In fact, as indicated in the previous chapter, the understanding of the diversity of religious and traditional forms from the point of view of the *philosophia perennis* is itself a sacred science and is needed in order to understand the interrelation of sacred sciences which have been cultivated in diverse traditional civilizations.

5. See Nasr, *Knowledge and the Sacred*, chapter seven, p. 221ff.; and O. Bakar (ed.), *Critique of Evolutionary Theory* (Kuala Lumpur, 1987).

6. Usually what has been missing in these discussions is the non-Western or Oriental traditional sciences with which we shall deal in the next chapter.

7. Trans. by M. Pallis and R. Nicholson (London, 1962).

8. Needless to say, these attitudes still prevail among many politicians and civil servants in the non-Western world and have hardly disappeared.

9. That is, it is not possible to adopt Western technology wholescale without suffering from consequences such as the destruction of the natural environment and impersonalization of means of production. What could be done is to develop alternative technologies which have only been tried on a small scale here and there, only where the situation has necessitated the preservation of nonmodern forms of technology, as for example in Indian villages, certain areas of China or the mountains of countries such as Afghanistan and Persia.

10. There is an extensive literature on this "new science" which is often seen to be closely intertwined with the principles and ideas of Oriental metaphysics and cosmology, although not all those who write on this subject understand fully the meaning of Oriental doctrines.
    For works dealing with the relation of contemporary science to Oriental doctrines, see the well-known book of F. Capra, *The Tao of Physics* (New York, 1977); J. Needleman, *Sense of the Cosmos* (New York, 1988); R. Ravindra, *Science and Spirit* (New York, 1991); and G. Zukav, *The Dancing Wu Li Masters: An Overview of the New Physics* (New York, 1980) M. Talbot, *Mysticism and the New Physics* (New York, 1981); and the more recent work of F. Capra, *The Turning Point* (New York, 1987). The works of the well-known physicist David Bohm, who speaks of the "implicate order" and a new natural philosophy for physics, reveal something of this "new science" itself. See his *Wholeness and the Implicate Order* (London, 1980).

11. The pseudo-scientific theory of evolution, which became a pseudo-religion replacing traditional faith in many circles in the West and even among modernized groups in the East has been challenged not only philosophically but also scientifically in recent decades. See O. Bakar, *Critique of Evolutionary Theory*; G. Sermonti and R. Fondi, *Dopo Darwin* (Milan, 1980); R. Fondi, *La Révolution organiciste* (Paris, 1986); and the debate between various scientists in *Krisis "Evolution"?*, no. 2 (April 1989).

12. Some of the profoundest philosophical and theological views today come from those scientists who are not imprisoned in the confinement of the limitations inherent to the modern scientific outlook. See, for example, W. Smith, *The Cosmos and Transcendence* (La Salle, Ill., 1984).

13. Published originally as the *Encounter of Man and Nature*, it was reprinted in later editions as *Man and Nature*.

14. We shall turn in chapter nine of this work to the environmental crisis and the role in this crisis of the traditional and sacred sciences, in this case the Islamic.

15. Needless to say, there are still those who hold this view and who are willing to go to war in far away regions of the earth as well as destroy what little remains of virgin nature to prove that they are right.

16. As far as the impact of technology upon the West is concerned, see the penetrating studies of J. Ellul: *The Technological Society*, trans. J. Wilkinson (New York, 1964); and *The Technological Bluff*, trans. G.W. Bromiley (Grand Rapids, Mich., 1990).

17. Limited war is still possible against a small country as the recent Persian Gulf War demonstrated, but even in this case the ecological consequences have been devastating.

18. Such books have proliferated during the past two decades since the Club of Rome Report was published and today there is a vast literature on the subject; some of them are quite influential but not as yet influential enough to change the perspective of the majority of Westerners toward the relation between man and nature and the limits upon human rights as far as the domination and plunder of nature is concerned. As an example of this type of literature see J. Rifkin, *Biosphere Politics* (New York, 1991): R.F. Nash, *The Right of Nature* (London, 1989); and for the more scientific type of literature dealing with the environment, the bibliography contained in G. Tyler Miller, *Environmental Science* (Belmont, Cal., 1988), pp. A10–A16.

19. See T. Burckhardt, "Traditional Cosmology and the Modern World," in his *Mirror of the Intellect*, trans. W. Stoddart (Albany, N.Y., 1987), p. 13ff; on the false premises of Teilhardism, see W. Smith, *Teilhardism and the New Religion* (Rockford, Ill., 1988).

20. See J. Needleman, *Consciousness and Tradition* (New York, 1982): and M. Ajmal, "Sufi Science of the Soul," in S.H. Nasr (ed.), *Islamic Spirituality—Foundations* (New York, 1987), pp. 294–307.

21. See, for example, Illich, *De-Schooling Society* (London, 1973); and his *Tools for Conviviality* (New York, 1971); also Roszak, *Where the Wasteland Ends* (New York, 1973); and *Unfinished Animal* (New York, 1975).

CHAPTER SEVEN

The Traditional Sciences

The world is a theophany, an epiphany of things themselves unseen.
—A.K. Coomaraswamy, "Chinese Painting"

Having dealt with Oriental and traditional civilizations in confrontation with Western science, which they are now adopting rapidly as their own, it is now necessary to delve more deeply into the meaning of traditional science which these very civilizations cultivated over the ages and which still survives here and there despite the onslaught of modern secular science.

For those whose understanding of the word 'science' is limited to its current English usage,[1] the phrase 'traditional science' might appear as a contradiction in terms. Science is understood as an ever-changing knowledge of the physical world based on ratiocination and empiricism, whereas tradition, as understood by contemporary masters of the exposition of traditional doctrines who have been mentioned already in this work, implies immutability, permanence and knowledge of a principial and metaphysical order. It is, however, meaningful to speak of traditional science as a knowledge which, while not pure metaphysics, is traditional, that is, related to metaphysical principles, and though a science in the sense of organized knowledge of a particular domain of reality, it is not divorced from the immutability which characterizes the principial order. In all traditional civilizations, especially sedentary ones, many forms of traditional sciences have been cultivated ranging from the study of the heavens to that of the anatomy of an ant. These sciences are distinct from metaphysics, or gnosis, the supreme science which, as already mentioned, is the ultimate *scientia sacra*. Yet they are related to metaphysical principles through various cosmological schemes of a strictly traditional character and are none other than 'sacred sciences' understood as knowledge pertaining to the manifested and created order.

The traditional sciences are also distinct from the social, juridical and theological dimensions of traditional civilizations. Although their fruit, whether it be architecture or pharmacology, is used by nearly all members of the society in question, the sciences themselves are related more to the esoteric rather than the exoteric dimension of each tradition. It was the Taoists and not Confucian rationalists who cultivated alchemy and physics in China. Likewise in Islam it was such esoteric groups as the Ikhwān al-Ṣafā' or metaphysicians such as

Quṭb al-Dīn Shīrāzī and Naṣīr al-Dīn Ṭūsī who were outstanding mathematicians and astronomers and not the jurists and theologians.[2] The very nature of the traditional sciences and the forms, forces, patterns and symbols with which they deal, require that the principles of these sciences be related to "the supreme science" and the esoteric dimension of the tradition in which they are nurtured. That is why when they are cut off from their roots and background they appear as "occult sciences," covered by an unpenetrable veil and often subject to arbitrary interpretations. Of course, in their traditional setting they are also in a sense "occult" or literally hidden,[3] but only to those not qualified to study them. For persons with the necessary spiritual and intellectual preparation, those for whom these sciences were originally meant, they are far from being occult in the sense of mystifying. They are in fact one of the means of access to the world of light which they reflect on their own particular domain in conformity with their nature and field of application. It must not be forgotten that in India treatises (śastras) were written on the traditional sciences which are called Vedāṅga, literally "limbs or powers of the Vedas."

One can also speak of sacred and profane science in distinguishing between the traditional and modern sciences.[4] From the traditional point of view, there is of course no legitimate domain which can be considered as completely profane. The universe is the manifestation of the Divine Principle and there is no realm of reality that can be completely divorced from that Principle. To participate in the realm of the Real and to belong to that which is real also implies being immersed in the ocean of the sacred and being imbued with the perfume of the sacred. The metaphysical and cosmological sciences of the traditional civilizations are certainly sacred sciences in that they are based on knowledge of manifestation not as veil or māyā but as symbol and "signature" of the Divine, as the vestigia Dei. As pointed out by a number of traditional authorities more than once,[5] however, not all the sciences cultivated in traditional civilizations are strictly speaking, sacred sciences. Not every page of Pliny, Strabon, Brahmagupta or al-Bīrūnī can be considered as sacred science. There is always at the core of the sciences cultivated in traditional civilizations an orientation toward the sacred, but there are also here and there purely human speculations or observations of a scientific order in the contemporary sense, elements which can hardly be neglected totally in speaking of the traditional sciences. The main difference between the traditional sciences and modern science lies in the fact that in the former the profane and purely human remain always marginal and the sacred central, whereas in modern science the profane has become central and certain intuitions and discoveries which despite everything reveal the Divine Origin of the natural world have become so peripheral that they are hardly ever recognized for what they are despite the exceptional views of certain scientists. The traditional sciences are essentially sacred and accidentally profane and modern science essentially profane and only accidentally aware of the sacred quality of the universe and, even in such rare instances, unable to accept the sacred as the sacred. Modern science shares fully the characteristic of modern man as a creature who has lost the sense of the sacred.

The traditional sciences of all traditional civilizations agree on certain principles of the utmost importance which need be reiterated in this age of forgetfulness of even the most obvious truths. These sciences are based on a hierarchic vision of the universe, one which sees the physical world as the lowest domain of reality which nevertheless reflects the higher states by means of symbols which have remained an ever open gate towards the Invisible for that traditional humanity which had not as yet lost the "symbolist spirit."[6] The psycho-physical world, which preoccupies modern science, is seen in the traditional perspective as a reflection of the luminous archetypes, and its stages of life, which have now become the subject of paleontological studies, as so many "consolidations of the dream of the World Soul," to use a formulation which belongs originally to Schuon.

The traditional sciences take place in a "space" which is related here and now to the higher levels of reality, without being unaware of the march of time, which is seen not as a continuous progression but as the rhythm of a series of cycles governed by laws as strict as those governing space.[7] The "great chain of being" has remained vertical for all the traditional sciences, relating the physical to the psychic, the psychic to the imaginal, the imaginal to the intelligible and the intelligible to the archangelic world.[8] The traditional civilizations were too aware of the Divine Origin of the world as well as the ontological dependence of material creation upon the higher orders of reality here and now to make the fatal error of subverting the "great chain of being" into a horizontal one and ending with the modern conception of evolution, which is a monstrosity from the traditional point of view.

Metaphysically speaking, whatever exists at the omega point must have been already present at the alpha point. No amount of material permutation or transformation can cause intelligence to issue forth from brute matter. Nor can the greater ever evolve from the lesser unless it is already present there in one way or another. When traditional doctrines speak of the Perfect or Universal Man, they mean man in his primordial reality and not what he might 'evolve' into in the future. When they speak of the perfection of creation, they mean the reestablishment of the paradisal perfection with the help of Heaven Itself and not through a gradual temporal process and by means of merely terrestrial means even if the 'terrestrial' extend to the galaxies.[9] No greater obstacle exists in the way of understanding traditional cosmologies and sciences than the theory of evolution as usually understood, a theory brought into being in the atmosphere of nineteenth-century secularism in order to compensate for the loss of the vision of God and the intuition of the everabiding presence of the archetypal realities in the physical world.

The goal of the traditional sciences has never been either purely utilitarian in the modern sense nor for the sake of science itself. Since in the traditional perspective man is seen as a totality encompassing body, soul and spirit, all the sciences which have been cultivated in traditional civilizations have catered to a particular need of this totality and have therefore not been developed with the aim of "science for the sake of science," as such a concept is understood today. But then neither have these sciences been utilitarian in the sense of being useful only to the needs of man considered as a purely terrestrial being. These sciences are in fact "useful" and "of utility" if man's spiritual as well as mental and physical needs are taken into consideration. In the perspective of the traditional sciences there is no complete dichotomy between contemplation and action or truth and 'usefulness.' While these sciences have had obvious practical applications connected with the active life, they have possessed and in fact continue to possess a contemplative aspect which provides food for the contemplative soul and helps man to see the cosmos not as a veil of opacity but as a mirror of light reflecting the Beauty of the One. These sciences, which from the external point of view may appear useless, are nevertheless most useful from an inner point of view, for what can be of greater use to man than that which nourishes his immortal soul and helps him to become aware of that Divine Spark in him by virtue of which he is man?

The language in which the traditional sciences have been expressed over the ages has not always been the same. Some traditions are mythological in nature, while others make use of a more abstract language to express the Truth which Itself is one and is to be found in all traditions. The same distinction can be seen in traditional sciences, some of which are expressed in mythological and others in mathematical and abstract language. In fact in certain traditions such as Hinduism both types of sciences can be found side by side. But in both cases the language is eminently symbolic. Whether the movements of the planets are described qualitatively in the form of myth[10] or mathematically as in the Ptolemaic model, the language involved is a language of symbolism which reveals a truth beyond the domain of the facts of the science in question. Every traditional science is metaphysically significant precisely because of its being able to relate a lower domain of reality to the higher planes through the language of symbolism. Traditional mathematics or astronomy *are* mathematics and astronomy but not *only* mathematics and astronomy in the limited modern sense of these terms. Rather, they are symbolic expressions of realities belonging to the metaphysical order. Without awareness of the language of symbolism, it is not possible to gain a full understanding of the traditional sciences, which make use of appearances in order to reveal the essential realities which the appearances at once veil and reveal.[11]

Nowhere is the presence of the two types of language of the traditional sciences more evident than in cosmology, which is in a sense the mother or matrix of the traditional sciences.[12] Traditional cosmology must not be confused with the speculations based on modern astrophysics that bear the same name today. Traditional cosmology is an application of metaphysical principles to the cosmic domain. The modern world simply does not possess a cosmology if cosmology is understood in this sense and not as inductions based on astronomical findings and subject to constant change. Traditional cosmology has been expressed in innumerable ways from the mythical accounts of the Australian aborigines and the Polynesians to the most elaborate schemes of Tibetan Buddhism, from qualitative descriptions to the mathematical elaborations of Islamic or medieval Christian cosmologists. But in all cases the purpose of cosmology is to reveal the hierarchic structure of the universe and the Divine Origin of the natural world, which is at once a remnant of the terrestrial paradise and an anticipation of the celestial one. Whether in the form of ancient Vedic myth of the sacrifice of *Puruṣa* or the Zoroastrian and Mythraic accounts of the dismemberment of the Primordial Man, Gayomārth, or yet the doctrine of Universal Man (*al-insān al-kāmil*) in Islam, the same truth can be observed, the truth that the terrestrial realm is itself the "remainder" of a sacrificed divinity or a reflection of an archetypal reality which is also the essence of man.

The world is at once order and beauty. The Greek *kosmos* means at once the world, order and beauty, while the Latin *mundus*, which has the same root as *maṇḍala*, also means both world and beauty. The word 'world' itself is etymologically related to Primordial Man and his sacrifice.[13] Traditional cosmology reveals this reality and the rapport of the realm of nature to the higher levels of existence, making use of a series of languages as diverse as the languages employed in the sacred art of various traditions. In fact cosmology *is* an art which transforms the world of multiplicity into an icon to be contemplated, as well as a crypt to be traversed and transcended. It must never be forgotten that if, according to the famous medieval dictum, *ars sine scientia nihil*, in a certain sense also *scientia sine arte nihil*. Traditional science and most of all traditional cosmology is an art as traditional art is a science. Cosmology is that universal, intelligible scheme, that vast tapestry within which each particular traditional science is woven as a particular form or figure whose meaning is unveiled only with reference to the whole of the tapestry, a whole which one cannot behold save through the light of metaphysics and gnosis.

God said, "Let there be light; and there was light," states the Book of Genesis (III.1) and the Quran confirms this universal truth in the verse, "His command, when He desireth a thing, is to say to it, 'Be!' and it is" (XXXVI.82, Arberry translation). Also, "In the beginning was the Word" (John I.1). Therefore the principle of cosmic manifestation is at once light and the Word or Logos. Sacred language, the sign of the sounds and utterances of such a language and the esoteric significance of its alphabet, stand at the heart of most of the traditional sciences and are in a sense the mother and progenitor of these sciences.

In Hinduism the first language is identified with Manu, the prototype of humanity, who conceived the archetypal or ideal forms (*mantras*) of objects and explained their relation to the objects in the physical world to mankind, thus creating the first language. These *mantras* are permanent and spiritual bodies of transient physical forms, so that the primordial language associated with the *mantras* is related to the principles or roots of the objects of the world. That is why utterances belonging to sacred or primordial language carry man beyond the physical world to the abode of the divinity residing at the heart of the particular *mantra* in question. In fact, as the *Yāmala Tantra* states, "Verily the body of the deity arises from its basic thought-form [or seed-*mantra*]."14

As for the alphabet, according to Hinduism it is derived from natural ideograms which are based on *yantras* or visual equivalents of *mantras*. As the *Kanlāvalīyam* states, "the *yantra* has the *mantra* as its soul. The deity is the soul of the *mantra*. The difference between the *yantra* and the divinity is similar to that between a body and its soul."15 The alphabet, like the sounds of the sacred language, is therefore related to the Divine Energies which have brought the cosmos into being, and the science which studies the symbolism of the alphabet is also concerned with the structure of the universe.

According to the Kabbala also, the sacred language, this time the language in question is Hebrew rather than Sanskrit, reflects the spiritual or inner aspect of the universe. The letters of the Hebrew alphabet are elements of creation so that a knowledge of the inner laws of the sacred language and the symbolism of its alphabet lead to a knowledge of the inner structure of the world. The *Sefer Yeṣira (Book of Creation)* mentions specifically the *sefirot* or ten primordial numbers which along with the twenty-two letters of the Hebrew alphabet provide the spiritual elements of the universe.16 Jewish esoterism, especially the German Hassidic tradition, developed elaborate sciences concerning the symbolism of the sacred alphabet, the most important of these sciences being *guematria*, concerned with the numerical value of the letters of the alphabet, *noṭarikon*, the interpretation of the letters of a particular word as initials of the words of a sentence, and *temurah*, the permutation of letters. These traditional sciences concerned with the sacred language and the Logos or Word "by which all things were made" were therefore also concerned with the nature of things. They related the domain of external reality to the Divine World through the study of the Word which is ultimately the substance or reality of the created order.

It is interesting to note that although traditional sciences of language are always concerned with the sacred language of the revelation with which the tradition in question in concerned, in the case of the Kabbala there exists also a Christian Kabbalistic school associated with such figures as Pico della Mirandola, Reuchlin, Agrippa von Nellesheim, Jacob Böhme, John Olearius, Robert Fludd and Athanasius Kircher. The teachings of this school are still based on the Hebrew language although in a Christian context.[17] This particular situation can be explained through the special relation of Christianity to Judaism and the fact that Christianity does not posses a sacred language of its own. This case, therefore, does not invalidate the general principle that the traditional sciences concerned with language and the alphabet are bound up in each tradition with the sacred language of that tradition and are in fact derived from the sacred sources of the tradition in question.

This relationship is perfectly evident in the case of Islam, where one can find elaborate esoteric sciences connected with the Arabic language and alphabet, Arabic being the sacred language of Islam, the 'form' in which the Quranic revelation reached mankind. According to Islam, the Quran in its inner reality is uncreated,[18] this archetypal Quran being at once the origin of the Noble Book or the composed Quran (al-Qur'ān al-tadwīnī) and the universe or the "cosmic Quran" (al-Qur'ān al-takwīnī). The traditional sciences concerned with both the sounds and alphabet of Arabic are therefore keys not only for the understanding of the Noble Book, but also for the penetration into the meaning of the cosmos.[19] The traditional science of al-jafr, said to have been established by 'Alī, is not only a means of unravelling the mysteries of the Quran, but also a gate through which one can enter into the inner chamber of the world of creation, whose external phenomena are related to the 'signs' or āyāt of the Quran, which can be deciphered by means of al-jafr. This science can be known only to the Islamic esoterists because it is itself concerned with the esoteric and the condition for understanding is familiarity with the inner dimension of the religion. Nothing can lead from the outward to the inward unless it has itself issued forth from the inward. Al-jafr, like similar sciences concerned with sacred languages and their alphabets in other traditions, is an esoteric science meant to guide man to an inward knowledge of both sacred scripture and the world, an inward knowledge which, however, is impossible to attain without penetration by the seeker into the inner chamber of his own being.

Closely allied to the traditional sciences of language and the alphabet is traditional mathematics, especially its main branches as enumerated in the

Pythagorean *quadrivium* consisting of arithmetic, geometry, music and astronomy.[20] Mathematics is itself a special language which speaks of the inner harmony of things. It deals outwardly with quantity but is inwardly the ladder leading to the intelligible world. Numbers are so many crystallizations of the qualities of being, symbols of spiritual quality for those qualified to perceive them as such. Numbers are a key to the understanding of the cosmos because they reveal the harmony which pervades all things. Not only the well-known Pythagorean tradition, but also the Egyptian and Babylonian sciences from which it derived, and Islamic mathematics, which reflects a Pythagorean intellectuality in an Abrahamic ambience, are based on the sacred conception of numbers and their symbolism.[21]

Traditional arithmetic conceives of numbers as so many elements of multiplicity which somehow never leave Unity. It sees arithmetic as applied metaphysics and at the same time as the quantitative aspect of a reality whose qualitative aspect is revealed in music. Musical melodies and harmonies cannot be reduced to numbers in the quantitative sense; rather, musical harmony presents to the human soul through the auditory faculty an irreducible reality whose intelligible structure is unveiled through mathematics.[22] Mathematics and especially arithmetic is thus both a key to metaphysics and a path to the understanding of the harmony pervading the created order whose auditory aspect is revealed in music. The beauty of music and of mathematics are aspects of the same reality.[23]

According to Hindu mythology the first art to have been revealed to mankind by Śiva was music. The harmony of music is also the key to the understanding of the universe, which is structured upon musical harmony.[24] The ratios of small integers which produce musical notes and harmonic scales are at the same time the ratios which determine the structure of God's creation from the shell of the snail to the planetary system, whose movements Johannes Kepler discovered through his knowledge of harmony (the Third Law is described for the first time in a work entitled *Harmonica mundi*). In the traditional world, music was inseparable from the other sciences of the Pythagorean *quadrivium*, namely arithmetic, geometry and astronomy. It accompanied man from the first moments of his venture on earth, and in a sense from music, or rather its harmonical principles, were born the other arts and sciences.

Among the most primordial of these sciences is geometry, many of whose principles are already displayed in the patterns to be found in works of Neolithic man not to speak of the remarkable stone monuments of such ritual sites as Stonehenge.[25] Traditional geometry is related to the symbolic configurations of space, reflecting so many aspects of the theophanies of the One, which is itself above space and is symbolized by the point. Geometric forms such as the triangle, square and various regular polygons, the spiral or the circle are seen in the traditional perspective to be, like traditional numbers, so many crystallizations of that multiplicity which never leave the fold of Unity. Through geometry, as through traditional arithmetic, multiplicity is brought back to Unity and Unity is seen as reflected in multiplicity.

Many traditions have asserted that if man lives in time and in a sense time belongs to man, space belongs to the gods. Metaphysically, space symbolizes the Divine Presence and the field for the actualization of the possibilities inherent in cosmic manifestation.[26] Its measurement, determination and the orientation which takes place in it are means whereby traditional man gains awareness of this Presence. Through sacred geometry, which exists in the rites as well as in the sacred architecture of all traditions, the profane space of everyday physical experience becomes transformed into the sacred space where man orients himself toward and becomes attached to the Center, which is at once everywhere and nowhere.

The *maṇḍala* is a "wordless symbol" of the inner structure of things and of man. In fact, its symbolic geometry not only aids man as an object of contemplation but also leads man to the discovery of himself. Man is in fact himself a *maṇḍala*, were he only to know who he is.[27] The sacred temples of all traditions, based on the symbolism of the directions of space and geometric proportions, are not only a space in which man experiences the sacred. Rather, they *are* themselves man in his inner reality as God's vice-gerent (*khalīfah* in the Islamic tradition), in this world, the *pontifex* uniting Heaven and earth.[28] Traditional geometry, like arithmetic, is inseparable from the fundamental harmonies upon which the macrocosm as well as man, the microcosm, are structured. That is why no traditional civilization has been without it and why both the rituals and sacred art of various religions are always related to it. In fact some of the purest and noblest forms of spirituality, such as that of the North American Plains Indians, reflect the purest form of geometrical symbolism in both their ritual practices and their art,[29] and the last of the major religions of the present cycle of humanity, Islam, has led to a sacred art based in certain of its aspects almost solely upon geometry.[30]

The last of the "mathematical sciences" to be enumerated in the Pythagorean *quadrivium* is astronomy, which is also the oldest of the so-called "exact sciences." Traditional astronomy has a long history antedating by millennia the schools of ancient Babylonia and India, where extensive treatises were written on the subject. In fact the study of the heavens and their motions was carried out in an age in which the mythological mode of thought prevailed over the mathematical and when knowledge of even complicated astronomical motions were transmitted in the form of mythical tales. The impressive astronomical works of the ancient Babylonians and Indians are based on millennia of observation of the heavens during the periods preceding the advent of these civilizations.[31]

There are many schools of traditional astronomy such as the Babylonian, the Indian, and the Greek, which was based on the Babylonian as well as the astronomy of the Egyptians. These traditions along with that of the Persians led in turn to Islamic astronomy, which after the Mongol invasion was to have profound mutual interactions with the independent school of Chinese astronomy and which of course influenced the West from the eleventh century onward. And outside of all these schools one finds remarkable astronomical studies carried out by the ancient Aztecs and Mayans. All of these schools remain faithful to the study of the heavens as they appear to man on earth, and not as they might appear to him were he to stand on the sun or outside the solar system. That is why their symbolism is not at all logically affected by the Copernican Revolution even if historically this revolution did in fact help to bring about the eclipse of that knowledge to which traditional astronomy points in its symbolic aspect.

Besides practical considerations of agriculture and the like, the "utility' of traditional astronomy was to enable man to orient himself in the cosmos with the purpose of preparing himself to journey beyond it.[32] The practical spiritual import of this aspect of astronomy is evident everywhere from the Australian aborigines' descriptions of the heavens to the *Divine Comedy* of Dante. As far as the great civilizations of antiquity and the Middle Ages are concerned, however, it is the system of concentric spheres developed in two different fashions by the Greeks, one by Aristotle and the other by Ptolemy, on the basis of the works of their predecessors such as Eudoxus, which are of particular interest.[33] These systems depict, through their symbolism, the hierarchic nature of cosmic reality and man's place in this hierarchic scheme as being located centrally but on the lowest level of reality, veiled from the splendor of the Divine Throne by the levels of cosmic manifestation symbolized by the various spheres associated with the planets and the fixed stars.

In traditional civilizations there was hardly a distinction to be made between the terms astronomy and astrology, as these words in Greek and *nujūm* in Arabic demonstrate. Gradually, however, the two became separated—one quantified completely and depleted of its symbolic significance and the other deprived of its metaphysical foundations and reduced for the most part to a superstition in the etymological sense of the term. Yet in its traditional sense astrology continues to reflect a symbolism of primordial significance, one which is of spiritual interest even if one puts aside completely the predictive element of astrology.[34] In its symbolic sense astrology unveils in a more direct fashion the symbolism inherent in traditional astronomy upon which the astrological art depends.

Astrology sees terrestrial phenomena as reflections of their celestial archetypes symbolized by the twelve zodiacal signs[35] and the possibilities inherent in them and actualized by the planets, each of which symbolizes an aspect of the cosmic intelligence.[36] The components of astrology are dominated by the numbers 3 and 4, symbolizing respectively heaven and earth. There are the three cosmic tendencies, the *gunas* which form the foundation of Hindu cosmology, and there are the four elements. Then there are the seven planets ($7 = 3 + 4$), the twelve signs ($12 = 3 \times 4$) and the twenty-eight stations of the moon ($28 = 7!$ and also 7×4). The moon, as the cosmic memory, "recapitulates" all of the cosmic influences and relays it to the terrestrial domain below. There are of course differences of emphasis. Hindu astrology atributes a somewhat different role to the lunar mansions than Western astrology, while the Chinese-Uighur system adds, to the calendar, a twelve-year cycle based on the symbolism of animals in such a way that time itself becomes so many repetitions of a twelve-year cycle, reflecting the twelve-fold "spatial" division of the signs of the Zodiac and repeating on a larger temporal scale the twelve-fold partition of the year into months.[37]

Through astrology, major events of the life of the individual and society, events such as marriage, coronation of a king or initiation, were made to conform to auspicious cosmic moments so that events and objects below conformed to their celestial archetypes and man lived according to cosmic harmony. But astrology also linked man through his horoscope to his cosmic reflection and to his "angelic being." Astrology in its symbolic aspect is also a kind of anthropology, a science as well as an art (*ṣinā'ah* as it is called in Arabic) which unveils the typology of man and reveals differing human types. It provides a key for understanding not on the level of everyday actions but on a higher plane which determines how various human beings act out their lives in this world. It helps to discover the patterns which link different types of men with the rhythms of the cosmos and the archetypes which determine the forms and events of the world of generation and corruption, without this denying either the Divine Will as it penetrates into human life or the free will bestowed by God to man.

Traditional civilizations developed yet another science related to astronomy, namely chronology, or the science of the divisions of time. Of course, all traditional calendars are based on sacred history and on repetitions which bring man once again to the sacred "events" of a transhistorical nature, "events" which periodically rejuvenate him and bestow meaning upon his life. Traditional chronologies are many, ranging from the remarkable Mayan and Aztec ones to those of the people of Central Asia and Siberia in ancient times, not to speak of the calendars of the Chinese, the Egyptians, the Babylonians and the Persians.[38] But the Hindus stand out particularly in this domain not so much for the devising of an exact calendar but for their elaborate study of the cosmic rhythms, which as *kalpas*, *manvantāras*, and *yugas* determine the various cycles of the life in this world. The traditional doctrine of cycles is one which lies completely beyond the grasp of modern science and cannot be understood save in the light of metaphysical doctrines and even a particular "grace" issuing from Heaven and aiding intellectual intuition. That is why the predictive element in the writings of even those contemporary authors who claim to write on cosmic cycles from a traditional point of view is often dominated by a sense of imprisonment which stifles the spirit as if it were to exclude the Will of God from acting in His creation.[39] That is also why a *ḥadīth* of the Prophet of Islam goes so far as to assert that "all those who predict the Hour [that is, the end of the world] are liars." The science of cosmic cycles and subcycles as developed so extensively in the *Purāṇas*, remains, nevertheless, an important traditional science linked with astronomy on the one hand and the devising of the calendar or chronology (which is itself also linked with astronomy) on the other. It is a science, moreover, which is found in one form or another in various traditions, as for example among Hermetic and Kabbalistic authors in the West as well as in the Far East, where a figure such as the Neo-Confucian Shao-Yung was particularly known for his treatise entitled *Cosmic Periods*.

In a sense the terrestrial image of astrology may be said to be alchemy, which deals with those "intelligent" forms of matter called metals. That is why metals in fact possess the same symbols in alchemy as their astrological counterparts (for example,   —/Saturn/lead,   —/Sun/gold and —/Moon/silver).[40] But traditional alchemy is not only a science or art which seeks to transmute various substances and metals into gold. Alchemy is one of the most extensive and encompassing of the traditional sciences. It is related at once to cosmology, medicine, the science of substances and psychology.[41] Alchemy, like astrology, is based on a primordial vision of the earth as a living being in whose bosom and with the help of celestial influences grow the metals which stand outside of the natural order. The metallurgist is like a gynecologist who delivers the metal from the womb of the earth and who, with the aid of spiritual forces, is able to quicken the process by which this event takes place.[42]

The major traditions of alchemy, namely the Alexandrian with its roots in the ancient Egyptian tradition, the Chinese, the Indian, the Islamic and the Western, all grew out of this ancient science (or once again "art," if we remember that most traditional sources, both Arabic and Latin, call it art— *ṣinā'ah* or *ars*). These later traditions, despite the differences between them, and including the Chinese, which emphasizes the gold-making juice as the elixer or immortality,[43] all shared the basic principles which saw metals as special states of "matter" with a common substratum, ready to be transmuted into the highest state, which is that of gold provided the Philosopher's Stone be present.[44] But they also knew that this external transmutation was no more than support for that inner transformation of the lead of the soul into the gold which alone can resist the withering influences of this world. They were also fully aware that this inner transformation is only possible through the presence of the spiritual master who is the real Philosopher's Stone. This does not mean that alchemists did not make use of the external substances for support to which many Hermetic authors bear witness.[45] Alchemy was certainly a way of enobling matter, hence its relation to sacred art. But this also means that alchemy is not just a prelude to chemistry, that it is a science of the soul in its relation to the cosmos and making use of external transformations for the sake of that inner transformation which is the ultimate goal of all traditional sciences.

More than most disciplines, medicine reveals the completely contingent nature of modern science, as well as the relativity of even the traditional sciences, in the light of the Absolute and the science of the Absolute. The efficacy of traditional schools of medicine proves in a practical manner that there are other ways of studying and treating the human body than what modern medicine has taken into consideration. Moreover, the fact that there is not one but several schools of traditional medicine based on different cosmological principles but all efficacious in their own ways, proves that there are many cosmological sciences of even a single reality, which in this case is the human microcosm, although these sciences all lead to the single science of the Real. Finally, the fact that no single school of traditional medicine is completely successful in the treatment of all diseases proves that not even a science of the traditional order can completely overcome illness and other physical handicaps, not to speak of aging and death, which are in the very nature of this world and which prove, if proof is necessary, that only God is good. *Samsāric* existence remains *samsāric* even if studied from the point of view of traditional medicine.

In all traditional civilizations, medicine has been closely related to the basic principles of the tradition in question. Its origin has always been seen to be divine. In Egypt the figure of Thoth and later Hermes was associated with the founding of the science of medicine as was Agathedemon in Greece, while in India *Ayurvedic* medicine was associated with the *Atharva-Veda*. In Egyptian medicine a clear distinction was already made between illnesses whose origin was spiritual, those which came from psychic imbalance, and those resulting from purely physical disorders. The psyche was seen to affect the body and the spirit the psyche. The hierarchy of these three fundamental "substances" within the human microcosm was fully recognized and an elaborate medicine developed upon its foundations, thereby making use of treatments ranging all the way from incantations to herbs.[46]

Greek medicine was to continue this tradition while developing through Hippocrates and his school the theory of the four elements and humors, which led to Galen's vast synthesis based upon humoral pathology.[47] Meanwhile herbs were widely utilized following Egyptian usage and also in part as a result of contact with Persian medicine, in which a vast pharmacoepia had been developed. These two traditions, the Greek and the Persian, were to merge later in Islamic medicine, but even in Dioscorides elements of both schools are to be seen.

Indian medicine called *Ayur-Veda*, meaning literally health knowledge, developed as a branch of purely traditional Hindu learning, although it too was influenced in its earlier phase by Persian medicine, as can be seen in the Indian word for medicine (*bheshaji*) which is of Avestan origin. *Ayurvedic* medicine, which continues as a living school today, sees disease as being caused by not one but numerous factors, ranging from divine or diabolical elements, to psychic forces associated with sorcery, astrological influences, hereditary factors and physical and climatic conditions. Like Greek and Islamic medicine, it makes use of the concept of hot and cold diseases (*ushman*) and is based on treatment by means of medicines of contrary nature. It is based on the atomic theory of matter (*paramāṇu*), the theory of the three *guṇas* or qualities within the physical world, the five traditional elements (*bhūtas*), the seven elements of physiology (*septa-dhātu*) and three rather than four human temperaments which are also understood as "sheaths." (*tri-dosha*). Through this "theoretical" basis, it is related to Hindu cosmology and metaphysics as well as eschatology. *Ayurvedic* medicine makes use of a bewildering range of cures including not only medicines which are taken by mouth, but diet, exercise, fumigation, blood-letting, scarification, not to speak of massage, bathing and sweating. *Ayurvedic* medicine remains in both practice and theory one of the notable systems of traditional medicine which have survived to this day.[48]

India's neighbor, China, was to develop a medical system no less efficacious and in a sense more remarkable in both its practice and results. The medicine based on acupuncture and acupressure, which developed in China and later spread to Japan, Korea, and Indo-China, is as closely related to the cosmological principles of the Chinese tradition as the *Ayurveda* is to the Indian. Chinese medicine is based on the basic Chinese doctrine of the masculine-feminine principles of *Yin* and *Yang*, two principles which are opposite yet complementary, the five elements also found in traditional Chinese cosmology and physics,[49] and the ether sometimes translated as energy or the principle of life (*ch'i*) which pervades the human microcosm. Centers of the psychic body which facilitate the flow of life energy and connect the psychic and physical elements of the human microcosm have been discovered by Chinese medicine in a most accurate fashion and a treatment is applied which deals directly with the principle of the physical body rather than the physical body itself. If there were any need of empirical proof of the validity of the Chinese cosmology which underlies acupuncture, one would only need to observe the remarkable results of treating certain types of illnesses through the methods of Chinese medicine. The revival of this school even in the modern West and in a context in which this medicine is often practiced in forgetfulness of its cosmological and metaphysical background is proof of the powerful means it has developed to deal with human illness by considering man in his total relationship with the cosmos about him, although the efficacy of this medicine cannot be total if it is severed from its cosmological principles.[50]

The Islamic world was touched by Chinese medicine only after the Mongol invasion, but it became heir to nearly every other great school of medicine of antiquity including the Indian, from all of which it created a vast synthesis associated with the names Rhazes and Avicenna. This school, which is also still alive, especially in the subcontinent of India, is again a science of the human body as a microcosm reflecting the hierarchy of cosmic existence and in harmony with parts of the universe. This medicine, therefore, while including a vast pharmacology and even resorting to complicated techniques of surgery, also employs such arts as music for the cure of illness and has developed a remarkable school concerning what has come to be known today as psychosomatic medicine. It was this tradition which formed the basis for traditional medicine in the medieval West and against which Paracelsus, the representative of the last school of medicine in the West which can still be called, properly speaking, traditional, nevertheless rebelled in the sixteenth century.[51]

The study of traditional medicine and pharmacology was always related to natural history, which saw man as part of the three kingdoms and a vast natural environment which, being the creation of God, was also a symbol of the spiritual world. Natural history was as much the subject of "natural science" as of mythology; it was as much a source for the knowledge of the relation of plants to their habitat as it was the source of the forests in which Krishna played the flute and the angels became transformed into various animal forms.

The importance of natural history for the specifically religious themes of various traditions can be best seen in that part of this science which deals with "sacred geography," for which the term geomancy is also sometimes employed.[52] Traditional civilizations envisaged the earth itself as a symbol reflecting the vertical hierarchy. The earth in a sense was an angel as the ancient Zoroastrians claimed.[53] The Hindus saw the earth as being comprised of four continents, Uttarakuru in the north, Pūrvavideha in the east, Jāmbudvīpa in the south and Aparagoyāna in the west, all surrounding the central Mount Meru, the cosmic mountain where Heaven and Earth meet.[54] Likewise, the Chinese envisaged the sacred mountain Khun-Lun as the center of the earth,[55] as traditional Christians and Jews have viewed Jerusalem and the Muslims Mecca.[56]

But there is another aspect to sacred geography which concerns the study of the subtle influences on the surface of the earth and symbolic forms which make a particular sight more conductive to the reception of the grace of Heaven, a science which is related to the location of sites for temples, sanctuaries, tombs and initiatic centers and also the creation of gardens and landscapes which maximize the presence of the *barakah* which runs through the arteries of the universe and which transform a natural environment into a reflection of paradise. Some of the Japanese and Persian gardens built with knowledge of the principles of this important traditional science are like an antechamber opening into the paradisal world. In fact they *are* paradise if only one were to remain recollected in the contemplation of their exquisite forms.

Finally, a word must be said about traditional technologies which are related to these sciences, although they need to be treated separately to do justice to the subject. Traditional technologies had to do with craftsmanship and art in its original sense (*techné* in fact like *ars* means "to make"), but precisely because in the traditional context, as shown so majestically by such contemporary traditional authors as T. Burckhardt and A.K. Coormaraswamy, *ars sine scientia nihil*, they were also concerned with the traditional sciences. For example, traditional architecture is at once a synthesis of art, building techniques and science. There are also other forms of traditional technology of remarkable character such as the chemical technology of ancient Egypt, the dyes made by the Chinese or the metallurgy of the Persians and the Arabs. There are also remarkable monuments to the technology of irrigation in the form of dams, canals, underground waterways, etc. found in lands as different ecologically and climatically as Sri Lanka and Persia. In traditional forms of technology the knowledge drawn from the traditional sciences was combined with practical methods to create results which affected the body *and* soul of the maker as well as the user and beholder of the object or work in question.

As asserted above, the traditional sciences are so many applications of metaphysical principles and for certain types of minds, ladders for reaching those principles. In the context of living traditions they were means whereby all facets of life and knowledge were integrated into the center of the tradition. But in the modern world, once they are divorced from the ray of a living spirituality which alone can make them transparent symbols of the supernal verities, they can no longer fulfill the same function. In the absence of this light they can become a diversion and a veil which can divert the seeker from "the one thing necessary," rather than being sciences which bestow ultimate meaning on the world which surrounds man. But for the "mindful" and those for whom the traditional universe is a living reality, these sciences can become, according to each person's vocation and destiny, a vital key for the understanding of the cosmos and aids his journey across and beyond the cosmos. Although they are sciences of the cosmic domain, they may become with the aid of the Spirit symbols which reveal rather than veil the spiritual reality beyond the forms and help man to reach, through the grace of Heaven, the state of "seeing God everywhere." They can be a support for the cleansing of man's perception of the world about him so that he can come to see things not as they appear to be in themselves but as they are in God, for as the English poet William Blake has said: "If the doors of perception were cleansed, everything would appear to man as it is, infinite." (*Marriage of Heaven and Hell*).

The highest function of the traditional sciences has always been to aid the intellect and the instruments of perception to see the world and in fact all levels of existence not as facts or objects but as symbols, as mirrors in which is reflected the face of the Beloved from Whom all originates and to Whom everything returns.

Notes

1. The English term science is even more limited in meaning than the French *science* or the German *Wissenschaft*, although it still carries the resonance of the Latin term *scientia*, a resonance which can always be used to revive the more universal meaning of the term which we are in fact using in this book.

2. We have dealt with this question in our *Man and Nature*, chapter 3.

3. In Arabic, in fact, many of the traditional sciences are classified under the category of *al-'ulūm al-khafiyyah*, literally "occult sciences." On the more general classification of the sciences in Islam, see Nasr, *Science and Civilization in Islam* (Cambridge, 1987), p. 63; and also our *Islamic Science: An Illustrated Study* (London, 1976), chapter II. In these classifications, which concern the formal curricula of teaching institutions, the "occult sciences" are sometimes excluded as a separate category and integrated into the scheme of the formal or "official" sciences.

4. On the distinction between sacred and profane science, see R. Guénon, "Sacred and Profane Science," trans. by A.K. Coomaraswamy, *Viśva-Bharati Quarterly*, vol. 1, (1935) pp. 11–24. Also in Guénon, *Crisis of the Modern World*, trans.by A. Osborne (London, 1975), chapter IV. Concerning the traditional sciences Guénon writes, "toute science apparaissait ainsi comme un prolongement de la doctrine traditionnelle elle-même, comme une de ses applications...une connaissance inférieure si l'on veut, mais pourtant encore une véritable connaissance." *Orient et Occident*, (Paris, 1930), chapter 2.

5. See, for example, Schuon's *Esoterism as Principle and as a Way*.

6. Numerous works of A.K. Coomaraswamy refer to the traditional doctrine of the states of being; for example, "The Inverted Tree," *Quarterly Journal of the Mythic Society*, vol. 29, (1938), pp. 111–49, also in R. Lipsey (ed.), *Coomaraswamy, 1: Selected Papers— Traditional Art and Symbolism* (Princeton, 1977), pp. 376–404; "Gradation and Evolution, I," *Isis*, vol. 35 (1944), pp. 15–16, and II, *Isis*, vol. 38 (1947), pp. 87–94. Coomaraswamy

also discusses the grades of being from the point of view of the soul's journey through them in his "Recollection, 'Indian and Platonic' " and "On the One and Only Transmigrant," *Journal of the American Oriental Society*, vol. 45, supplement no. 3 (1944), also in Lipsey (ed.), Coomaraswamy, vol. II, pp. 49–87. This doctrine is also summarized in R. Guénon, *The Multiple States of Being*, trans.by J.Godwin (Burdett, N.Y., 1984).

7. On the traditional doctrine of the cycles of time which has been expounded most extensively in Hinduism, see R. Guénon, *The Reign of Quantity and the Signs of the Times*, trans. by Lord Northbourne (Baltimore, 1972); Guénon, *Formes traditionnelles et cycles cosmiques* (Paris, 1970); M. Eliade, *The Myth of the Eternal Return*, trans. by W. Trask (New York, 1959); and H. Zimmer, *Myths and Symbols in Indian Art and Civilization*.

8. On the historical and philosophical background of this idea, see A. Lovejoy, *The Great Chain of Being* (Cambridge, Mass., 1957). On the "great chain of being" itself, see H. Smith, *Forgotten Truth: The Primordial Tradition*, chapter 3.

9. The belief of some modern authors about the extraterrestrial origin of man from outer space is in reality a caricature of the traditional doctrines in a world in which, as a result of the loss of intellectual intuition, the higher states of reality have become so forgotten that they have become replaced by galaxies in outer space in the same way that the intelligences of the celestial hierarchies have given their place to aliens with super "intelligence" invading the planet earth.

10. On astronomy in mythological form see G. di Santillana and H. von Dechend, *Hamlet's Mill* (Boston, 1969).

11. For traditional man in whom the "symbolist spirit" was still alive, an object was not only symbol of a higher reality. Rather, it *was* that reality on a lower level of existence. This is particularly true of those people who have been called primitive without an awareness on the part of those who use this term usually in a pejorative sense of the primacy of intuitive power among them and their greater consciousness of the essential and noumenal rather than the phenomenal in contrast to modern man who has chosen to give them this seemingly pejorative name. A.K. Coomaraswamy has dwelt extensively on this matter in many of his writings and especially in his well-known essay, "On the Primitive Mentality," *Quarterly Journal of the Mythic Society*, vol. 20, (1940), pp. 69–91. On the traditional meaning of symbols, see M. Lings, *Symbols and Archetype* (Cambridge, 1991).

12. On the cosmological perspective, see T. Burckhardt, "Nature of the Cosmological Perspective," in his *Mirror of the Intellect*, trans. by W. Stoddart (Cambridge, 1987), pp. 13–16.

13. "An archaic traditional creation myth recounts that God, the One, was sacrificed and dismembered by demons or that he offered himself up as a victim to himself. From his dead limbs sprang up the various parts of the visible world. The visible world is his dead body.

"The word *world* bears witness to the myth; it comes from the Old English *weorld*, which probably stems from *wer*, 'man' (still found in *werewolf*, 'man-wolf') and *ald*, 'full-grown', 'big' (hence *old*). The world is a dead giant or god." E. Zolla, "Traditional Methods of Contemplation and Action," in Y. Ibish and I. Marculescu (eds.), *Contemplation and Action in World Religions* (Seattle and London, 1978), p. 117; also in Y. Ibish and P. Wilson (eds.), *Traditional Modes of Contemplation and Action*, (London and Boulder, 1977), p. 60.

14. Quoted in A. Daniélou, *Hindu Polytheism* (New York, 1964), p. 334.

15. Ibid., p. 350.

16. On the Jewish Kabbala, see L.Schaya, *The Universal Meaning of the Kabbala*, trans. by N. Pearson (Baltimore, 1973); G. Scholem, *Major Trends in Jewish Mysticism*, trans. by M.M. Davy (New York, 1954); G. Vajda, *Recherches sur la philosophie de la kabbale* (Paris, 1962); and P. Vulliard, *La Kabbale juive* (Paris, 1964). The doctrine of the correspondence between the sacred alphabet and the cosmic order has been developed elaborately by many Islamic esoterists, notably Ibn 'Arabī, who devotes many pages to the relation between letters of the Arabic alphabet and cosmic elements in his *al-Futūḥāt al-makkiyyah*, vol. II (Cairo, 1293 A.H., pp. 426–60. See also J. Canteins, "The Hidden Sciences in Islam," in S.H. Nasr (ed.), *Islamic Spirituality—Manifestations* (New York, 1991), pp. 447–468.

17. On the Christian Kabbala, see M.J.L. Blau, *The Christian Interpretation of the Cabala in the Renaissance* (New York, 1944). See also J. Godwin, *Athanasius Kircher* (London, 1979).

18. See F. Schuon, *Understanding Islam*, trans.by D.M. Matheson, (London, 1981), chapter 2.

19. We have dealt with this question extensively in our *Introduction to Islamic Cosmological Doctrines*, especially chapter 12. See also L. Massignon, *Essai sur les origines du lexique technique de la mystique musulmane* (Paris, 1954); and his *The Passion of al-Hallāj: Mystic and Martyr of Islam*, trans. by H. Mason (Princeton, 1982), vol. 3, (1975), pp. 91–107; also Schuon, *Esoterism as Principle and as Way*, p. 65ff.

20. On the traditional conception of mathematics, see Fabre d'Olivet, *The Golden Verses of Pythagoras*, trans. by N.L. Redfield (London, 1925); M. Ghyka, *Le Nombre d'or*, 3 vols. (Paris, 1931); *Introduction to Arithmetic*, trans. by M.L. D'Ooge in *Great Books in the Western World*, vol. II (Chicago, 1952); K. Critchlow, *Order in Space* (London, 1969); K. Critchlow, *The Soul as Sphere and Androgyne* (Ipswich, 1980); N. Pennick, *Sacred Geometry* (Wellingborough, 1980); and R. Lowlor, *Sacred Geometry, Philosophy and Practice*, (New York, 1982); E. Levy, "The Pythagorean Concept of Measure,"*Main Currents in Modern Thought*, vol. 2, no. 3 (January-February 1965), pp. 51–57; E. McClain, *The Pythagorean Plato: Prelude to the Song Itself* (Stonybrook, N.Y., 1978); and Nasr, *An Introduction to Islamic Cosmological Doctrines*, p. 47ff. See also K.S. Guthrie, *The Pythagorean Source Book* (Grand Rapids, Mich., 1987).

21. Arithmetic is related to language and the alphabet, but it antedates the alphabet, for as G. di Santillana and H. von Decheud have written: "Number gave the key. Way back in time, before writing was even invented, it was *measures* and *counting* that provided the armature, the frame on which the rich texture of real myth was to grow." *Hamlet's Mill*, p. ix.

22. On the relation between traditional music and mathematics, see R. Brumbaugh, *Plato's Mathematical Imagination* (Bloomington, Ind., 1954); A. von Thimus, *Die harmonikale Symbolik des Altertums* (Cologne, 1868 and 1876), which is the source of instruction and inspiration for the many works of H. Kayser (see especially his *Akróasis: The Theory of World Harmonics*, trans. by R. Lilienfeld [Boston, 1975] and E. Levy most of whose works have remained unpublished. M. Schneider, A. Daniélou and E.G. McClain have also made notable studies of traditional music in its relation to mathematics. See also J. Godwin, *Harmonies of Heaven and Earth* (Rochester, Vt. 1987).

23. This Platonic teaching is strongly reflected in the writings of Neopythagoreans and Neoplatonists such as Nichomachus and Proclus. It is also to be found in other traditions, especially Hinduism, where an elaborate science of sound is related in certain schools to its mathematical symbolism. See, for example, E.G. McClain, *The Myth of Invariance* (Boulder and London, 1978); also A. de Nicholás, *Avatāra* (New York, 1976), where a new translation of the *Bhagavad-Gita* is accompanied by the study of sound-*maṇḍalas*.

24. Keyser has applied the Pythagorean table to numerology, botany and zoology and shown how the major proportions of natural forms are based on musical harmony. The same is of course true of traditional architecture, which some like M. Schneider have called "frozen music." On the musical proportions involved in one of the greatest masterpieces of Western architecture, the Chartres cathedral, see the appendix by E. Levy "On the Proportions of the South Tower of Chartres Cathedral" in O. von Simson, *The Gothic Cathedral: The Origins of the Gothic Cathedral and the Medieval Concept of Order* (London, 1956).

25. The sacred geometry of Stonehenge and other Neolithic monuments have been studied extensively in recent years by scholars aware of the significance of sacred science. See for example, K. Critchlow, *Time Stands Still* (London, 1979). The author is one of the foremost students of traditional mathematics in the West and has made a major contribution to the rediscovery of traditional geometry, especially as it applies to architecture.

26. The symbolic aspect of geometry is naturally related to Euclidean geometry because this particular type of geometry corresponds to the immediate experience of spatial reality to which the symbolic sciences of nature always appeal. The appearance of non-Euclidean forms of geometry do not in any way destroy the significance of the symbolic geometry associated with the name of Euclid.

27. On the significance of the *maṇḍala*, see G.Tucci, *The Theory and Practice of the Mandala*, trans.by A.H. Broderick (New York, 1978); and M. Danielli, *The Anthropology*

of the Mandala (Amherst, N.Y., 1974). As for the relation of the *maṇḍala* to the sacred architecture of India, see S. Kramrish, *The Hindu Temple* (Calcutta, 1946).

28. The Egyptian temple, which displays in a remarkable fashion the application of the knowledge of traditional geometry to architecture, has been studied in this light by R. Schwaller de Lubicz, *Le Temple de l'homme*, 3 vols. (Paris, 1957–58). See also his *The Temple in Man*, trans. R. and D. Lawlor (Brookline, Mass., 1977).

29. See F. Schuon, *The Feathered Sun* (Bloomington, Ind., 1990).

30. On geometric symbolism in Islamic art, see, T. Burckhardt, *The Art of Islam* (London, 1976). See also K. Critchlow, *Islamic Patterns* (London, 1976).

31. In their masterly work *Hamlet's Mill*, Di Santillana and von Dechend have recorded in a unique manner this "protohistory" of the science of the heavens in its relation to myth and metaphysics.

32. We have dealt with this theme in as much as it concerns the Islamic tradition in our *Introduction to Islamic Cosmological Doctrines*, chapter 15.

33. The monumental work of P. Duhem, *Le Système du monde*, 10 vols. (Paris, 1913–1959), remains still the most thorough study of this subject, although numerous major studies by such men as O. Neugebauer, E.S. Kennedy, D. Pingree, D. King and others have added enormously to our knowledge of Babylonian, Greek, Indian, Islamic and medieval Latin astronomy.

34. On the two kinds of astrology, genethliac and judicial in their Islamic context, see Nasr, "The Wedding of Heaven and Earth in Astrology," in *An Introduction to Islamic Cosmological Doctrines*, p. 151ff.

35. Di Santillana has shown the extremely ancient character of the signs of the Zodiac, which along with other heavenly signs were considered by traditional man to have been revealed by God to mankind.

36. For a profound study of the metaphysical symbolism of astrology, see T. Burckhardt, *Mystical Astrology According to Ibn ʿArabī*, trans. by B. Rauf (Gloucestershire, 1977). The literature on astrology is vast, although few works are from the traditional point of view. The following works concerning various schools of astrology are of scholarly interest: H. Lewy, *Chaldaean Oracles and Theurgy* (Cairo, 1956); F. Cumont, *Astrology and Religion Among Greeks and Romans* (New York and London, 1912); D. Pingree, *Census of the Exact Sciences in Sanskrit* (Philadelphia, 1970); W. and H.G. Gundel, *Astrologumena* (Wiesbaden, 1966); C.A. Nallino, *Raccoltá di scritti edite e inediti*, vol. I (Rome, 1944); and the monumental collection of L. Thorndike, *A History of Magic and Experimental Science*, 8 vols. (New York, 1923–58), which contains a great deal of material on many of the "occult" sciences including astrology.

37. After the Mongol invasion, the Chinese-Uighur practice entered into Islamic astrology, at least among the Turks and Persians, and is still to be found in popular astronomical

and astrological works. On this cycle, see J. Needham, *Science and Civilization in China*, vol. III (Cambridge, 1959); and F. Boll, *Kleine Schriften zur Sternkunde des Altertums* (Leipzig, 1950).

38. No work of the premodern period has recorded with greater care this reckoning of time among various peoples of antiquity than al-Bīrūnī's *Chronology of Ancient Nations*, trans. by C.E. Sachau (London, 1879).

39. As F. Schuon has mentioned more than once, to predict future events from traditional accounts of the unfolding of various parts of the historic and cosmic cycle is like seeing an image in a broken mirror. The image is there yet not exactly as one would detect its contours in a normal situation. See his *Logic and Transcendence*, trans. by P. Townsend (London, 1984), p. 155ff.

It is of some interest to note that Coomaraswamy was opposed to an overliteral interpretation of traditional teachings concerning the various *yugas*, despite his affirmation of their great metaphysical significance, one which was exposed fully for the first time in the Western world by R. Guénon.

40. For this correspondence and in fact the principles of alchemy in general, see the unrivaled work of T. Burckhardt, *Alchemy: Science of the Cosmos, Science of the Soul*, trans. by W. Stoddart (Longmead, Dorset, 1987).

41. The latter connection has turned many modern students of psychology to the study of alchemy. But although there is a profound link between the two, it must be emphasized that this link is not at all to be discovered through the Jungian interpretation of "archetypes" which belong more to the garbage can of humanity than to the luminous world of the Spirit. Jung's work on this subject, *Psychology and Alchemy*, trans. R.F.C. Hull (New York, 1953), despite its interesting illustrations, is devoid of the metaphysical foundations necessary for the understanding of the subject from the traditional point of view.

42. See M. Eliade, *The Forge and the Crucible*, trans. by S. Corrin (New York, 1962).

43. On Chinese alchemy, see N. Sivin, *Chinese Alchemy: Preliminary Studies* (Cambridge, 1968).

44. See Nasr, *Science and Civilization in Islam*, chapters nine and ten.

45. On this as well as the cosmological and medical facets of alchemy, see E. Zolla, *La meraviglie della natura: Introduzione dall'alchimia* (Milan, 1975). See also the works of Canseliet and Fulcanelli.

46. Older standard histories of medicine such as those of M. Neuburger, *Handbuch der Geschichte der Medizin*, vol. I, (Jena, 1902); and the history of J.L. Pagel and K. Sudhoff contain major sections on Egyptian medicine as do the extensive histories of H.E. Sigerist and M. Laignel-Lavastine. For more recent works see the monumental work of H. Grapow, *Grundriss der Medizin der alten Aegypter*, 8 vols. (Berlin, 1954–62). Some of these and other sources cited in the following footnotes concerning various

schools of traditional medicine are not written from a traditional point of view, but they nevertheless contain valuable documentation of traditional medical ideas, themes and practices.

47. See G. Sarton, *A History of Science*, vol. I (1952); vol. II (1959), C. Kerenyi, *Asklepios: Archetypal Image of the Physician's Existence* (London, 1960); F.B. Lund, *Greek Medicine* (New York, 1936), J. Schumacher, *Antike Medizin* (Berlin, 1963).

48. On Indian medicine see Giridranath Mukhopadhyaya, *History of Indian Medicine*, 3 vols. (Calcutta, 1923–29); H. Zimmer, *Hindu Medicine* (Baltimore, 1948); J. Jolly, *Hindu Medicine* (Poona, 1951); A.F.R. Hoernle, *Studies in the Medicine of Ancient India* (Oxford, 1907); V.W. Karambelkar, *The Atharvavedic Civilization* (Nagpur, 1959).

49. Chinese cosmology and physics based on the theory of *yin* and *yang* and the five elements was developed especially by the Neo-Confucian philosophers of medieval China such as Chou Tun-i, but always on the earlier foundations of Taoism and Confucianism. See C. Chang, *The Development of Neo-Confucian Thought* (New York, 1954); J. Needham, *Science and Civilization in China*, vol. II (Cambridge, 1956), especially section 13, "The Fundamental Ideas of Chinese Science"; and M. Granet, *La Pensée chinoise* (Paris, 1934)

50. On Chinese and Japanese medicine, see F. Mann, *Acupuncture: Cure of Many Diseases*, *(London* 1971); M. Hashimoto, *Japanese Acupuncture* (New York, 1968); A. Chamfrault and Ung Kang Sam, *Traité de medecine chinoise*, 4 vols. (Angouleme, 1954–61); Y. Fugikawa, *Japanese Medicine* (New York, 1934); E.H. Hume, *The Chinese Way in Medicine* (Baltimore, 1940); and K. Chunin Wong and Wu Lien-Teh, *History of Chinese Medicine* (Shanghai, 1936).

51. A fine bibliography of works on various branches of Islamic medicine can be found in M. Ullmann, *Die Medizin im Islam* (Leiden, 1970).

On the "philosophy" of this medicine see O. Gruner, *A Treatise on the Canon of Medicine* (London, 1930); Nasr, *Islamic Science: An Illustrated Study*, p. 159ff. *Philosophy of Medicine and Science* (New Delhi, 1972); M.S. Khan, *Islamic Medicine* (London, 1986), chapter two; and M.H. Shah, *The General Principles of Avicenna's Canon of Medicine* (Karachi, 1966).

52. On geomancy as sacred geography see Needham, *Science and Civilization in China*, vol. II (Cambridge, 1969), pp. 359–63. Geomancy as understood in this sense should not be confused with the divinatory art of the same name which Muslims call *al-raml* and associate with the Prophet Daniel. In fact, the use of geomancy in this second sense entered the West through Hugo Sanclilliensis from Muslim sources. On Islamic geomancy, see R. Jaulin, *La Géomantie, analyse formelle* (Paris, 1966), in which the author tries to show that the sixteen geomantic figures form a mathematical group known as the Abelian group in modern mathematics. His study has been taken to task by M.B. Smith in "The Nature of Islamic Geomancy," *Studia Islamica*, vol. 49 (1979), pp. 5–38.

53. See H. Corbin, *Spiritual Body and Celestial Earth: From Mazdean Iran to Shi'ite Iran*, trans. by N. Pearson (Princeton, 1991), where this theme is elaborated extensively.

54. See L. Renou and J. Filliozat, *L'Inde classique; manuels des études indiennes*, vol. II (Paris, 1953), p. 377ff. This cosmography is described fully in the third book of *Abhindharmakośa*.

55. See Needham, *Science and Civilization*, vol. 3 (1959), p. 565.

56. Of course Muslims also believe in Mount Qaf, where the mythical Sīmurgh, the symbol of the Divine Intellect, resides. Many Sufi treatises such as the *Manṭiq al-ṭayr* of 'Aṭṭār are based on this symbolic geography. See Nasr, *Islamic Art and Spirituality* (London, 1987), p. 98ff.

CHAPTER EIGHT

The Spiritual Significance of Nature

There are not only traditional and sacred sciences cultivated within various traditional civilizations and concerned with the study of the cosmos in the light of metaphysical principles. There is also a dimension of sacred science which concerns nature as a whole in as much as the spiritual significance of nature is concerned. Nature possesses a spiritual meaning of the utmost importance with which every integral spiritual tradition is concerned in one way or another, although the emphasis on this dimension of reality has not been the same in various traditions over the centuries. There is a need to come to know of this spiritual significance, as there is a need to rediscover sacred science. In fact a sacred science of nature leads ineluctably to an understanding of the spiritual significance of nature and any treatment of sacred science must include a treatment of the spiritual message which nature provides through her rhythms and harmonies, forms and movements, through her symbols and the grace which emanates from the Origin through her varigated manifestations.

It needs to be asserted here that to the extent that the modern cancer of urban growth and the destruction of nature even beyond the boundaries of the ever-expanding city lay waste to what remains of the natural order on earth, to that extent does the spiritual message of virgin nature become more vital for the very survival of man. The spiritual significance of nature has begun to dawn upon modern man much like the importance of fresh air, which is appreciated only when unpolluted air becomes difficult of access and pollution begins to affect the very foundations of biological and terrestrial life for the sake of which heaven was so easily sacrificed by the Promethean man of the Renaissance and its aftermath. Today one can no longer be seriously concerned with the spiritual well-being of man without turning to the spiritual significance of nature, no matter how somewhat more diluted forms of present-day technologies seek to make a virtue of the suffocating ugliness that modern man has substituted for the harmony, beauty and peace of the natural environment within whose bosom man lived and breathed in bygone ages.

The spiritual significance of nature manifests itself on many levels and through many channels. Virgin nature possesses order and harmony. There exists within this vast domain of immediately perceptible reality of nonhuman origin an order, an interrelation of parts, a complementarity of functions and roles and an interdependence which, for the mind not paralyzed by the reductionism inherent in the modern scientistic worldview, cannot but lead to a sense of wonder and awareness of the spiritual character of that Light which turned chaos into cosmos and which still reveals itself in the natural order.

This order is, moreover, related to an incredible harmony which in the technically musical sense pervades all the realms of nature from the stars to subatomic particles. The proportions of the parts of animals and plants, of crystal structures or of the planetary movements, when studied mathematically from the point of view of traditional or Pythagorean mathematics, reveal the presence of a harmony pervading all orders of the universe. It is as if the whole cosmos were music congealed into the very substance of things, which not only have their existence according to the laws of harmony but also move and live according to the rhythm of that cosmic dance, symbolized by the dance of Śiva, which is the very embodiment of the dynamic power that makes possible the "cosmic play." The whole of nature still echoes that Primordial Word which is both silence and the fullness of sound, containing within itself the harmony pervading all existence.

The life of nature not only displays harmony and order but also laws which make the harmony and order possible. To modern science such laws may appear as being "merely" mechanical or biological, but this reduction does not at all obliterate the spiritual significance of these laws, save for those who have become blinded by the all too pervasive reductionism of today and who have lost their sense of wonder. For what is the source of these laws and why do they exist? Why does calcium continue to behave as calcium or the apple tree to bear apples rather than pears? The "laws of nature" are but the laws of God for His creation, the *Sharī'ah* of each order of existence, to use an Islamic term. Or to turn to the nontheistic language of Buddhism, the "laws of nature" are the *dharmas* of things. To observe how each aspect of nature follows fully the laws that govern its existence is to become aware of the *dharma* which man must also follow. Moreover, the perfect submission of nature to its *dharma* is a lesson for man to submit himself perfectly to that norm which is *his dharma*, and which is none other than the quest for enlightenment. Virgin nature in a sense reflects sanctity, albeit in a passive mode, for, like the saint, the forms of nature remain in perfect submission to the Will of the Creator or to their *dharma*. They are perfect *muslims* in the sense of being completely submitted to the Divine Order. One of the greatest lessons which nature can teach the spiritual person is this perfection of submission to the laws governing things, to the principle that rules over creation, to the Tao. From this submission arises the harmony of all things which the Far Eastern sages have emphasized in their quest to integrate themselves into the at once natural and supernatural rhythms of the world of nature.

The spiritual significance of this submission is also reflected in the moral lessons which nature teaches man, provided he is willing to observe the overwhelming harmony, cooperation and complementarity that can be observed in nature far above and beyond the strife and discord that is so much emphasized by modern biologists and zoologists. Of course, strife also exists in nature, but even strife and struggle, which are real on their own level and which never destroy the harmony of the whole, are pregnant with meaning of an ethical nature. If sacred scriptures of the East and the West as well as traditional literature and lore—ranging from the Sanskrit *Pañca-tantra* to medieval European bestiaries to the animal lore of the American Indians—draw so much from the world of animals and plants, from the movements of the heavens and the creatures of the earth, to point to moral lessons which man must master, it is because this moral quality of the natural order is an aspect of its spiritual significance, although not as central as those ontological realities in the realm of nature which reflect Divine Qualities. The observation of moral lessons in nature might appear excessively anthropomorphic in the eyes of those who have adopted the mechanistic point of view opposed to all purpose and entelechy in nature, but these themes are far from being confined to the theistic perspective with its anthropomorphic language. The vision of nature as man's moral mentor in is universal and appears in Hindu and Buddhist sources as well as in Jewish and Christian ones.

The 'submission' of nature to its *dharma* and the harmony which pervades the realm of virgin nature not only lead to the 'moral quality' pervading the natural order when this order is viewed from the traditional point of view; they also result in that incredible beauty that is to be observed everywhere in nature. It is remarkable how in virgin nature beauty dominates in a complete manner over ugliness. The ugly is passing accident, while the beauty is abiding substance. The beauty of nature at its highest level is a direct theophany of Divine Beauty and an echo of a paradise whose interiorizing and integrating beauty is still reflected in the natural order. Nearly all normal human beings have a sense of the wholesomeness of this beauty of nature and its healing function. In nature the function of healing is combined with wholeness and ultimately holiness.

It is not an accident that so many Westerners, wary of the debilitating ugliness of the modern world and the products of the machine, turn to natural foods, water and air as a means of not only gaining bodily health but also spiritual wholeness. Although it is not possible to read the pages of the cosmic book without the aid of the grace issuing from revelation, the very attempt on behalf of so many contemporaries to combine the healing qualities and properties of nature with wholeness and even holiness testifies to a spiritual presence in nature manifested in a beauty which heals the soul as well as the body. The yearning of human beings for the beauty, peace and tranquility of nature is in reality a yearning for the paradise which nature reflects, which it *is* in its essence and which man carries at the depth of his being.

The beauty of nature has, however, a more esoteric and directly spiritual function for the person who, through spiritual discipline or by the gift of Heaven, is able to discern beyond forms the presence of the Formless. The beauty of virgin nature is at once interiorizing and absorbing. It brings recollection of the spiritual Reality from which man has originated and in fact aids man in returning to that ever present-Reality. The beauty of nature at its highest level and in conjunction with methods of spiritual realization inebriates the soul with spiritual drunkenness, resurrects man's inner being and finally aids in man's sanctification by bearing witness to the immortal paradisal substance within him. The beauty of nature is the direct reflection of the beauty of God; it is therefore an interiorizing beauty which, although seemingly outward, does not disperse but brings man back to the Center wherein abides the ineffable beauty of the One.

The spiritual message of nature is not contained, however, only in the overall beauty of its forms, movements and qualities, but also in the symbols which are direct reflections of various Divine Qualities. The symbolist spirit shared by all traditional peoples and especially by those belonging to different primal and archaic traditions, see in certain forms of nature, ranging from the sun, the eagle and the lion to the river and the sea, direct symbols of Divine Qualities and even in a sense those Qualities themselves. The forms of nature are for them letters and words of a sacred language written by the creating power of the Divinity upon the tablet of cosmic existence. To read this cosmic book requires a special kind of literacy which is in fact very different from the literacy taught through modern education, the literacy that often causes many people to become impervious to the symbolic significance of nature and illiterate regarding the primordial message written upon the face of majestic mountains, withering autumn leaves or the shimmering waves of the sea.

The spiritual message of the symbols of nature is based on neither sentiment nor some kind of vague nature mysticism. It is based on a sacred science which is itself a science of cosmic correspondences and is concerned with the ontological reality of the natural forms in question. The reality of the sun as the symbol of the Divine Intellect is certainly not less than the reality of its mass measurable by methods of modern astrophysics. If this symbolic reality is no longer perceived by a particular segment of humanity, it is not because there is so such reality, but because the symbolist spirit has been lost as a result of a kind of education which trains the mind and the eye to perceive certain accidents while blinding them to the substance, leaving the inner faculties and even the other outer senses practically completely neglected. The spiritual message of the symbols found in nature do not become unreal because a particular society fails to take cognizance of it anymore than the existence of the aroma of a rose ceases to exist because it is lost in the biochemical analysis of the cells of the flower in a laboratory.

While in most traditions certain symbols are sanctified directly by revelation with the aid of which natural symbols in general are comprehended and viewed, there are some primal traditions, like that of the Plains Indians of North America and certain other branches of Shamanism, where natural symbols *are* the symbols sanctified by revelation. In such cases the various animals and plants become direct manifestations of Divine Powers and in a sense the bridge between man and the world of the Spirit whereas from the general metaphysical point of view, it is man who, as the central being in the terrestrial realm, acts as the bridge between Heaven and earth and the channel through which the light of the Spirit shines upon the earthly realm and its creatures.

The science of the symbols of the natural order has been developed in the bosom of numerous traditional cosmologies, ranging from those of the Australian aborigines to the cosmologies of an Ibn Sīnā or the medieval Jewish Kabbalists. In all these cases the spiritual significance of nature has been recapitulated in an intelligible language in such a manner as to enable traditional man, living in the sacred universe which gives rise to the cosmology in question, to discover a map with which he can orient himself in his spiritual journey beyond the cosmos and to contemplate the entire cosmos as an icon reflecting the power and wisdom of the Divine Artisan. Traditional cosmologies are many, even within a single tradition such as the Islamic or Buddhist, but their goal is one. It is to reveal multiplicity in the light of Unity, *samsāra* as *nirvāṇa*, *māyā* as the creative power of *Ātman*. Its goal is to help man save himself from the indefinite multiplicity of the cosmic labyrinth by integrating this unending and ever-changing realm of becoming into an intelligible pattern which has the power of freeing man from undue fascination and concern with the ever-flowing stream of change and the withering influence of time. To have read the pages of the cosmic book is to be able to close that book and put it aside. And once the cosmic scroll is folded up, to use the Sufi image, there remains but the Face of the One who never perisheth. The spiritual significance of the various traditional cosmological sciences lies in fact in leading man beyond the cosmos to that metacosmic Reality wherein alone is the spiritual significance of nature perceived on the highest level.

Virgin nature is also the workshop of the Divine Artisan, wherein are to be found the greatest masterpieces of sacred art. In the same way that sacred art as usually understood is produced by supra-individual inspiration emanating from revelation and based on a science of an ultimately Divine Origin of forms, symbols and substances, the forms of nature are direct products of the work of that Demiurgic Power which draws from the treasury of Divine Possibility those archetypes that externalized become the forms of nature. Virgin nature is the counterpart of sacred art, conveying a Divine Presence and having a soteriological function. In certain traditions such as the Chinese and Japanese, in fact, a landscape painting or garden *is* sacred art playing the same role as an icon does in Christianity. For those Westerners sensitive to the saving grace and beauty of sacred art as found in a Chartres cathedral or a Byzantine Madonna and Child, the perception of nature as sacred art is a powerful means of bringing out its spiritual significance. Such a comparison might make it more comprehensible for us why the American Indians fought so valiantly for virgin nature which they saw as their sanctuary and cathedral. But for those who hail from the primal traditions, the primacy of nature as sacred art par excellence is so evident that no sacred art created by human hands, even if inspired, can be compared in their eyes with the beauty and perfection of natural forms. For them, nothing ever made by man is worth the destruction of nature and the profanation of virgin nature is more heinous than the destruction of the greatest works of human art.

It is in fact as sacred art that nature and its forms lend themselves to contemplation. The spiritual man, the contemplative, not only seeks shelter in nature against the trivialities of human life and frivolities of worldliness, but is also able to contemplate in the forms of nature the spiritual realities which these forms hide from the eyes of the profane but reveal to those who have gained intimacy with the world of the Spirit. The contemplative hears in the silence of virgin nature the call of the Spirit and the music of the heavenly abode, which is also the call of his Origin. The rhythms of night and day and the seasons, the contrast between the rigor and generosity of nature, the unending transformations which continue within all realms of nature, the perfection of the flower which reflects a paradisal reality and yet the rapid withering of the same flower because it is in fact the reflection of that reality in the world of transience and not that reality itself, the masculine immutability of the crystal and the feminine growing power of the plant, these and numerous other features of the natural order are contemplated by man of a spiritual nature. They reveal to him not only the transient and refractory character of terrestrial existence, but also the permanence of the spiritual realities which the forms of nature at once veil and reveal. For the contemplative every tree is a reflection of the tree of paradise and every flower a mirror of the paradisal innocence for which man yearns because he still carries that primordial nature in the deepest recesses of his being.

On the highest level virgin nature can be contemplated as a theophany which possesses its own metaphysical message and spiritual discipline. Nature reveals the One and Its multiple qualities. It prays and invokes. The air of the mountain top at the moment of dawn or the vast deserts and prairies at sunset are filled with that ether which is not only the substratum of the visible elements but also the substance of quintessential prayer or invocation. But to participate in nature's prayer and to read the profound gnostic message which she conveys through her forms and qualities requires prior possession of a high degree of spiritual realization.

Nature, however, is generous even to those as yet not so accomplished in matters spiritual but who are sensitive to her beauty and spiritual presence. For them, as for the person who is able to read her metaphysical message and participate in her incantatory rhythms, nature offers a sanctuary of the greatest value at a moment when the storm caused by modern man, out to conquer nature, is wreaking havoc upon the surface of the earth. Strangely enough, while from the metaphysical point of view to speak of the human is to speak of God, from the vantage point of the secularized world of modern man, to leave the world made by Promethean man is to enter into the realm of spiritual presence. Virgin nature in fact gives the lie to that agnosticism, secularism, skepticism and the cult of ugliness and unintelligibility which characterize the modern world. It provides a vivid reminder of what is "really" real and what we are at our deepest level of being. The very word 'nature,' from the Latin root *nat*, meaning "to be born," not only means that she is the progenitor of forms which are born from her. It also signifies her regenerating power for man's spirit, for in her bosom and within the embrace of her spiritual presence, which is the reflection of the Spirit Itself, man's spirit is rejuvenated and he is reborn.

For this reason the protection of virgin nature, against the onslaught of covetous and greedy men attached to only worldly ends, is indeed a spiritual duty. That is why, in fact, so many of those who have sought to revive the spiritual heritage of mankind to rekindle the light of tradition for contemporary man have loved nature so deeply and have written about it with such sympathy and insight. Such men have unveiled the grandeur and beauty of that cosmic mountain and that sublime peak which touches the Void and which reverberates with that spiritual presence that constitutes both the goal of human life and the very substance of what constitutes the human state.

PART FOUR

Tradition, Sacred Science
and the Modern Predicament

Sacred Science
and the Environmental Crisis—
An Islamic Perspective

O Lord, show us things as they really are.
—*Saying [ḥadīth] of the Prophet*

When one looks at the Islamic world today, one sees blatant signs of the environmental crisis in nearly every country from the air pollution of Cairo and Tehran to the erosion of the hills of Yemen to the deforestation of many areas of Malaysia and Bangladesh. Environmental problems seem to be present everywhere, especially in urban centers and also in many parts of the countryside, to a degree that one cannot distinguish the Islamic world from most other areas of the globe as far as acute environmental problems are concerned. If one were to study the situation only superficially, one could in fact claim, in the light of present-day conditions, that the Islamic view of nature could not have been different from that of the modern West which first thrust the environmental crisis upon the whole of mankind. But a deeper look will reveal an Islamic view of the environment very different from what has been prevalent in the West during the past few centuries. If that view has now become partly hidden, it is because of the onslaught of Western civilization since the eighteenth century and the destruction of much of Islamic civilization, due to both external and internal factors, although the Islamic religion itself has continued to flourish and remains strong.

In fact the Islamic world is not totally Islamic today and much that is Islamic lies hidden behind the cover of Western cultural, scientific and technological ideas and practices emulated and aped to various degrees of perfection, or one should rather say imperfection, by Muslims during the past century and a half. The Islamic attitude toward the natural environment is no more manifest than the Buddhist one in Japan or Taoist one in China, all as a result of the onslaught upon these lands of a secular science based upon power and domination over nature and a technology which devours the natural world with no respect for the equilibrium of nature, a science and technology of Western origin which have now become nearly global, eclipsing for the most part what has remained of the sacred sciences in various non-Western civilizations.

Despite this situation, however, Islam continues to live as a powerful religious and spiritual force and its view of nature and the natural environment still has a hold upon the mind and soul of its adherents, especially in less modernized areas and also in some of the deeper attitudes toward nature. The role of this survival of the traditional view of nature can be seen in the refusal of Islamic society to surrender completely to the *dicta* of the machine despite the attempt of leaders of that world to introduce Western technology as much as and as soon as possible. This view is, therefore, significant for a global consideration of the environmental problem, not only because of its innate value but also because of its continuous influence upon Muslims, who comprise a fifth of the world's population.

The Islamic view of the natural environment is furthermore of significance for the West itself since Islam shares with the West a religion of the Abrahamic family and the Greek heritage which played a major role in the history of both Western and Islamic science, in the first mostly through the agency of the second. The Islamic view of nature presents a precious reminder of a perspective mostly lost in the West today and based upon the sacred quality of nature in a universe created and sustained by the One God of Abraham to whom Jews and Christians also bow in prayer.

The Islamic view of the natural order and the environment, as everything else that is Islamic, has its roots in the Quran, the very Word of God, which is the central theophany of Islam.[1] The message of the Quran is in a sense a return to the primordial message of God to man. It addresses what is primordial in the inner nature of men and women; hence Islam is called the primordial religion (*al-dīn al-ḥanīf*).[2] As the "Primordial Scripture," the Quran addresses not only men and women but the whole of the cosmos. In a sense, nature participates in the Quranic revelation. Certain verses of the Quran address natural forms as well as human beings, while God calls nonhuman members of His creation, such as plants and animals, the sun and the stars, to bear witness in certain other verses. The Quran does not draw a clear line of demarcation between the natural and the supernatural, nor between the world of man and that of nature. The soul which is nourished and sustained by the Quran does not regard the world of nature as its natural enemy to be conquered and subdued but as an integral part of man's religious universe sharing in his earthly life and in a sense even in his ultimate destiny.

The cosmic dimension of the Quran was elaborated over the centuries by many Muslims sages who referred to the cosmic or ontological Quran (*al-Qur'ān al-takwīnī*) as distinct from and complementing the composed or "written" Quran (*al-Qur'ān al-tadwīnī*).[3] They saw upon the face of every creature letters and words from the pages of the cosmic Quran which only the sage can read. They remained fully aware of the fact that the Quran refers to the phenomena of nature and events within the soul of man as *āyāt* (literally signs or symbols), a term that is also used for the verses of the Quran.[4] They read the cosmic book, its chapters and verses, and saw the phenomena of nature as "signs" of the Author of the book of nature. For them the forms of nature were literally *āyāt Allāh*, *vestigia Dei*, a concept that was certainly known to the traditional West before, with the advent of rationalism, symbols were turned into brute facts and before the modern West set out to create a science to dominate over nature rather than to gain wisdom and joy from the contemplation of its forms.

The Quran depicts nature as being ultimately a theophany which both veils and reveals God. The forms of nature are so many masks which hide various Divine Qualities, while also revealing these same Qualities to those whose inner eye has not become blinded by the concupiscent ego and the centrifugal tendencies of the passionate soul.

In an even deeper sense, it can be claimed that according to the Islamic perspective God Himself *is* the ultimate environment which surrounds and encompasses man. It is of the utmost significance that in the Quran God is said to be the All-Encompassing (*Muhīt*), as in the verse, "But to God belong all things in the heavens and on the earth: And He it is who encompasseth (*muhīt*) all things" (1V.126), and that the term *muhīt* also means environment.[5] In reality, man is immersed in the Divine *Muhit* and is only unaware of it because of his own forgetfulness and negligence (*ghaflah*), which is the underlying sin of the soul, only to be overcome by remembrance (*dhikr*). To remember God is to see Him everywhere and to experience His reality as *al-Muhīt*. The environmental crisis may in fact be said to have been caused by man's refusal to see God as the real 'environment' which surrounds man and nourishes his life. The destruction of the environment is the result of modern man's attempt to view the natural environment as an ontologically independent order of reality, divorced from the Divine Environment without whose liberating grace it becomes stifled and dies. To remember God as *al-Muhīt* is to remain aware of the sacred quality of nature, the reality of natural phenomena as signs (*āyāt*) of God and the presence of the natural environment as an ambience permeated by the Divine Presence of that Reality which alone is the ultimate 'environment' from which we issue and to which we return.

The traditional Islamic view of the natural environment is based on this inextricable and permanent relation between what is today called the human and natural environments and the Divine Environment which sustains and permeates them. The Quran alludes in many verses to the unmanifested and the manifested worlds ('*ālam al-ghayb wa'l-shahādah*). The visible or manifested world is not an independent order of reality but a manifestation of a vastly greater world which transcends it and from which it issues. The visible world is like what one can observe around a camp fire during a dark desert night. The visible gradually recedes into the vast invisible which surrounds it and for which it is the veritable environment. Not only is the invisible an infinite ocean compared to which the visible is like a speck of dust, but it permeates the visible itself. It is in this way that the Divine Environment, the Spirit, permeates the world of nature and of normal humanity, nourishing and sustaining them, being at once the origin (*al-mabda'*) and entelechy and end (*al-ma'ād*) of the manifested order.[6]

As a result of this view of nature as delineated in the Quran and accentuated by the sayings (*Ḥadīth*) and wonts (*Sunnah*) of the Prophet, the traditional Muslim always harbored a great love for nature, which is a reflection of paradisal realities here below. This love is reflected not only in Arabic, Persian and Turkish literature—not to speak of the literatures of other Islamic peoples from Swahili to Malay—but also in Islamic religious thought, where no clear distinction is made between what Western theology has come to call the natural and the supernatural. This love is also reflected in many pages of the works of Islamic philosophers, but finds its most profound and also universal expression in Sufi poetry. It was the Persian poet Sa'dī who composed the famous verse,

> I am joyous with the cosmos
> For the cosmos receives its joy from Him.
> I love the whole world, for the world belongs to Him.

It was another Sufi, this time the great folk poet of the Turkish language, Yunus Emre, who heard the invocation of God's Blessed Name in the sound of flowing streams, which brought a recollection of celestial realities and so he sang,

> The rivers all in Paradise
> Flow with the word Allah, Allah,
> And ev'ry loving nightingale
> He sings and sings Allah Allah

(Trans. A.M. Schimmel, *As Through a Veil*, [New York, 1982], p. 150.)

Muslim contemplatives and mystics have loved nature with such intensity[7] because they have been able to hear the prayer of all creatures of the natural world to God. According to the Quran, "Nothing is, that does not proclaim His praise" (XVII.44). This praise, which is also the prayer of all things, is the root of their very existence. Fallen man who has forgotten God has become deaf to this ubiquitous prayer as a result of this very act of forgetfulness. The sage, on the contrary, lives in remembrance of God (*dhikr Allāh*) and as a result hears the prayers of flowers as they turn toward the sun and of the streams as they descend from hills toward the sea. His prayer has, in fact become one with the prayers of the birds and the trees, of the mountains and the stars. He prays with them and they with him and in contemplating their forms not only as outwardness but as theophanies or as "signs of God," he is strengthened in his own recollection and remembrance of the One. They in turn draw an invisible sustenance from the human being who is open to the grace emanating from the realm of the Spirit and who fulfills his or her role as the *pontifex*, the bridge between Heaven and earth.

This contemplative attitude towards nature and love for it is of course reserved at its highest level for the few who have realized the full possibilities of being human, but throughout the centuries it has percolated into the Islamic community as a whole. Traditional Islamic society has always been noted for its harmonious relation with the natural environment and love for nature, to the extent that many a Christian critic of Islam has accused Muslims of being naturalistic and Islam of being devoid of the grace which is usually so trenchantly separated and distinguished from nature in the mainstream of Christian theology.

This Islamic love of nature as manifesting the "signs of God" and being impregnated with the Divine Presence must not be confused with naturalism as understood in Western philosophy and theology. Christianity, having been forced to combat the cosmolatry and rationalism of the ancient Mediterranean world, branded as naturalism both the illegitimate nature worship of the decadent forms of Greek and Roman religion and the very different concern and love for nature of northern Europeans such as the Celts, a love which nevertheless survived in a marginal manner after the Christianization of Europe, as one can see in the works of a Hildegard of Bingen or in early medieval Irish poems pertaining to nature. Now, one must never forget that the Islamic love for nature has nothing to do with the naturalism anathematized by the Church Fathers. Rather, it is much closer to the nature poetry of the Irish monks and the addresses to the sun and the moon by the patron saint of ecology, St. Francis of Assisi. Or perhaps it should be said that it is he who among all the great medieval saints is the closest to the Islamic perspective as far as the love of nature is concerned. In any case the Islamic love of nature and the natural environment and the emphasis upon the role of nature as a means to gain access to God's wisdom as manifested in His creation, do not in any sense imply the negation of transcendence or the neglect of the archetypal realities. On the contrary, on the highest level it means to understand fully the Quranic verse, "Whithersoever ye turn, there is the Face of God" (II.115). It means, therefore, to see God everywhere and to be fully aware of the Divine Environment which surrounds and permeates both the world of nature and the ambience of man.

The Islamic teachings concerning nature and the environment cannot be fully understood without dealing with the Islamic conception of man, who has been always viewed in various traditional religions as the custodian of nature and who has now become its destroyer, having changed his role, thanks to modern civilization, from the being who had descended from Heaven and who lived in harmony with the earth to a creature who considers himself as having ascended from below and who has now become the earth's most deadly predator and exterminator. Islam considers man as God's vice-gerent (al-khalīfah) on earth and the Quran asserts explicitly, "I am setting on the earth a vice-gerent (khalīfah)" (II.30). This quality of vice-gerency is, moreover, complemented by that of servantship (al-'ubūdiyyah) towards God. Man is God's servant ('abd Allāh) and must obey Him accordingly. As 'abd Allāh, he must be passive towards God and receptive to the grace that flows from the world above. As khalīfat Allāh, he must be active in the world, sustaining cosmic harmony and disseminating the grace for which he is the channel as a result of his being the central creature in the terrestrial order.[8]

In the same way that God sustains and cares for the world, man as His vice-gerent must nurture and care for the ambience in which he plays the central role. He cannot neglect the care of the natural world without betraying that "trust" (al-amānah) which he accepted when he bore witness to God's lordship in the pre-eternal covenant (al-mīthāq), to which the Quran refers in the famous verse, "Am I not your Lord? They [that is, members of humanity] uttered, Yea, we bear witness" (VII.172).

To be human is to be aware of the responsibility which the state of vice-gerency entails. Even when in the Quran it is stated that God has subjected (sakhkhara) nature to man as in the verse, "Hast thou not seen how God has subjected to you all that is in the earth" (XXII.65), this does not mean the ordinary conquest of nature, as claimed by so many modern Muslims thirsty for the power which modern science bestows upon man. Rather, it means the dominion over things which man is allowed to exercise only on the condition that it be according to God's laws and precisely because he is God's vice-gerent on earth, being therefore given a power which ultimately belongs to God alone and not to man who is merely a creature born to journey through this earthly life and to return to God at the moment of death.

That is why also nothing is more dangerous for the natural environment than the practice of the power of vice-gerency by a humanity which no longer accepts to be God's servant, obedient to His commands and laws. There is no more dangerous a creature on earth than a *khalīfat Allāh* who no longer considers himself to be *'abd Allāh* and who therefore does not see himself as owing allegiance to a being beyond himself. Such a creature is able to possess a power of destruction which is truly Satanic in the sense that "Satan is the ape of God"; for such a human type wields, at least for a short time, a godlike but destructive dominion over the earth because this dominion is devoid of the care which God displays towards all His creatures and bereft of that love which runs through the arteries of the universe.

As traditionally defined by Islam, man is seen as being given power even to the extent of finally causing corruption on earth as predicted in the Quran. But this power is seen in the traditional Islamic perspective to be limited in normal circumstances by the responsibilities which he bears not only towards God and other men and women, but also towards the whole of creation. The Divine Law (*al-Sharī'ah*) is explicit in extending the religious duties of man to the natural order and the environment. One must not only feed the poor but also avoid polluting running water. It is pleasing in the eyes of God not only to be kind to one's parents, but also to plant trees and treat animals gently and with kindness. Even in the realm of the Divine Law, and without turning to the metaphysical significance of nature, one can see the close nexus created by Islam between man and the whole natural order. Nor could it be otherwise, for the primordial character of the Islamic revelation reinstates man and the cosmos in a state of unity, harmony and complementarity, reaffirming man's inner bond to the whole of creation, which shares the Quranic revelation in the deepest sense with man.

There is so much talk today of human rights that it is necessary to mention here the basic truth that according to the Islamic perspective responsibilities precede rights. Man has no rights of his own independent of God, whether these rights be over nature or even over himself since he is not the creator of his own being. Man is not in fact capable of creating anything from nothing. The power of *fiat lux* belongs to God alone. What rights man does possess are given to him by God as a consequence of his having accepted the covenant with God and fulfilled his responsibilities as God's vice-gerent on earth.

The Islamic attitude towards man differs profoundly not so much from traditional Jewish and Christian ones, although even here there are some notable differences, as from postmedieval forms of humanism, to which much of the later religious thought in the West gradually succumbed. Islam sees God alone as being absolute. One of the meanings of the testimony of Islam (*lā ilāha illa'Llāh*) is that there is no absolute unless it is the Absolute. Man is seen as a creature who, as a theomorphic being, reflects all of God's Names and Qualities in a direct and central fashion, but he is not absolute in himself especially in his transient earthly state. In fact whatever positive qualities man possesses come from God. That is why in the Quran it is asserted, "God is the rich and ye are the poor" (XLVII.38). Man's greatest glory lies in fact in the realization of this poverty, through which alone he is able to reach the Absolute.

In contrast, since the advent of Renaissance humanism Western civilization has absolutized earthly man. While depriving man of his center and creating a veritable centerless culture and art, Western humanism has sought to bestow upon this centerless humanity the quality of absoluteness.[9] It is this purely earthly man defined by rationalism and humanism who developed seventeenth century science based upon the domination and conquest of nature, who sees nature as his enemy and who continues to rape and destroy the natural environment always in the name of the rights of man, which are seen by him to be absolute. It is this terrestrial man, now absolutized, who destroys vast forests in the name of immediate economic welfare, without thinking for a moment of the consequences of such action for future generations of men or for other creatures of this world. It is such a creature who, in seeing his earthly life as being absolute, tries to prolong it at all costs, creating a medicine which has produced both wonders and horrors, including the destruction of the ecological balance through human overpopulation. Neither God nor nature have any right in the eyes of a humanity which sees itself as absolute even when talking about man being an insignificant observer on a small planet on the periphery of a minor galaxy, as if all this superficial humility were not also based upon the absolutization of the sense-experience and rational powers of earthly man.

Now Islam has always stood strongly opposed to this absolutization of what one might call the Promethean and Titanic man. It has never permitted the glorification of man at the expense of either God or His creation. Nothing is more detestable to traditional Muslim sensibilities than some of the Titanic art of the Renaissance created for the glorification of a humanity in rebellion against Heaven. If modern science and with it a civilization which gave and still gives itself absolute right of domination over the earth and even the heavens did not come into being in the Islamic world, it was not because of the lack of mathematical or astronomical knowledge. Rather, it was because the Islamic perspective excluded the possibility of the deification of earthly man or of the total secularization of nature. In Islamic eyes, only the Absolute is absolute.

The consequence of this perspective upon the relation between man and the environment has been immense. In the traditional Islamic world, since the human state was never absolutized, man's rights were never made absolute in total forgetfulness to the rights of God and also of His other creatures. Modern Western man, in contrast to the traditional Muslim or for that matter the traditional Christian, owes nothing to anyone or anything. Nor does he or she feel responsible to any other being beyond the human. In contrast, the traditional Muslim or *homo islamicus* has always lived in awareness of the rights of God and the rights of others which includes the nonhuman realm. He has remained aware of his responsibility to God and also responsibility for His creatures. Islam has been always strongly opposed to rationalism while being rational, to naturalism while being aware of the sacred quality permeating the natural order and to humanism while being concerned with human beings and their entelechy in the deepest manner possible. These attitudes, moreover, exercised an immense influence upon the Islamic attitudes towards nature and the natural environment, especially until the domination of the Islamic world by the West.

Many secularists in the West today blame what is now called the Judeo-Christian tradition, to which Islam is also added in this context and not elsewhere, for the present ecological crisis, forgetting the fact that neither Christian Armenia nor Ethiopia nor even Christian Eastern Europe gave rise to that science and technology which in the hands of secular man has led to the devastation of the globe, and that therefore other factors must have been involved. Moreover, it must first of all be remembered that if one chooses not to speak of Judaism and Christianity but of the Judeo-Christian tradition, one should speak of the Judeo-Christian-Islamic tradition, which would thus include the three members of the Abrahamic family of religions. Secondly, one must remember that each of the religions of the Abrahamic family has its particular doctrinal and theological emphasis and spiritual contour. As far as the question of the spiritual and metaphysical significance of nature is concerned, Islam has placed greater emphasis upon it than the mainstream theological tradition of Western Christianity and has always emphasized and preserved even to this day teachings which have been either forgotten or marginalized in religious thought in the West.

This does not mean, however, that Judaism or Christianity are in themselves responsible for the environmental crisis. Moreover, this marginalization, combined with the acceptance of the secular view of the cosmos and even condonation if not out and out approval of the rape of nature by secularized man was the result of Christianity's battle for five centuries with humanism, rationalism and secularism, although Western Christianity did fail to emphasize the spiritual significance of nature in its mainstream theology even before the Renaissance. The result of this acquiescence has been the success of the forces of secularism and the science and technology which are based upon it in depleting nature of its sacred quality and causing the forgetfulness of that metaphysics which alone can explain who man is, why his rights are limited and why he is the bridge between Heaven and earth, called by his human vocation to be custodian of the earth and its creatures.

It must now be asked that if the traditional teachings of Islam concerning the natural order as outlined above are still alive, why are they not more evident in the voices from the Islamic world which have been and are heard in the West, nor more effective in the practical realm in averting ecological disasters and why it is that the environmental crisis is no less acute in the Islamic world than in other parts of the globe? Let us first of all turn to the voices from the Islamic world which the West has heard during the past century and a half and still hears and through which it interprets the Islamic view concerning the natural environment.

During the last century and half two voices from the Islamic world have been most vociferous and easily heard in the West: the voice of the so-called fundamentalist reformers and that of the modernists.[10] The first includes such schools as the Wahhābīs and Salafīs who have stood opposed to the West and defended the sacrosanct character of the Divine Law, seeking to reestablish a society in which this Law would be promulgated thoroughly and completely. At first, its proponents were against Western technology, as can be seen in the attitude of the Wahhābī supported Saudis in Arabia during the first decades of this century. But this opposition was more juridical than intellectual. These movements were not usually concerned with the traditional Islamic philosophy of nature and dealt with the environment according to *Sharī'ite* norms but without the critical knowledge of Western science and technology necessary to realize the catastrophic effects of modern science upon the religiously inspired views of nature and of modern technology upon the environment. Furthermore, they were too engrossed in combatting Western colonial influences and in what they considered to be "cleansing" Islamic society of alien accretions to be much concerned with the natural environment.

It was this lack of knowledge and critical judgment which led to an open espousal of Western science and technology by later followers of this very group during the second half of this century. Again this can be seen in Saudi Arabia, which began to embrace rapid industrialization from the 1950s onward while maintaining its close links with Wahhābism. Concern with the environment there did not in fact became an issue until very recently.

The second voice is that of the modernists who have expressed a staunch defence of Western science and technology from the early nineteenth century. The defeat of Egypt by Napoleon in 1798, followed by the defeat of the Ottomans and the Persians by European powers and the British conquest of India in the early decades of the nineteenth century, led to a crisis within the Islamic world which was not only political but also cultural and religious. As political leaders like Muḥammad 'Alī of Egypt sent students to Europe to master Western military arts, modernist thinkers began not only to accept but to practically idolize Western science and technology, which they saw as the secret of the West's power. From Sir Sayyid Aḥmad Khān in India to Muḥammad 'Abduh in Egypt, from Zia Gökalp in Turkey to Seyyed Hasan Taqizadeh in Persia, modernists stressed the importance of Western science and technology which could do no wrong and which would lead to the material and even spiritual happiness of Muslims. A figure such as Jamāl al-Dīn al-Afghānī simply equated Western science with Islamic science, to which it owes a great deal historically but whose philosophical framework Western science does not accept at all to say the least. For over a century, teachers in classrooms and even preachers from pulpits of mosques repeated this view, extolling Western science and technology and considering its mastery as practically a religious duty. If there were a few dissenting voices here and there, such as Sayyid Aḥmad Kasrawī in Persia, who openly criticized Western science and technology, they were brushed aside by the modernists as being simply obscurantists.[11]

Meanwhile, a third voice, that of traditional Islam, especially in its sapiental and not only juridical dimension, survived but was hardly heard in the West until quite recently. Poets still expressed the traditional love of nature and those devoted to the inner dimension of Islam still studied and continue to study the cosmos as a book to be deciphered and understood by penetrating into the inner meaning of its symbols. But until recently the West hardly heard this voice. Occasionally a poet such as Muhammad Iqbal would become well known in the West, but he would not be the type of poet to sing primarily of the love of nature. As for the specific case of Iqbal, he was too deeply engrossed in the current problems of the Islamic community and too profoundly influenced by nineteenth century European philosophy to emphasize that science of nature which leads to the contemplation of nature and spiritual perfection rather than dominion and power over nature with the aim of reaping from it all that one can to satiate the unending demands of a purely earthly man. Yet, even in his case, here and there in his poetry, rather than his prose, one can gain a glimpse of that attitude towards nature which Sufis and Islamic philosophers have cultivated over the centuries on the basis of the clear message of the Quran.

In any case the voice of traditional Islam in its sapiental dimension, wherein is to be found the Islamic doctrine of the ultimate meaning of nature and the natural environment, continued to resonate within the Islamic world, although it was now no longer the dominating voice. Nor was it heard by the West, which devoted its study of the Islamic world until recently almost completely to the fundamentalist reformers and modernists, two opposing groups who during the past few decades have disagreed on many issues but who have met eye to eye in more recent times in their blind acceptance of modern science and technology and their total neglect of the traditional Islamic views concerning science and nature. As the ecological crisis has become a major global issue, however, the voice of traditional Islam has begun to be heard ever more clearly and loudly It is this voice which speaks of the millennial wisdom of the attitudes of Islam and its science toward the natural environment and which insists that the role of religion in the present environmental crisis is not only ethical but also intellectual, providing a critique in depth of the totalitarian and monopolistic contention of modern science to be the only valid form of knowledge of the natural domain.

As stated already, there are also practical reasons why the Islamic world has not been more successful on the operational level in avoiding an environmental crisis, despite the religiously positive and caring attitude of Islam towards nature. These reasons are related to the global domination of the West and the need felt not only by Muslims but by what is wrongly called "Third World countries" to overcome the economic consequences of this domination. This need cuts across several continents and can be seen in Islamic Egypt and Buddhist Thailand, Hindu India and Christian Ethiopia. This worldwide need, added to common human nature which seeks everywhere the forbidden fruit of Faustian science, has caused Shinto-Buddhist Japan with its remarkable appreciation of nature, and the Navajo nation with its incredible spiritual insight into the significance of natural forms, to suffer almost as much from the destruction of their natural ambience as what one finds in formerly Communist and now Catholic Poland or half-secularized and half-Christian northern New Jersey. The fact that Cairo or Karachi suffer from environmental decay does not negate the traditional Islamic doctrines concerning the love and appreciation of nature any more than does the pollution of Tokyo negate the spiritual significance of the Zen gardens of Kyoto.

The economic and political factors which have prevented Muslims from paying greater attention to their own traditional teachings concerning the environment are very complex and need a separate treatment. Suffice it to say here that when the pollution of the Hudson River can be measured in the Azores, when every American born will use over a hundred times more raw materials than a Muslim from Bangladesh, when the West refuses to be put its own house in order through a sane energy and raw materials policy and instead invades another part of the globe to preserve "the Western way of life," which in this context means the wasteful use of energy, without thought of the consequences of its actions for future generations, then it should not be too difficult to understand why the environmental issue does not possess much priority in the Islamic world at the present moment.

Furthermore, there is the question of innovation and reception of a Western technology which until now has been very destructive of the natural environment. The Islamic world is on the receiving end of an ever-changing technology which guarantees its domination through constant innovation. There is no breathing space to adapt an existing technology with the minimum environmental impact without economic pressure which is simply unbearable for most Islamic countries. If "catching up" with the West, which is the goal of many Muslim governments, were possible, such an achievement would simply expand the circle of the virulent and agressive destruction of the environment caused by such technology, as the case of Japan, Korea and Taiwan bears out. Such countries have certainly not become ecologically safer havens since joining the industrialized world. One wonders what would happen to the world's biosphere were people from Nigeria to Indonesia to spend the same amount of energy and use the same amount of raw materials as citizens of the so-called advanced countries!

On the practical level there is finally one other important factor to mention as far as the Islamic world is concerned. The colonial domination of the West not only brought about economic exploitation and introduced a second-rate Western technology into the Islamic world. It also resulted in many Muslim countries discarding much of the Divine Law or *al-Sharī'ah*, with its numerous teachings concerning responsibility towards the natural environment, in favor of secular Belgian, French or British codes which had little to say concerning nature. And even if laws relating to the environment were passed in the framework of the new secular laws imported from the West, these did not carry any religious weight and remained divorced from ethical considerations whose sole origin and source for Muslims is the Islamic revelation. This change in the significance of law in many Islamic lands, added to the migration of a large number of people from the countryside to urban areas with its concomitant cultural dislocation, poses a major obstacle to propagating the traditional Islamic teachings concerning the environment among certain groups in many Muslim cities. The callousness toward domestic animals and trees in many of the large Middle Eastern cities bears evidence of the existence of these factors to which great poverty must be added in many areas. The problem of the preservation of the natural environment seems simply too far removed from the immediate concerns of life for those influenced by these factors, while many political leaders simply relegate it to a position of secondary importance and consider it to be simply a Western problem despite the blatant evidence to the contrary.

Of course, the environmental crisis is not only Western but global. And although the Muslims for the most part endanger themselves in their heedless attitude towards the environment, while the highly industrialized countries threaten the ecology of the whole globe, it is absolutely essential for the Islamic world to face this issue in a most serious manner.[12] It is also important for everyone to realize that since the environmental crisis is global, it requires global attention. The Islamic world must do its utmost to bring its rich intellectual and ethical tradition to bear upon this problem, as the West must realize that there is a wisdom within the Islamic tradition concerning nature and the natural environment which can be of great significance for those in the West who are in quest of reformulating a theology of nature.

At this point it is necessary to point to some of the elements which distinguish the situation of Islam today from that of the West as far as the environmental crisis is concerned. In the West there is need to reformulate a Christian theology of nature in a society in which for several centuries religious faith has weakened and where theology had surrendered the realm of nature to science and shied away from any serious concern with the sacral dimension of natural forms and phenomena. There is also the need to dethrone the humanistic conception of man which makes of man a demigod who determines the value and norm of things and who looks upon all of nature from only the point of view of his self-interest. This dethronement means a death of the type of man who almost instinctively views nature as the enemy to be conquered and the birth of the man who respects and loves nature and receives spiritual as well as physical sustenance from it, while also giving something of himself to the multifarious species of the natural kingdom. Anything short of this death and rebirth of modern Western man is cosmetic as far as the environmental crisis is concerned and no amount of clever engineering based on the current secular science of the natural order will be able to avoid the catastrophe created by the applications of this science.

This task is an extremely difficult one, seeing how deeply aliened from nature as well as from the supernatural source of the natural order is the psyche and mind of secularized Western man. But there is a compensation in the fact that the forces with which the religious and spiritual elements in the West have to contend come for the most part from within Western civilization itself and not from the outside, the economic and now technological challenge of Japan being the only exception.

In contrast, in the Islamic world the origin of the technological problems bearing upon the environment is to be sought outside that world. The intellectual and spiritual leaders of the Islamic world must deal not only with their own problems but with ever continuing challenges which originate beyond their borders. There are, however, also certain advantages in the Islamic situation. There, religion is still very strong and one can appeal more easily to the people's religious sensibilities in seeking to solve the environmental crisis. Moreover, what would be called a theology of nature in Christian terms has never been forgotten in Islam; nor has the sacred view of the cosmos been totally replaced by a view based upon a purely quantitative science, as has occurred in the West. Finally, the ethical dimension of life as grounded in revelation is still strong among Muslims and can be appealed to more easily than is the case of many but of course not all sectors of Western society. The task of saving the natural

order from that humanity which has lost its vision of who man is and has thus
become useless from a spiritual point of view is daunting in both worlds, but
it is a task which must be carried out if human life is to even continue not
to say to have a qualitative dimension.

In conclusion it is necessary to mention what it is, exactly, that the Islamic
world must do in the face of the devastating environmental crisis, leaving the
agenda of the West to others who speak for it and who are specifically concerned
with it. The Islamic world must carry out two extensive programs despite all
the obstacles placed before it by external factors.[13] The first concerns formulating
and making clearly known in a contemporary language the perennial wisdom
of Islam concerning the natural order, its religious significance and intimate
relation to every phase of man's life in this world. This program must of necessity
include a critical appraisal of both modern science and scientism as well as
the significance of traditional Islamic science not only as part of the Western
history of science but as an integral part of the Islamic intellectual tradition.[14]

The second program is to expand the awareness of *Sharī'ite* teachings
concerning ethical treatment of the natural environment and extend their field
of application whenever necessary according to the principle of the *Sharī'ah*
itself. In addition to passing laws of a civil nature against acts of pollution similar
to what is done in the West, Islamic countries must bring out the *Sharī'ite*
injunctions concerning the care for nature and compassion toward animals and
plants, so that environmental laws will be seen by Muslims to be impregnated
with religious significance. The ethical treatment of the environment in the
Islamic world cannot take place without emphasis upon the teachings of the
Divine Law and hence the ethical and religious consequences for the soul of
man if he treats the natural environment with impunity and seeks simply to
rape it with unbridled ferocity.

In traditional times there existed not one but several humanities, each
dominated by a religious and spiritual norm which could be called "the presiding
Idea" of the civilization in question. Religions remained impervious to other
universes of religious discourse with exceptions which only proved the rule.[15]
Today, as already pointed out earlier in this book, the boundaries of those
traditional universes have been broken and there is need for them to understand
each other and to reach a harmony which is in fact possible only in the "Divine
Stratosphere." Meanwhile, however, the members of these different human
collectivities have become nearly all participants, some more actively than
others, in the destruction of the earth. It is, therefore, essential for those who
speak for religion and the world of the Spirit, to collaborate and apply that
inner unity and harmony which binds them together to the terrestrial realm
and the question of saving the planet from a humanity in rebellion against both

Heaven and earth. The person who speaks for the life of the Spirit today cannot remain indifferent to the destruction of that primordial cathedral which is virgin nature nor maintain silence concerning the harm that man does to himself as an immortal being by absolutizing the "kingdom of man" and as a consequence brutalizing and destroying everything else in the name of the earthly welfare of members of that kingdom.

Islam has certainly its share of responsibility in drawing the attention of its own adherents as well as the world at large to the spiritual significance of nature and the necessity to live in peace and harmony with the rest of God's creation. The Islamic tradition is particularly rich in preserving to this day its sacred sciences, a sapiental knowledge combined with love of the natural environment, a metaphysics of nature which unveils her role as the grand book in which the symbols of the world of Divine Majesty and Beauty are engraved. It also possesses a system of ethics, rooted in the revelation and bound to the Divine Law, which concerns the responsibilities and duties of man towards the nonhuman realms of the created order. It is incumbent upon Muslims to resuscitate both of these dimensions of their tradition in a contemporary language which can awaken and lead men and women to a greater awareness of the spiritual significance of the natural world and the dire consequences of its destruction.

It is also the duty of those who speak for traditional Islam to carry out a dialogue with followers of other religions on an issue which concerns men and women everywhere. By sharing the wisdom of their tradition with others and learning from them, they can contribute a great deal not only to the Islamic world itself as it struggles with the consequences of the environmental crisis, but to the whole of humanity. As the sun shines upon all men and women from east to west and the night stars reveal their mysterious beauty to those with eyes to see whether they behold them in Japan, India, Arabia or America, so does the wisdom concerning nature and the compassionate care for nature as taught by various religions belong to human beings wherever they might be, as long as they are blessed with the gift of appreciation of the beauty of the rose and the song of the nightingale. The Quran asserts that "to God belong the East and the West" (II.115). This statement possesses many levels of meaning, one of which is that where the sun rises and where it sets, where forests cover the land and where sand dunes rove over empty spaces, where majestic mountains touch the void of heaven and where deep blue waters reflect the Divine Infinite, all belong to God and are hence interrelated. The destruction of one part of creation affects other parts in ways that the science of today has not been able to fathom. In such an interdependent natural environment in which all human beings live, it is for men and women everywhere to unite, not in an agnostic humanism which kills the Divine in man and therefore veils the reflection of the Divine in nature, but in the one Spirit which manifests itself in different ways in the vast and complex ocean of humanity.

To rediscover this Spirit and its reflection in oneself is the first essential step. To see the reflection of this Spirit in the world of nature is its natural consequence. Man cannot save the natural environment except by rediscovering the nexus between the Spirit and nature and becoming once again aware of the sacred quality of the works of the Supreme Artisan. And man cannot gain such an awareness of the sacred aspect of nature without discovering the sacred within himself and ultimately the Sacred as such. The solution of the environmental crisis cannot come but from the cure of the spiritual malaise of modern man and the rediscovery of the world of the Spirit, which being compassionate always gives of Itself to those open and receptive to Its vivifying rays. The bounties of nature and her generosity to man are there, proofs of this reality, for despite all that man has done to destroy nature, she is still alive and reflects on her own ontological level the love and compassion, the wisdom and the power which belong ultimately to the realm of the Spirit. And in this crisis of unprecedented proportions, it is nature as God's primordial creation that will have the final say.

Notes

1. Concerning the Islamic view of nature, see S.H. Nasr, *An Introduction to Islamic Cosmological Doctrines* (Albany, N.Y., 1993); *idem, Science and Civilization in Islam*; and *idem Islamic Life and Thought* (Albany, N.Y., 1981), especially chapter 19.

2. On the concept of Islam as the primordial religion, see F. Schuon, *Understanding Islam*, and S.H. Nasr, *Ideals and Realities of Islam* (London, 1989). Islam is also called *dīn al-fiṭrah*, which means the religion that is in the very nature of things and engraved in man's primordial and eternal substance.

3. See our "The Cosmos and the Natural Order," in S.H. Nasr (ed.), *Islamic Spirituality—Foundations*, vol. 19 of *World Spirituality: An Encyclopedic History of the Religious Ouest* (New York, 1987), p. 345ff. See also S.H. Nasr, *Ideals and Realities of Islam*, p. 53ff.

4. See Nasr, *An Introduction to Islamic Cosmological Doctrine*, p. 6ff. Also *Ideals and Realities of Islam*, p. 55.

5. See W. Chittick, " 'God Surrounds all Things': An Islamic Perspective on the Environment," *The World and I*, vol. I, no. 6 (June 1986), pp. 671–678.

6. It is of great significance that the Islamic paradise is not constructed of only precious stones from the mineral realm, but contains also plants and animals. Certain later Islamic philosophers such as Ṣadr al-Dīn Shirāzī in his *al-Asfār al-arba'ah* and *Risālah fi 'l-ḥashr* speak at length of the resurrection of animals and plants as well as of men.

7. On the Sufi attitude towards nature, see F. Meier,"The Problems of Nature in the Esoteric Monism of Islam," in *Spirit and Nature: Papers from the Eranos Yearbooks*, trans. R. Mannheim (Princeton, 1954), p. 203ff.; and Nasr, *Islamic Life and Thought*, chapter 19.

8. On the Islamic concept of man, see G. Eaton, "Man," in *Islamic Spirituality—Foundations*, chapter 19; also Nasr, *Knowledge and the Sacred*, pp. 358–377.

9. For a profound study of this loss of center in Western man as a result of the advent of humanism, see F. Schuon, *Having a Center* (Bloomington, Ind., 1990), p. 160ff.

10. This categorization is somewhat simplified for the sake of argument. There are, needless to say, shades of opinion and a certain amount of diversity in each category, although the general characteristics of each voice as outlined below holds for members of the category in question.

11. Kasrawī, who died in 1946, held many views which are problematic from a traditional Islamic point of view, but he was perhaps the first Muslim writer to have thoroughly criticized European science and technology and their effect upon society.

12. We say "for the most part" since most of the environmental problems of the Islamic world concern the health and physical well-being of its own citizens and do not affect the pollution of the global environment in the same way and to the same degree as do the actions of highly industrialized nations. There are, however, actions taken by certain Islamic or for that matter so-called Third World countries which do have dire consequences for the globe as a whole. These include the destruction of tropical forests and the use of pesticides which are of course the products of modern chemistry and part and parcel of modern agricultural practice. Strangely enough, because of such practices and their global consequences, for the first time since the beginning of the period of European expansion, the life of the industrialized West depends in a basic way upon the actions of those who live in what used to be European colonies.

13. We would be the last person to advise inaction by Muslims because of the technological and economic domination of the West. Even under the difficult conditions of today, much can be done by Muslims themselves. Moreover, some of the ecologically catastrophic actions taken in various Islamic countries ranging from agricultural to architectural fiascos did not have to be carried out and certainly the West cannot be blamed for all the wrong planning and action or for that matter inaction within Islamic countries despite the West's grave responsibility as the main agent in the creation of the present global environmental crisis.

14. We have dealt extensively with this question in several of our writings, such as *Islamic Life and Thought* and *Science and Civilization in Islam*, and cannot deal with it at any length here.

15. See F. Schuon, *The Transcendent Unity of Religions*, especially chapter 2 and 3. See also Part Two above.

CHAPTER TEN

The Concept of Human Progress Through Material Evolution: A Traditional Critique

One of the consequences of the loss of sacred science in the modern world is the development of the concept of indefinite human progress through material evolution, a concept which became almost worshipped for nearly two centuries as a dogma in a pseudo-religion which only now is being exposed as the illusion that it always was. The modern dilemma is due to a large extent to this central superstition of the modern world whose consequences in the destruction of the natural environment and much of the social structure of societies for which it became the sole guiding principle is evident everywhere today. Criticism of it is therefore of the utmost importance if one is to assert the reality of tradition and to rediscover and reformulate the sacred science of which the contemporary world is in such a great need.

There is little doubt that the idea of human progress, as it came to be understood since the eighteenth century in Europe, is one that was at first confined to Western thought, especially in the form of the wedding of the idea of progress with material evolution, and only later spread to other parts of the globe. Moreover, this idea was a latecomer upon the scene of Western civilization, although some have tried to find its roots among the Greeks.[1] Traditional Western man, like his fellow human beings in various Eastern civilizations, saw the flow of time in a downward rather than upward direction, whether this was conceived of as cycles, as among the ancient Greeks and Romans, or in a linear fashion, as in the Jewish and Christian traditions. Nor was the moving force of history seen in purely materialistic terms except in rare instances, such as in ancient antiquity. But even in such cases the concepts involved were very different from those held today since the ancients did not have the conception or even the word for matter as this term is used today. For most premodern peoples of the West the moving forces which governed human existence and its history were in any case nonmaterial, whether these forces were seen as *moira* or *dyké*[2] by the Greeks or the Will of God and various angelic hierarchies in Judaism and Christianity.

As for the non-Western world, among all of the civilizations which this world embraces, the perfection of the human state has always been seen as being at the beginning or the origin which is of course also reflected perpetually in the ever-present now. The perfect state of things, for both individual and collective man, has been envisaged as being at the time of the first Emperor in the Far East, or at the beginning of the last Golden Age or *Kṛta Yuga* in Hinduism and the like. Likewise in Islam, which is closer to the Jewish and Christian traditions, perfection is associated with the origin of the religion. The most perfect man is the Prophet of Islam and the most perfect society that of Medina. Even in cases where perfection has been described as belonging to the future it has always been associated with another Divine intervention in human history, with the coming of the Saoshyant in Zoroastrianism, or Kalki, the Kali Avatāra, in Hinduism or the Mahdī in Islam. The traditional East joined the traditional West in distinguishing clearly between a messianic vision based on Divine Agencies and a messianism which is reduced to purely human proportions.

To discuss the idea of human progress through material evolution in Western philosophy is therefore to deal with a recent phenomenon in Western intellectual history. It is also to deal with an idea which is confined to modern civilization as it developed in the West, although it has spread during the past century beyond this geographical area. The ideas and concepts which served as the background for the rise of the typically modern idea of human progress through material evolution are, however, somewhat older. Some reach back to the origins of the Western tradition, although these ideas were in every case distorted and even subverted to make it possible for the idea of progress based on material factors to be created from them.

Perhaps the most basic factor which gave rise to the modern idea of human progress through material evolution was that reduction of man to the purely human which took place in the Renaissance. Traditional Christianity saw man as a being born for immortality, born to go beyond himself, for, as St. Augustine had stated, to be human is to be more than merely human. This also means that to seek to be purely human is to fall below the human level to the subhuman level, as the history of the modern world has demonstrated so clearly. Renaissance humanism, which is still spoken of in glowing terms in certain quarters, bound man to the earthly level and in doing so imprisoned his aspirations for perfection by limiting them to this world.[3]

Until that time, and of course for a short period afterwards, since no major change of this order can come about so abruptly, progress had been associated with the perfection of the human soul and not the perfection of society as a whole except with the coming of the kingdom of God on earth, identified with the coming of the Messiah and the establishment of the New Jerusalem.

Renaissance and post-Renaissance humanism and secularism made the traditional idea of the progress of the human soul towards its perfection, which resulted in its ultimate wedding with the Spirit, of secondary concern, and the actual reality of the eschatological events associated with the descent of the Celestial Jerusalem and the coming of the Messiah even more "far-fetched" and inaccessible, until both became reduced to the category of illusion, superstition or some form of psychological subjectivism. But the imprint of the idea of progress and perfection in human nature was too profound to be obliterated so easily. Man still lived and breathed with these ideas in his heart and soul.

Meanwhile, the conquest of the New World, Africa and Asia was bringing great wealth into Europe and creating a new mercantile society which saw in its power to manipulate the world, the possibility of perfecting it in a material and economic sense. Certain forms of Protestant theology in fact saw moral virtue in economic activity and were associated with the rise of capitalism and its well-known link until very recent times with the idea of material progress.[4]

With this new confidence gained by European man in his ability to conquer the world and to remold it, the human background was prepared for the transfer of the idea of perfection and the progress of the soul from its upward, vertical dimension towards God to a purely this-worldly and temporal one. These ideas, thus suppressed, had to find an outlet in the worldview of modern man since they were so deeply ingrained in the human soul. The natural outlet was provided by this exceptional chapter of European history during which, despite incessant wars between Catholics and Protestants, Spain and England, England and France, etc., European man as a whole found himself mastering the earth rapidly and being able apparently to mold the destiny of humanity. It took but a single step to see in this very process of the expansion of European civilization and the amassing of wealth which accrued from it, the road to human progress and the confirmation of the secularized conception of man which had made such a domination possible in the first place.[5] This success was due to the secularization of man and in turn hastened the process of secularization and this-worldliness by encouraging human beings to devote all their energies to worldly activities as the hereafter became more and more a distant concept or belief rather than an immediate reality. Moreover, the belief in human progress in history provided a goal which aroused men's fervor and faith and even sought to satisfy their religious needs. Perhaps there is no modern ideology which has played as great a role in replacing religion and, as a pseudo-religion, attracting the ultimate adherence of human beings as the idea of progress which later became wed to evolutionism.[6]

Another element of great importance whose secularization and distortion contributed a great deal to the rise of the idea of human progress through material evolution was the Christian doctrine of incarnation and the linear conception of history associated with it and especially with the type of Christology adopted by the Western Church. For Christianity the Truth entered into history, into the stream of time and, through this event, time and change gained significance beyond the domain of time itself. In other religions also, time is of course of significance. What human beings do affects their immortal souls and the state of their being in the worlds which lie beyond time. Whether the world is seen as *māyā* as in Hinduism or as mirrors reflecting God's Names and Qualities as in Islam, there is not the concern in these religions with the "historicity" of the incarnation of the Truth in the way that one finds in Christianity. This statement would also include Zoroastrianism, although it sees time itself as an angel and would hold true even in later developments of the religion in the form of Zurvanism, where Zūrvān or "boundless time" is seen as the principle of the universe itself.

As long as the integral Christian tradition was alive in which Christ was seen as the eternally present Logos and not only as an "historical personality," the doctrine of incarnation was preserved from desecration, distortion and perversion, but as suprasensible levels of being began to lose their reality for Western man and Christianity became bound solely to an historic event, history itself became impregnated with ultimate significance affecting the Truth as such. From this position there was but a single step to take to arrive at nineteenth century European philosophy, which with Hegel converted the philosophy of history practically into theology itself. The secularization of the Christian concept of incarnation removed Christ in one degree or another from the center of the arena of the historical and cosmic drama but preserved the idea of the ultimate significance of temporal change for human existence. Belief in human progress through temporal and historical change replaced to a large extent the central role occupied by the doctrine of incarnation in traditional Christian theology. One cannot imagine a philosophy which makes changes in human history the ultimate determining factor of human destiny and even of the Truth Itself arising anywhere but in a world in which the historical flux had been impregnated with theological significance to an extraordinary degree. In a way Hegelianism and Marxism could have arisen only in a world whose background was Christian and Marxism could only be a Christian heresy as far as its philosophical aspect is concerned, although its concern with every aspect of life makes it in a sense a parody of Judaism with its all-embracing notion of Divine Law as incorporated in the Talmud.

As for the linear conception of time which is to be found in traditional Christian sources such as St. Augustine, it saw history as a single line or movement punctuated by that one great event which was the descent of the Logos or the Son into time. Time had three points of reference, the creation of Adam, the coming of Christ and the end of the world associated with his second coming. History had a direction and moved like an arrow towards that target which is described so powerfully in the *Revelations of John*. There was no cyclic conception of rejuvenation, gradual decay and decomposition followed by a new period of rejuvenation resulting from a new intervention by Heaven upon the human plane as one finds in so many Oriental religions. Nor was there an emphasis upon the cycles of prophecy as we see in Islam, although the more metaphysical and esoteric forms of Christianity were certainly aware of the ever-lasting and ever-present nature of the Logos. But as these more profound teachings became less accessible and theology more rationalistic, it became easier for the secularist thinkers to take the one step needed to convert the Christian conception of linear time to the idea of continuous and linear human progress and the popular idea that things simply *must* become better every day simply because time moves on.

As the Celestial Jerusalem became replaced by a vaguely defined perfect society in the future, the Christian conception of linear time became replaced by the secular one which preserved the idea of the linear character of time moving towards the goal of perfection in some undefined future, but rejected the transhistorical significance of historical events as envisaged by Christianity. In a sense historicism, and the idea of progress associated with it in many philosophical schools, are the result of the secularization and perversion of a particular Christian view of history adopted by the mainstream of Western Christianity.

It is in this context that one must understand the rise of the idea of utopianism, which is another important element among the array of factors and forces that gave rise to the idea of progress in the modern West. Traditional teachings had always been aware of the ideal and perfect society, whether it was the *civitas Dei* of St. Augustine or *al-madīnat al-fāḍilah* of al-Fārābī, not to speak of Plato's well-known description of the perfect state described in the *Republic*, which antedates both. But in a profound sense these "cities" were not of this world, at least not in the ordinary sense of the term "world." The word *utopia* itself, used by Sir Thomas More as the title of his famous work, reveals the metaphysical origin of this concept. Utopia means literally no-where (*u* which denotes negation and *topos* space in Greek). It is the land that is beyond physical space, in the eighth clime as the Muslim philosophers would say.[7] It belonged to the spiritual world and was not realizable on earth unless it were to be the descent of this celestial city upon the earthly plane.

The secularization which took place in the West after the Middle Ages gradually transformed the idea of utopia to create utopianism in its modern sense.[8] In this transformation messianic ideas emanating from Judaism, and to a certain extent Christianity, were also to play an important role. Through this religious zeal to establish a perfect order on earth, the already secularized notion of utopianism gained much momentum and became a major force in Western society. It is not accidental that the most dogmatic ideology based on the idea of inevitable human progress to issue from the West, namely Marxism, was to combine a pseudo-religious fervor deriving in many ways from a subversion of messianic ideas with utopianism. The role of the Messiah to establish the Kingdom of God on earth became converted into that of the revolutionary to bring about the perfect social order through revolutionary and violent means. In this way also religious eschatology was converted, or rather perverted, into the secular vision of the perfect order established by means of human progress through material evolution or revolution, for both views existed among the Western philosophers of the eighteenth and nineteenth centuries.

As far as material evolution in concerned, it too is the result of transformations which began during the Renaissance and reached their peak in the seventeenth century Scientific Revolution, although the evolutionary idea itself was not to appear until two centuries later. The science of the Renaissance was still medieval science based on symbolism, correspondence between various levels of being, concern with the totality and the whole rather than parts and other features associated with the traditional sciences which have been discussed already.[9] The scientists of the age were concerned with Hermeticism and the Kabbala and the sciences dealing with names such as Marciglio Ficino, Pico della Mirandola, Nicola Flamel, and even Leonardo Da Vinci and Giordano Bruno recall more wholistic sciences of nature than the mechanistic natural philosophy which came to the fore in the seventeenth century.

Yet it was during this period that the cosmos was becoming gradually desacralized following upon the nominalistic perspective of the late Middle Ages which had already succeeded to some extent in depleting the cosmos of its sacred presence. This was also the period of the eclipse of a serious philosophy based on certainty and the vision of Being.[10] The result was the quest after a new science and a new philosophy, a science based on a mechanistic conception of the universe as developed by Galileo, Kepler and Newton, and a philosophy based upon the certainty of one's individual consciousness divorced from the world of extension or "matter" as developed by Descartes. The two went hand in hand in creating a view of things in which the knowing subject or the mind was totally other than the known object or "matter" which then became reduced to a pure "it" or "thing" in a mechanistic world where quantitative laws were to explain the functioning of all things.[11]

This new transformation of the European mentality was itself responsible for the birth of the very concept of "matter" as it is known to modern man today. Neither the ancients nor the medieval people had the conception of matter which is taken for granted now, nor in fact do so to this day those sections of the human race which have not been affected by the influence of modernism. Neither the Greek *hylé*, the Sanskrit *prakṛti*, the Arabic *māddah*, nor even the Latin *materia* means exactly matter in the modern sense. It was the seventeenth century Scientific Revolution combined with the philosophical changes associated with Cartesianism which made possible the very idea of something being "material" and materialism in its current sense. Even the so-called materialistic philosophers of the Hellenistic period or the Hindu atomists cannot be considered, strictly speaking, as materialists since the modern concept of matter had no meaning for them.

Although the birth of mechanistic science and a purely material conception of the world is associated with the seventeenth century, the worldview of this period was still a static one. Even radically materialistic philosophers such as La Mettrie envisaged the material world as a static order with change occurring within it but not with the directed movement which would be associated later with the idea of evolution. This later idea was to come not from the domain of physics but from the temporalization of the ancient philosophical idea of the "great chain of being" which was applied to the world of living things and was the paradigm through which natural historians since Aristotle had explained the chain of life, relating the creatures of the three kingdoms to each other and to the whole of creation.

Traditional man saw a scale of perfection in existence ranging from the angels to the dust beneath the feet of earthly creatures. As long as the intuition of the world of Platonic Ideas on the one hand and living faith in a Divine Being who created and ordained all things on the other remained alive, man had no problem envisaging this "chain of being" in a "spatial" manner, so that the hierarchy of the planes of being was a living reality for him here and now. This static vision of the cosmos did not of course preclude the possibility of cosmic rhythms stated explicitly by the Indian and Greek sages and philosophers and alluded to by certain Jewish and Christian authorities, but such a vision did definitely preclude the possibility of a gradual growth in time and through only temporal means from one state of being to another. Such a growth was possible inwardly in the life of man but not for the species as a whole.

The eclipse of faith, the spread of secularism, the loss of intellectual intuition, the forgetfulness of sacred science and the mechanization of the cosmos combined to make the hierarchy of universal existence appear as unreal. Having lost the vision of the Immutable, Western man could not but turn to the parody of the concept of the chain of being in time. The vertical "great chain of being" was made horizontal and temporal, resulting in the birth of the idea of evolution.[12] Wallace and Darwin did not arrive at the theory of evolution simply from their observations. Rather, in a world in which the Divinity had been either denied or relegated to the role of the maker of the clock which the seventeenth century conceived the universe to be and where sapiential wisdom based on the contemplation of the higher states of being had become practically inaccessible, the theory of evolution seemed the best way of providing a background for the study of the amazing diversity of life forms without having to have recourse to the creative power of God. The theory of evolution soon turned to a dogma precisely because it rapidly replaced religious faith and came to provide what appeared to be a "scientific" crutch for the soul to enable it to forget God. It has therefore survived to this day not as a theory but as a dogma among many scientists as well as nonscientists whose worldview would crumble if they were but to take evolution for what it is, namely a convenient philosophical and rationalistic scheme to enable man to create the illusion of a purely closed universe around himself. That is also why logical and scientific arguments against it have been often treated by its defenders not at all rationally and scientifically but with a violence and passion that reveals the pseudo-religious role played by the theory of evolution among its exponents.

This loss of the vision of the Immutable was to generalize the idea of evolution and extend it far beyond the domain of biology. At the same time Hegelian dialectic was introducing change and becoming into the heart of reality as it was conceived by nineteenth century European man. It did not take much to transformd Hegel's idealism into materialism, considering how prevalent were the various materialistic schools at that time. The new form of materialism announced by Marx, however, differed from its predecessors in its insistence upon the dialectical process to which was grafted the idea of progress whose development has been already mentioned. In the crucible of nineteenth century European thought the strands of the ideas of human progress, materialism and evolution became welded together under the general banner of human progress through material evolution. Of course, there were major differences of view among Marx and his followers, the French exponents of progress, the English evolutionists—not all of whom were "materialists" strictly speaking—and others. But all these schools harped upon variations of the same themes of central concern which had grown out of the experience and thought of postmedieval European civilization and which had reached a point of view that was totally different from that of other civilizations in either East or West.

During the nineteenth century Christian theology remained in general opposed to this amalgamation of ideas and forces outlined above, especially the theory of evolution and materialism. But as it was not able to marshal evidence of a truly intellectual—rather than simply rational or sentimental—order, it fought a continuously defensive battle. The opposition to these forces and ideas usually relied either solely on faith or remained on the emotional level often associated with various fundamentalist positions bereft of intellectual substance. Nevertheless, evolutionary concepts remained for the most part outside the citadel of Christianity.

One had to wait for the twentieth century to witness a fusion—which can also be called a perversion—of these ideas with Christian theology itself, of which perhaps the most radical and far-fetched example is Teilhardism.[13] This phenomenon is particularly strange in that the idea of progress itself has ceased to attract the attention of the most perceptive of Western thinkers for several decades and many people in the West seek to rediscover the nature of man beyond the image of the evolving mammal striving through evolution to higher states of consciousness or a more perfect society as presented in so many nineteenth century schools of thought. It is a parody that at the moment when the idea of progress through material evolution is itself becoming a victim of historic change and going out of vogue, the force of religion in the West which had for so long resisted this idea is becoming influenced to an ever greater degree by its theses. The direction of life of contemporary man itself will be determined by the degree to which he is able to distinguish once again, with the help of metaphysics and sacred science, between the immutable and the changing, the permanent and the transient, and between the apparent in contrast to the real progress available and possible for man as a being who no matter how much he changes remains in the depth of his being the same creature he has always been and will always be, a being born for the immortal empyrean of the Spirit.

Notes

1. See, for example, the study of R. Nisbet, *History of the Idea of Progress* (New York, 1980), which has brought a great deal of historical research to bear upon the subject but which overemphasizes the Greek origin of this idea.

2. *Moira* and *dykė* are both key Greek philosophical and religious terms, the first associated with the Olympian and the second with the Dionysian-Orphic schools, and both imply destiny or justice or a principle which dominates over the world and is responsible for its functioning. The exact meaning of the two terms is, however, very different because of the basic differences between the two worldviews to which they belong. See F. Cornford, *From Religion to Philosophy: A Study in the Origins of Western Speculation* (New York, 1957).

3. On the significance of this event which, from the traditional point of view, implied a new "fall" for man, see F. Schuon, *Light on the Ancient Worlds*, especially p. 28ff.

4. This theme has been treated by many social, economic and cultural historians, perhaps the most famous works being the classical ones by R.H. Tawney, *The Acquisitive Society*

(New York, 1920); and M. Weber, *The Protestant Ethic and the Spirit of Capitalism* (London, 1930).

5. Had not Europe rejected its own traditional civilization, it would not have been able to develop all the means and techniques which made the conquest of non-European civilizations possible.

6. On the pseudo-religious character of the idea of progress, see M. Lings, *Ancient Beliefs and Modern Superstitions* (London, 1980).

7. The Persian philosopher Suhrawardī refers in fact to this land as *nā-kujā ābād*, which in Persian means literally utopia. See H. Corbin, *En Islam iranien*, vol. IV (Paris, 1972) p. 384ff.; and D. Shayegan, *Henry Corbin: La Topographie spirituelle de l'Islam iranien* (Paris, 1990), pp. 195–97.

8. On utopianism see J. Servier, *L'Histoire de l'utopie* (Paris, 1960); and F.E. Manuel and F.P. Manuel, *Utopian Thought in the Western World* (Cambridge, Mass. 1979).

9. On Renaissance science see A. Debus, *Man and Nature in the Renaissance* (New York, 1978).

10. The absence of serious philosophical schools which would lead to intellectual certainty between the end of the Middle Ages and Descartes is studied and described in E. Gilson, *The Unity of Philosophical Experience* New York, (Westminster, MD, 1982).

11. On how this process of the mechanization of the universe and of nature occurred, see S.H. Nasr, *Man and Nature,* and Th. Roszak, *Where the Wasteland Ends* (New York, 1972).

12. The classical work of A. Lovejoy, *The Great Chain of Being,* is still of much value in tracing the history of this perennial idea in the West.

13. See the penetrating analysis of W. Smith in his *Teilhardism and the New Religion.*

CHAPTER ELEVEN

Reflections upon the Theological Modernism
of Hans Küng

One of the major dilemmas in the modern world from the point of view of tradition and sacred science is theological modernism, which represents the intrusion of the secularizing and desacralizing tendencies of modernism into the heart of Christian theology itself. The loss of the supreme science or *scientia sacra* along with a sacred science of nature could not but affect theology itself, that "science of God" whose role it had always been to protect the citadel of faith. As a result, modernistic formulations of theology have appeared upon the scene which are far removed from the traditional theology of a St.Thomas or even Bossuet, not to mention that theology of the Eastern Church where the very term theology means no less than the indwelling of God in man.

Among the best-known and most influential voices of theological modernism in recent years has been Hans Küng, to whose views the critique that follows is devoted. More particularly the comments below are in reference to an essay by Küng entitled, "Toward a New Consensus in Catholic (and Ecumenical) Theology," which summarize his general views concerning theology.[1]

The observations and commentaries on Hans Küng's essay made here come from the point of view of tradition itself, although some of the comments are also related more specifically to the Islamic tradition. To have lived and experienced any religion fully is in a sense to have experienced all religions. To have meditated on the basic intellectual problems concerning a particular religious community is to have confronted these problems as they face people of religion everywhere. The unity of the human race and the universality of the intellect as it functions in human beings are such as to permit the followers of one religion to think about and comment on the theological perspectives of another religion, especially in a world such as ours where traditional barriers between various civilizations have been lifted.

Yet precisely because it is religion which actualizes the potentialities of those who follow it and provides an objective cadre for the functioning of that inner revelation within humanity, which is the intellect in its original rather than debased meaning, particular problems of each religion remain its own.

In commenting upon Küng's theses, we are therefore fully aware that we have no right to deal with the specific religious and dogmatic problems of Catholicism and might be accused of being simply an intruding outsider were we to deal with specific issues of the Catholic faith and practice in a purely Catholic context. Still, it is amazing how religious issues in one religion are also confronted by other religions and how the weakening or foundering of a particular religious universe can affect others. It is with full awareness of these factors and in humility as an outsider to the scene of present-day Catholic theology that the following comments are offered:

At the beginning of his essay Küng writes: "However, the Second Vatican Council demonstrated that this [neo-Scholastic] theology was unable to deal effectively with the contemporary problems of humanity, the church and society." The question to ask is whether the neo-Scholastic theology, which is a revival of Thomism, is unable to deal with contemporary problems because of innate flaws in Thomism, or because its principles have not been applied to contemporary problems or because these problems are for the most part pseudo-problems brought into being as a result of ill-posed questions. Is Thomism true? If it is true, that is, if it is an expression of metaphysical truth in its Christian form, then it cannot cease to be true. Its language might need modification, but its message and content must continue to possess validity. And if there are other forms of theology necessary in the present context, are these other forms of theology different ways of explaining the eternal message of Christianity in a particular historical context with full consideration of the contingent factors involved, or are they no more than theologizing about passing and ephemeral experiences or so-called scientific "truths" which often cease to be of any great relevance from a theological point of view by the time the theologians have finished theologizing about them?

Truth must always come before expediency and even timeliness, especially as far as theology is concerned. Theology is after all literally "the science of God." It should explain the temporal with reference to the Eternal and not the Eternal in the light of temporality which is made to sound very *real*, central, and important by being baptized as the human condition, the modern world, or urgent human problems. There is no more urgent a human problem than the task of distinguishing between the Real and the Eternal on one hand and the illusory and ephemeral on the other. The plurality of theologies is valuable only if it means different paths opening unto the same Truth, as was in fact the case in early Christianity, and not of relativizing the Absolute and positing pseudo-philosophies based upon the confusion between the Eternal and temporal orders alongside authentic forms of theology which remain conscious of the basic mission of theology as the study of God and of creation in the light of God and His Wisdom and Power.

Küng is not even satisfied with post-Conciliar theology because, in his words, "since modern exegesis was generally neglected in otherwise productive movements of theological renewal, such as the patristic-oriented *'resourcement'* (H. De Lubac, J. Daniélou, H.U. von Balthasar) as well as the speculative transcendental mediation of Karl Rahner, their insufficiency became more and more apparent." Would a theology inspired by St. Augustine and Origen be insufficient because it does not take into account modern exegesis, by which is usually meant the so-called "higher criticism"?

This issue is quite sensitive especially from the Islamic point of view since Islam is based wholly on a sacred book. For it, "higher criticism" can only mean the unveiling of the inner meaning of the sacred book (*ta'wīl* or the *kashf al-maḥjūb* of the Islamic esotericists). Moreover, this process can only be achieved through the use of the higher faculties of man associated with the Intellect which resides at the heart or center of man's being. It implies an inwardness and drawing into the "book" of one's own being in order to reach the inner meaning of the Sacred Book. It certainly has nothing to do with archaeology or rationalistic analysis of texts or documents. The so-called "higher criticism," which in fact reduces the really "higher," which can be nothing but revelation, to the level of human reason, is based on the twin error which in fact characterizes so much of modern historicism and also science.

These two errors are, first of all, the presupposition that that concerning which there is no historical document did not exist, and secondly, that there is a kind of "uniformitarianism" in the laws and conditions of human society and the cosmos similar to what is posited as the key for the interpretation of the past by geologists and paleontologists. According to this thesis, the system, laws, and relations between cause and effect must have existed in days of old, let us say at the time of Christ, in the same way and mode that they can be observed today. To walk on water must be "understood" and explained away because no one can walk on water today. There is no better way to kill the inner meaning of a sacred text and the very elements which allow the human mind to ascend to higher levels of being than the so-called "higher criticism," whose result is the death of the meaning of sacred scripture as revealed meaning and the closing of the gate to the spiritual world.

Neither "higher criticism" nor the exegesis of sacred scripture, based on the common experience of a humanity that has been cut off from spiritual nourishment and lives in a world of ugliness, which stultifies the heart and the mind, can cause a theology based on the eternal truths of any religion to fail. If such a theology does exist and it appears to have "failed," the failure must be laid at the feet of those who have not succeeded in understanding it rather than being attributed to the theology itself, provided the theology in question is a veritable "science of God." It would be better to have a true theology understood by just one person than a diluted or distorted theology based on compromising the truth but accepted by the multitude. Surely in the question of religious truth it cannot be numbers that reign; otherwise what could one say concerning the lives and actions of that very small minority known as the early Christian martyrs?

The author believes that the only theology that could survive the future would be one which blends the two elements of "a 'return to the sources' and a 'venturing forth on to uncharted waters' or . . . *a theology of Christian origins and center enunciated within the horizon of the contemporary world.*" We could not agree more with the author concerning the doctrine that God is at once the Origin and the Center, the Beginning and the "Now." Therefore, theology must obviously be concerned with origins and the "Now" which is the reflection of Eternity in time, binding man to the Eternal. But religion is also tradition. It is a tree with its roots sunk in Heaven but also with a trunk and branches and laws of growth of its own. Also, like a living tree, a living religion is always amenable to a revivification and rejuvenation. Every "back to the roots" movement, however, which negates the existing trunk and branches, the long tradition which binds the particular person or community wanting to return to the roots or the Origin, only weakens the tree as a whole. There are many examples of this phenomenon in nearly all the major religions of the world, and their result has almost always been a much impoverished version of that religion which resembles the Origin outwardly but is never actually able to return to it. An awareness of the Christian Origin and Center is exemplified most positively in the history of Western Christianity by a St. Francis of Assisi who was called "the second Christ." If by returning to the Origin and Center such an event or reality is implied, then certainly what it would produce would not only live through the future but in fact shape and make the future. What such a return needs, however, which is most difficult to come by, is another St. Francis.

As for the "uncharted waters," as a result of the rampant secularism of the Western world, the water is first charted by nonreligious forces and then religion is asked to take the map of a secularized cosmos and navigate through it. From the traditional point of view, however, it is religion itself which must lead the way and charter the course. Theology as the intellectual expression of religion must be able to make the future and not simply follow the secularized disciplines with the hope of guaranteeing some kind of survival for itself by placating the "enemy" or even ceasing to call a spade a spade. Today there are many physicists who wish theologians would take theology a bit more seriously and modern science somewhat less so as far as its theological implications are concerned.

It is in the light of this statement that Küng's emphasis on the "two sources" necessary for the creation of a "scientific theology" must be examined.[2] These sources are "the traditional experience of the great Judeo-Christian movement on the one hand, and on the other the contemporary human experiences of Christians and non-Christians." First of all, in the term "non-Christians" two very disparate elements are covered in an indiscriminate fashion. A non-Christian can be a Muslim, Hindu, or Buddhist or he or she can be an agnostic or atheist, who in fact is, to say the least, as far removed from the followers of other religions as he or she is from Christianity or Judaism. There are then three groups or sources to consider rather than two: the Judeo-Christian tradition,[3] the other religions, and modern secularism. There is no doubt that the time has come for serious theology in the West to take cognizance of the religious and metaphysical significance of other religions, whose presence in a less mutilated and secularized form than much of contemporary Christianity, is in a profound sense a compensation sent by Heaven to offset the withering effect of secularism and pseudo-religious ideologies. A veritable dialogue in the spirit of authentic ecumenism which would respect the totality of each tradition and not reduce things to their common denominator would certainly be a great aid to future theological formulations among Christians. The writings of such figures as Frithjof Schuon have already made accessible the remarkable richness of this undertaking.[4]

But as far as the experience of the secular, or even modern science itself, is concerned, we do not believe that this can be a "source" for theology. Rather, it must be an element which contemporary theology must seek to explain in the light of its own principles. It is not theology which must surrender itself to modern science and its findings. Rather it is modern science which must be critically appraised from the metaphysical and theological points of view and its findings evaluated in this light. As the basic role of religion is to save the human soul from the world and not simply to carry out a dialogue with the world, the role of theology is to cast the light of the Eternal upon the experiences of mankind's terrestrial journey. Since modern humanity has experienced the void and nihilism, theology can explain the reason for such an experience and the meaning that this type of experience can have in bringing humanity back to God, for as Meister Eckhart has said, "the more they blaspheme the more they praise God." But this experience of the void or despair or injustice cannot be a "source" of theology without doing grave injustice to theology and destroying the sense of the sacred which alone can render meaning to human life.

There are a few other particular points in Küng's statements, which corroborate the views of Schillebeeckx, and which need to be commented upon in a few words. Küng states, *"divine revelation is only accessible through human experience.*" "Human experience," yes, but not ordinary human experience. There is much more to consciousness than what we usually experience. There is a hierarchy of consciousness as there is a hierarchy of experience leading ultimately to the concrete experience and consciousness of the spiritual world. Genuine revelation certainly involves experience but not one which is on the same level as everyday experience. It has been said of the messenger of Divine revelation in Islam, namely Muḥammed, that he was a man among men but not an ordinary man. Rather, he was like a jewel among stones. For Christianity, which is based on the doctrine of the incarnation and the God-man, surely Divine revelation cannot be reduced to the level of ordinary human experience, especially in a world where the higher modes of experience available to man as a theomorphic being have become so rare.

As for revelation coming, in Küng's terms, "in a lengthy process of events, experiences and interpretations and not as a supernatural 'intrusion'," what is meant by revelation here can only be the disciples' faith in Christ and not Christ himself who *is* the revelation in Christianity. But even on the level of the apostles, this secondary mode of "revelation" was not necessarily always a lengthy process. It could certainly have been an immediate "intrusion" and illumination if the substance of the soul of the disciple in question were already prepared. For people living today it is hardly conceivable to imagine what it would mean actually to encounter a great saint, not to speak of the Abrahamic prophets or Christ himself.

Closely allied to this assertion is the second point of agreement between Küng and Schillebeeckx in the above-cited essays, namely that revelation is always reached through human experience, which is never "pure." This would negate the "supernaturally natural" function of the Intellect in man which is able to know objectively and to discern between the Absolute and the relative. It would also negate the possibility of "annihilation" or what the Sufis call *al-fanā'*, through which the soul becomes "nothing" and removes itself as a veil, allowing the Supreme Self within to say "I." If humanity could not know the Truth in Itself, truth would have no meaning as either the source of objective revelation or that inner revelation which is the illumination of man's inward being. To say that there is no such thing as "pure experience" or knowledge of the truth is in a sense a negation of the very reality of the Truth. We must first accept that there is such a thing as pure knowledge and experience unveiling the Truth in its pristine purity in order to be able to decide that our experience is not pure experience in comparison with this pure experience—of which we must have some kind of knowledge if we are going to compare something with it.

The third point of agreement between Küng and Schillebeeckx[5] involves the significance of the "*living Jesus of history*" as "*the source, standard and criterion of Christian faith.*" While not at all questioning this distinctly Christian position, we would only like to add that one cannot at the same time forget or neglect the central significance of that transhistorical Jesus who said, "I am before Abraham was." Islamic Christology, which emphasizes the transhistorical Jesus, is more akin to certain early forms of Christology rejected by the later councils. It is strange that, now that there is so much attention paid to the "origins" and patristic-oriented theology, contemporary theologians do not emphasize more the Christ as the eternal Logos to which in fact many young Christians in quest of the rediscovery of integral Christianity are strongly attracted.

Finally, a comment must be made on each of the ten "guiding principles for contemporary theology" which Küng had formulated in his *Existiert Gott?* and which he repeats in the essay under review, here:

1. "Theology should not be an esoteric science only for believers but should be intelligible to non-believers as well."

Comment: First of all every living tradition *does need* an esoteric science which, however, is not usually called theology. As for theology, it should of course be written in such an intelligible manner that even the intelligent nonbeliever would be attracted to it. But it would be better for theology not to lead believers to unbelief in its attempt to be intelligible to unbelievers.

2. "Theology should not exalt simple faith nor defend an 'ecclesiastical' system but strive for the truth without compromise in intense scholarly fashion."

Comment: Certainly the goal of theology must be the truth, but if current scholarly methods are sufficient to attain the truth, then what is the difference between theology and humanistic and rational scholarship? The role of theology cannot but be the defense of the truth as revealed in God's religion. Then there is the basic question of what guarantee there is in each religion for the protection of the truth. Each religion has a different response. In Christianity, at least in its Catholic form, it has always been the *magisterium*. How can one prevent the truth from becoming reduced to mere individualistic whim and fancy if the authority of the *magisterium* be denied?

3. "Ideological opponents should not be ignored or hereticized, nor theologically co-opted. Rather their views should be set out in a fair and factual discussion and interpreted *in optimam partem* as tolerantly as possible."

Comment: Views of opponents should certainly be studied factually and objectively without passion. But truth is one thing and charity another. We must love other people, but that does not mean that we must be indifferent to the truth. Where truth is no longer of any consequence, the question of agreement or opposition is of little importance. It is easy to be tolerant when there are no immutable principles for which one stands. The situation becomes much more difficult when we have faith in a particular form of the truth which we call our religion and then either come face to face with those who possess other forms of truth which also come from God (a tree is judged by the fruit it bears),[6] or simply live in error from the point of view of the truth we accept as truth. It is this much more delicate problem that all "living theologies" of today and tomorrow face and will face not only in Christianity but in other religions as well.

4. "We should not only promote but actually practice an interdisciplinary approach. Along with a concentration upon our own field, we must maintain a constant dialogue with related fields."

Comment: This is indeed sound advice provided it is not carried out from a position of weakness and with an inferiority complex and that theology remains faithful to its own nature, mission and genius. Physicists should also follow the same advice, but that does not mean that tomorrow they will go into the laboratory and study subatomic particles through theological methods, even if they draw theological conclusions from their physical studies.

5. "We need neither hostile confrontation nor easy co-existence, but rather a critical dialogue especially between theology and philosophy, theology and natural science: religion and rationality belong together!"

Comment: This is certainly true, but it can come about only if theology stops its retreat before the onslaught of both modern philosophy and natural science. Dialogue is possible only among equals or those nearly equal. Theology has as much a right to study nature and the mind as do science and philosophy. Each discipline has a different approach and hence reaches different aspects of the truth which in its wholeness can only be seen by the science of the whole or of the totality, which is metaphysics in its original sense or the *scientia sacra*.

6. "Problems of the past should not have priority over the wide-ranging, multi-faceted dilemmas of contemporary humanity and society."

Comment: It is mostly as a result of neglecting the past as a source both of tradition and of experience for mankind that present-day humanity is faced with so many problems. Of course, theology must deal with contemporary dilemmas, but always in the light of the truth, which *is* and does not *become*, and the *scientia sacra* to which we have referred to so often in this book as well as in the light of the profound aspects of human nature, which despite appearances remains remarkably the same. It is in the light of this permanence that apparent change should be explained.

7. "The criterion determining all other criteria of Christian theology can never again be some ecclesiastical or theological tradition or institution, but only the Gospel, the original Christian message itself. Thus, theology must everywhere be oriented toward the Biblical findlings analyzed by historical-critical analysis."

Comment: Without in any way denying the central role of the Gospels, we cannot but be astonished at how this Holy Book could serve as the source for the truth of the Christian faith without the church, the oral teachings, the traditions and all that in fact connects a human being who calls him or herself Christian to the origin of this religion. If the Gospels sufficed, how could there be so many different schools all basing themselves on the same book? Although the phenomenon of the proliferation of schools and "sects" is similar in all religions, nowhere has it been as great as in Christianity when the Gospels were considered by certain schools as the main source for Christianity. But even in most of these schools, until now, certain other aspects of Christianity such as the reality of the historical Christian community have also been accepted. If the Gospels were to be taken as the sole source of theology, again the question would come up as to what guarantees the truth of the conclusions reached by a particular theological study of the Gospels and what is the origin of the faith in the light of which the Christian reads the Gospels.

8. "The Gospel should not be proclaimed in Biblical archaisms nor in Hellenistic scholastic dogmatisms nor in fashionable philosophic-theological jargon. Rather, it should be expressed in the commonly understood language of contemporary humanity and we should not stay away from any effort in this direction."

Comment: We disagree completely with this thesis. The so-called commonly understood language of contemporary humanity is itself no more than a debased jargon, influenced by the mass media and often deprived of the beauty of the language in question. Sacred books are too sublime to be cast in the molds of a language formed by the lower psyche of a humanity which is being dragged downward by the very "civilization" it has created. Religious texts have always been works of beauty which have adorned human life, and today humanity is in need of this saving beauty more than ever before. Why should the words of God sound like the outpourings of a football announcer? In other religions such as Islam where the Sacred Book is couched in the immutable beauty of a sacred language, the unchanging nature of the language has certainly not made people any less religious over the ages, even people whose mother tongue was or is not Arabic. The experience of Islam should be of some value for those who believe that catering to contemporary jargon will somehow draw people more to religion and the study of the Gospels. Let us not forget that even on the American frontiers the Bible survived in the language of Elizabethan England and was probably more widely read than many of its Americanized descendants are read by the "better-educated" descendants of those pioneers.

9. "Credible theory and livable practice, dogmatics and ethics, personal piety and reform of institutions must not be separated but seen in their inseparable connection."

Comment: We can only agree with this thesis, for in all religions method and doctrine must go hand in hand. But as far as reform is concerned, it is most of all the reform of ourselves that is at stake. Modern humanity wishes to reform everything but itself. That is why most of its reformations become deformations.

10. "We must avoid a confessionalistic ghetto mentality. Instead we should express an ecumenical vision that takes into consideration the world religions as well as contemporary ideologies: as much tolerance as possible toward those things outside the Church, toward the religious in general, and the human in general, and the development of that which is specifically Christian belong together."

Comment: Expressing an ecumenical vision in the sense already mentioned, is certainly commendable, but considering together world religions and contemporary ideologies which are the products of the secularized West, is really an insult to those religions. The much more logical and meaningful position would be to place all the religions, including Christianity, in one camp before which stand the forces of agnosticism and secularism. In fact Christianity, already scarred by several centuries of battle against humanism, secularism, and rationalism, has the choice of either returning to the universe of religion as such, to the sacred cosmos in which Islam, Hinduism, Buddhism, etc. still breathe, or attempting to bring about some kind of a marriage with secularism, which itself was born from a void created by the loss of the all-embracing Christian vision in the West. For the sake of humanity, let us hope that the first alternative will be followed and that the West will rejoin the rest of mankind spiritually, for from the marriage with secularism there cannot come into being anything but those beasts which shall lay the earth in ruin and to which the *Book of the Apocalypse* has referred so majestically.

We feel somewhat embarrassed criticizing a well-known Catholic theologian, but perhaps this exercise can be seen as a counterpart to the voluminous works written by Western Orientalists on the past, present and even future of Islam and even Islamic theology. In contrast to some of these works, however, our intentions have derived not from hatred but respect and love for Christianity and the followers of Sayyidnā 'Isā, as the Quran calls Christ. Moreover, an aspect of the experience of contemporary humanity necessitates a universal perspective on religion and an awareness of the interrelated nature of the spiritual destiny of all mankind, which makes an interest in other religions imperative for any religiously oriented person, including a Muslim concerned with the future of his own religion as well as religion as such.

Notes

1. See the essay of Küng under this title in L. Swindler (ed.), *Consensus in Theology? A Dialogue with Hans Küng and Edward Schillebeeckx* (Philadelphia, 1980), pp. 1–17.

2. A point in which he expresses his agreement with Schillebeeckx whose views are expressed in another essay in the above-cited volume entitled "I Believe in Jesus of Nazareth: The Christ, The Son of God, The Lord," pp. 18–32.

3. As already stated, the term Judeo-Christian, although now widely used, is really inappropriate. One should either refer to the Judeo-Christian-Islamic, that is, the Abrahamic traditions, or to each member of this family of religions separately. If we have used this term here, it is because we wish to remain faithful to Küng's terminology.

4. See chapter four above.

5. All these points of agreement concern the two essays cited above.

6. Here one needs to develop universal criteria for discerning the truth from error in such a way as not to overlook the truth as manifested in forms other than one's own nor to accept error parading as truth on the pretext of "openness" or pseudo-universality. Universality is meaningless without truth. We have discussed this matter fully in chapter four above.

Postscript

The Need for a Sacred Science

The world today is most of all in need of wisdom, of that supreme knowledge or science of the Real which is none other than metaphysics in its traditional sense or *scientia sacra* as we have defined this term in this book and elsewhere. But the world is also in need of a sacred science pertaining to the domain of manifestation and contingency but nevertheless dependent upon the Supreme Science or metaphysics, a science which can relate the various levels of knowledge once again to the sacred. Moreover, the principle that nature abbors a vacuum applies to both the domain of metaphysics and the cosmological and traditional sciences. In the same way that the disappearance in the West of authentic metaphysics led to its "replacement" by all kinds of feable philosophical replacements which have finally led to the suicide of philosophy in postmodernist thought, the eclipse of sacred science in the modern world has led to numerous substitutes ranging from occultism to "new age" treatments of the traditional sciences to the trivialization of the various forms of traditional and sacred sciences by their assessment through the eyes of positivism. The consequence is the appearance of a whole array of misinterpretations and caricatures of the sacred sciences which have become practically part and parcel of the present-day cultural scene.

The most obvious of these substitutes are the occult sciences, which, contrary to what was predicted by the positivist sociologists and historians of days gone by, have hardly disappeared from the concerns of modern humanity. On the contrary, these "sciences" seem to grew by leaps and bounds to the extent that the mental landscape of modern man becomes ever more secularized as a result of the ever greater spread of the modern scientific outlook with its innate opposition to the very meaning of the sacred especially as a category related to knowledge. Many of these occult sciences contain residues of authentic traditional sciences, while many other are devoid of any traditional interest whatsoever. Even in cases where something survives of the symbolic significance of the traditional science, which constituted the foundation of the occult science in question, the real significance of this symbolic reality is, however, lost because of the lack of the metaphysical knowledge necessary to interpret the sciences in question and also because of the loss of vision of that sacred universe where the traditional sciences and their symbolism possessed and even now continue to possess meaning.

There is, moreover, a whole new wave of interest in residues of traditional sciences associated with the so-called "new age spirituality," which seeks to go beyond the confines of the positivistic sciences and enter into the world of the traditional and sacred sciences, which it treats, however, in a most cavalier and usually superficial fashion. In the hands of many of its followers, the *I-Ching* or Hindu astrology becomes simply an alternative form of knowledge not at all related to the sacred and the transcendent. The traditional sciences are simply brought in to fill the vacuum created by the demise of the sacred in the worldview of modern man, but they are treated in a manner which is not profoundly different from the so-called positive sciences eschewed by so many new-age "thinkers" and gurus.

Closely associated with this phenomenon is the psychologization of traditional teaching à la Jung by many who have been drawn to the study of such traditional sciences as alchemy and astrology through psychology. No doubt such traditional sciences possess a dimension related to the realm of the psyche, but they cannot be reduced to a form of psychology without the destruction of their cosmological and ultimately metaphysical significance. Yet today's world bears witness to a continuous proliferation of such treatments of the traditional and sacred sciences in order to fulfill a need which is deeply felt by many people, especially those who can no longer find an intellectual home for themselves in the mental landscape created by modern rationalism, empiricism and scientism.

Paradoxically enough, this desire to go beyond the confines of positivistic science is to be found among a number of practitioners of modern science itself, especially physicists, some of whom have indicated the necessity of turning to traditional cosmologies and philosophies of nature to create a wider framework into which the findings of contemporary physics could be integrated. There is a vast range of views on this matter ranging from those of people who are at once respectable metaphysicians and scientists to serious physicists who are seeking to bring about a synthesis of the latest discoveries of physics and caricatures of traditional cosmological doctrines of a usually Oriental origin. Rapidly a new intermediate zone is being created between physics and a kind of "cosmic mysticism" of rather dubious authenticity, a zone which nevertheless caters once again to the need of certain types of human beings for an authentic sacred science. In this context the so-called "new gnosis" (*la nouvelle gnose*), which has been spreading so much during the past two decades especially in France is most telling.

There is, of course, in addition to all these activities stated above, the still continuous attempt of many official historians of science, fed by the positivism of E. Mach and other fathers of this discipline since the early decades of this century to simply explain the traditional sciences of nature away as childish preludes to the glorious discoveries of the Scientific Revolution and its aftermath. But a cursory study of the contemporary intellectual and cultural landscape shows to what extent such a view fulfills or fails to fulfill the need of man today for a sacred science, despite the laudable scholarship by numerous historians of science which has made available the written sources along with analyses in various modern languages of so many of the traditional and sacred sciences.

Our aim here is not to provide a thorough criticism of these and other modes of treating the traditional and sacred sciences in the modern world. Such a criticism would require a separate study. In mentioning these ways of viewing such sciences, the spread of such ways of thinking, and their success or lack thereof, our goal is to point to the reality of the need for the sacred sciences in the present-day situation. Neither the positivistic treatment of such sciences nor their treatment in opposition to positivism but also outside of the context of sacred tradition, has proven to be fully satisfactory, any more than profane philosophy has succeeded in quenching the thirst of contemporary man for wisdom. The need for the cultivation and mastery of the sacred sciences continues and will continue until authentic sacred sciences are reestablished in the light of the metaphysical principles which of necessity govern them. In the chapters of this book we have sought to indicate something of the nature of the sacred sciences, how they concern the world of nature as well as the world of the Spirit and how they are inexorably wed to and derive from that Supreme Science which is concerned with the Source of all reality, with the Real as such. It is our hope that these pages will incite further interest in both the rediscovery of that Supreme Science and the cultivation of authentic forms of the sacred sciences which alone can satisfy in depth the need of human beings for that knowledge which is wed to the sacred, that mode of knowing which is inseparable from sanctity, and that form of sanctity which accompanies knowledge as noesis.

As the Sufi poet Rūmī has said, "Do not seek water but seek thirst." It is first necessary to understand and experience the need for a sacred science. Once the nature of the need is fully realized and the nonauthentic substitutes for such a science are seen to be what they really are, a veritable sacred science derived from the Supreme Science and yet concerned with the domain of manifestation, both microcosmic and macrocosmic, cannot but be reformulated and reconstituted. May the present book be a humble step towards the achievement of this end, whose attainment is necessary for the intellectual revival of tradition in its totality and for the intellectual and spiritual welfare of those whose inner vocation beckons them to seek knowledge of the Absolute as well as the relative in the light of the Absolute.

wa'Llāh^u a'lam

Index

abad, al-, 38, 39
Aborigines, Australian, 57, 99
Abraham, 58, 163
Absolute, 56, 62, 134, 158, 162, 171; as absolute, 7, 62; God as, 8; relatively, 61, 68*n17*
acupuncture, 108
Adam, 20, 30, 32, 91, 150
aeons, 28
Afghanistan, 93*n9*
agnosticism, 9, 86, 125, 161
agriculture, 90
aḥad, al-, 10
Aḥmad, 62
Aitareya Āraṇyaka, 71
'ālam al-ghayb wa'l-shahādah, 129
alchemy, 38, 95, 106, 107, 116*n41*, 170
alphabet, 100; numerical value of letters, 100; relation to arithmetic, 114*n21*; sacred, 113*n16*
amānah, al-, 132
ammārah, al-, 19
ana'l-Ḥaqq, 17
angels, 109
anima, 15
animism, 78
annihilation, 49
anthropos, 64
Aparagoyana, 109
Apocatastasis, 31
architecture, 35, 89, 90, 95, 103; Islamic, 89; as sacred art, 35, 103; traditional, 89, 110, 114*n24*
Aristotle, 27, 30, 104, 153
arithmetic, 102, 103; relation to language, 114*n21*
art, astrological, 104
art, sacred, 34, 55, 63, 103, 107, 123, 124; architecture as, 35; differs from religious art, 35; forms of, 35, 36; music as, 35; poetry as, 35; symbols of, 35
art, traditional, 35
astrology, 104–105, 105, 106, 170; Islamic, 115*n37*; signs of, 115*n35*
astronomy, 87, 98, 102, 103–104, 104, 106, 112*n10*
astrophysics, 87
atheism, 161
Ātman, 16, 27, 38, 56, 84, 123
'Aṭṭār, 21
Augustine, Saint, 148, 151, 159
autology, forms of, 19
avatāra, 34
āyāt, 129
āyāt-Allāh, 129
azal, al-, 38

Balthasar, Hugo von, 159
baqā', 19
barakah, 35, 84, 110
beauty, 36, 42*n22*; of nature, 121, 122; from sacred art, 38
Being, 152; angelic, 105; in cosmos, 27; Divine, 153; formless, 91; levels of, 29; universal, 91
Beyond-Being, 27, 68*n17*
bhakti, 38
bhakti marga, 58
bhūtas, 108
biology, 86–87
Böhme, Jacob, 101
Bonaventure, Saint, 8
Book of Creation, 100
Book of the Apocalypse, 166
Brahma, 27, 29, 47
"Breath of the Compassionate," 11
Bruno, Geordano, 152
Buddha, 21

177

Buddhism, 12, 14*nl2*, 18, 35, 63, 67*nll*, 73, 99, 120, 121, 123, 127, 138, 161, 166; nature of ego in, 18
Burckhardt, Titus, 54, 110

Chardin, Teilhard de, 87
Chartres cathedral, 35, 124
chemistry, 107
China, 3, 93*n9*, 95, 105, 108, 124, 127
Christianity, 18, 30, 31, 35, 40*n7*, 41*nl8*, 51*nl*, 54, 57, 58, 63, 64, 86, 99, 101, 109, 121, 124, 128, 131, 133, 135, 138, 147, 148, 150, 151, 155, 157, 158, 160, 162, 164, 165, 166; coming of Christ in, 30, 151; concept of time in, 30; contemplative schools in, 18; doctrine of incarnation in, 150; ethical heritage of, 86; metaphysics in, 8; relation to Judaism, 101; Resurrection in, 41*nl8*; secularization of incarnation, 31; view of immortality, 148; weakening of, 140
Christology, 150, 163
chronology, 105, 106
civilization: Asian, 35, 71; Chinese, 3; Christian, 3; Indian, 71; modern problems of, 45–51; Oriental, 71–92, 89; Western, 3, 50, 76, 82, 86, 87, 89, 127, 134
civitas dei, 151
Club of Rome, 94*nl8*
consciousness, 37, 55–56; center of, 16, 21; levels of, 15, 28, 72; and matter, 77; of self, 18; states of, 56
Coomaraswamy, Ananda K., 14*nl0*, 16, 25, 54, 63, 72, 95, 110
Copernican Revolution, 104
Corbin, Henry, 64
cosmic: becoming, 30; cycles, 27, 30, 33, 34, 106; domains, 99; dualism, 73; existence, 16, 26, 27, 29, 109; harmony, 105, 132; illusion, 8; intelligence, 105; manifestation, 34, 100, 104; mysticism, 170; order, 38,

46, 72, 113*nl6*; Quran, 101, 128; reality, 36, 104; rhythm, 30, 153; time, 37; universal, 16; veil, 16, 27, 32
Cosmic Periods (Shao-Yung), 106
cosmology, 55, 63, 87, 93*nl0*, 96, 105, 106, 117*n49*, 170; as art, 99; Hindu, 108; traditional, 19, 99
cosmos: being in, 27; creation of, 16; as external reality, 19; meaning of, 101; mechanization of, 153; numbers as key to understanding, 102; sacred, 166; secular view of, 72, 135; understanding of, 110
creation, perfection of, 97
Creator, 11
crises. *See also* environment: ecological, 78, 79, 83, 84, 85, 89; economic, 85; energy, 79, 89, 138; environmental, 127–143; ethical, 84–85; raw materials, 89
Crisis of the Modern World, The (Guénon), 74
culture: anthrocentrism in, 84; Asian, 74, 77, 79, 80, 83, 84, 86, 92; centerless, 134; dislocation in, 139; ethics in, 84; metaphysics in, 73; non-Western, 83, 87

dahr, 28
Dā'irat al-nubuwwah, 31
Daniélou, Jean, 159
Dante, 32, 35, 41*nl6*, 104
darma, 38
Darwin, Charles, 153
Da Vinci, Leonardo, 152
death, 17, 18, 28, 35; awareness of, 27; time leading to, 25
De Lubac, Henri, 159
Descartes, René, 15, 29, 92*n3*, 152
dharma, 120, 121
dhikr, 129
dhikr Allāh, 131
dīn, al-, al-ḥanīf, 128
dīn al-fiṭrah, 143*n2*

Divine: Agency, 148; Alpha, 32;
    Archetype, 45; Artisan, 123; Beauty,
    121; Being, 153; Creativity, 11, 14n10;
    Empyrean, 3, 28; Energy, 100;
    Environment, 129, 130, 132; Essence,
    10; Eternity, 40n9; Infinitude, 27, 28,
    40n9, 142; Infinity, 9, 10; Intellect,
    17, 56, 60, 61, 122; Law, 133, 136,
    139, 141, 142, 150; Logos, 16, 60;
    Majesty, 142; Manifestation, 58, 60;
    Message, 64; Nature, 9, 10, 11;
    Norm, 49, 50, 56–57, 57;
    Omnipresence, 40n9; Oneness, 13;
    Order, 8, 26, 84, 120; Origin, 4n3,
    10, 35, 56, 62, 65n4, 96, 97, 123;
    Peace, 64; Play, 14n10; Possibility,
    124; Power, 123; Presence, 11, 17, 56,
    103, 124, 129, 131; Principle, 1, 8, 10,
    26, 27, 28, 61, 96; Proximity, 26;
    Quality, 36, 121, 122, 129; Reality,
    27; Spark, 38; Spirit, 50;
    Stratosphere, 50, 65, 141; Union, 36;
    Unity, 12; Will, 105; Word, 101
Divine Comedy (Dante), 104
Divinity, 41n9, 48, 73, 122, 154;
    creative power of, 11; manifestation of,
    62; nontheistic view, 73; as Reality, 7
Dogen, 18, 20–21

Eckhart, Meister, 8, 12, 20, 161
eclecticism, 88
ecological crisis, 78, 79. See also
    Environment
ecumenism, 59, 64, 65
Edenic state, 77
ego, 21; in Buddhism, 18; conflict, 20;
    perception of, 15
Eliot, T. S., 74
empiricism, 2, 12, 13n2, 57, 95, 170; in
    modern science, 2
energy: conservation, 89; crisis, 79,
    894 138; life, 108; matter and, 29;
    natural sources, 89; relation to time,
    31; wasteful use of, 138

environment: crisis in, 34 127–143;
    destruction of, 73, 77, 78, 79, 84, 90,
    93n9, 139; disasters caused by
    modern science, 71; ethical treatment
    of, 141; interdependent, 142; Islamic
    view of, 127, 128, 130, 131, 132, 133,
    137; man's power over, 46; responsi-
    bility toward, 139; urban, 46, 74, 78
epistemology, empirical, 7
equilibrium: of nature, 127; recreating,
    82; reestablishing, 50; state of, 46,
    47
Erigena, John Scotus, 8, 12, 42n21
Eskimos, 57
esoterism, 100
Eternal: Now, 32, 33, 34, 38, 39,
    41n16; Order, 26, 33, 34, 35, 36, 37,
    39; Principle, 28; Realm, 32, 36
Eternity: awareness of, 25; distinct
    from time, 28; Divine, 40n9; levels
    in, 28; moving image of, 25–39; as
    Reality, 32, 33; relation to time, 25;
    spiritual significance of, 40n9; in
    Western thought, 31
Eudoxus, 104
evil, 14n5, 40n9, 49; creation of, 9;
    eradication of, 47
evolution, 31, 73, 93n11, 97, 98, 148,
    149, 152, 153, 154, 155; material, 3,
    147–155; pseudo-scientific theory, 73,
    93n11; theory of, 98, 154
existence: cosmic, 16, 26, 27, 29; levels
    of, 30, 56; phenomenal, 29; samsāric,
    107; trajectory of, 39; universal
    hierarchy of, 27

fanā', 19
Fārābī, al-, 151
Ficino, Marsiglio, 152
Flamel, Nicholas, 152
Fludd, Robert, 101
forms, 29; diversity of, 51, 53, 154;
    Divine Origin of, 123; external, 59,
    60; geometric, 102–103; natural,

114n24; in nature, 119, 124, 129; physical, 100; religious, 47, 48, 51, 53, 60, 92n4; revealed, 33; in sacred art, 35; symbolic, 68n24, 109–110; in time, 34; traditional, 92n4

forms, sacred, 3, 33, 45; multiplicity of, 3, 55; revealed, 3; truth as, 45

France, 35, 64, 149

Francis of Assisi, Saint, 131

Freudianism, 88

Galileo, 92n3, 152

Gandhi, Mahatma, 83, 90

Genesis, Book of, 100

geography, 109–110, 117n52

geomancy, 2, 117n52

geometry, 102, 103, 114n26; sacred, 114n25; symbolic aspect, 114n26

George, Saint, 48

ghaflah, 129

Ghazzālī, al-, 40n8

gnosis, 54, 66n7, 80, 95, 99, 170

God, 45, 65n3, 100, 120, 125, 131, 142, 143, 149, 158, 159, 163, 164; as All-Possibility, 9, 10; as Being, 14n5; as Beyond, 14n5; creative power of, 154; Face of, 13, 48; goodness of, 107; hierarchy of ways to, 59; as Infinite, 8, 9, 15; Islamic doctrine of, 10, 14n6; knowledge of, 7; laws for creation, 120; and light, 100; love of, 20; names of, 91, 133; nature of, 3, 8, 9; as perfection, 10; as Reality, 7–13; reduction to abstract, 11; rights of, 135; seeing, 111; signs of, 129; as ultimate environment, 129, 132; Western understanding of, 9

Gospels, 164, 165

grace, 62, 84, 106, 121, 132; in tradition, 66n4

guematria, 100

Guénon, René, 54, 64, 72, 74, 95

guṇas, 108

Ḥadīth, 16, 106, 130

Ḥāfiẓ, 25, 32

Ḥallāj, al-, Manṣūr, 17

ḥaqīqah, al-, 12

Ḥaqq, al-, 12

Harmonica mundi, 102

Hebrew, 100

hedonism, 33

Hegel, Georg Friedrich, 150, 154

Heisenberg, Werner, 78

Hermeticism, 152

Hierarchy: angelic, 147; reality of, 58; in religion, 58; universal, 56

ḥijāb, al-, 8, 16

ḥikmah, al-, 12

ḥikmat, al-, al-khālidah, 65

Hildegard of Bingen, 131

Himpi Temple, 35

Hinduism, 27, 29, 30, 37, 38, 40n9, 41n10, 58, 63, 65, 79, 98, 100, 102, 105, 109, 121, 138, 148, 150, 153, 161, 166; cosmic cycles in, 30; cosmology in, 108; doctrine of time in, 41n12; knowledge in, 81; margas, 38; yoga in, 18

Hiroshima, 83

historicism, 63

"Hollow Men, The" (Eliot), 74

humanism, 45, 51n1, 133, 134, 135, 142, 148, 149, 166; classical, 45; secular, 45

humanity: continued existence of, 46; denial of sacred forms, 45; fallen nature of, 33, 48; family of, 45, 49, 50; passions of, 48; present condition of, 45–51; progress through material evolution, 147–155

Huxley, Aldous, 53

Ibn Sīnā, 73, 109, 123

I-Ching, 170

iḥsān, 170

ikhlāṣ, al-, 10

Ikhwān al-Ṣafā', 95

Illich, Ivan, 89
illness: factors causing, 108; spiritual, 107
images, 54; in *philosophia perennis*, 55
īmān, 67*n12*
imkān, 40*n8*
India, 35, 58, 60, 93*n9*, 96, 103, 108, 109, 142
industrialization, 78, 85, 86, 88, 90, 136; crises caused by, 80
Industrial Revolution, 78
Infinite, 56
insān, al-, al-kāmil, 16, 90, 99
intellection, 7, 40*n3*; denial of, 13*n2*; inner, 10; knowledge from, 12; and reality, 13*n1*
irrationalism, 12
Islam, 12, 30, 36, 37, 40*n7*, 41*n18*, 48, 50, 51*n1*, 57, 58, 63, 64, 67*n12*, 71, 73, 79, 80, 95, 101, 120, 123, 127, 128, 131, 132, 133, 134, 136, 137, 138, 139, 141, 148, 161, 166; astrology in, 115*n37*; astronomy in, 104; contemplative schools in, 18; doctrine of God in, 10; mathematics in, 102; medicine in, 108; metaphysical doctrine, 12, 90; nature of God in, 12; Prophet of, 33, 62, 106, 148; traditional, 3
"isms," 64, 80

jafr, al-, 101
Jāmbudvīpa, 109
Jāmi' Mosque, 35
jāwīdān-khirad, 65
Jerusalem, 109; Celestial, 149, 151
jñāna, 38
jñāna marga, 58
Judaism, 18, 40*n8*, 51*n1*, 64, 100, 101, 109, 121, 123, 128, 133, 135, 147, 148, 150, 151, 161; contemplative schools in, 18; esoterism in, 100; Hassidic tradition, 100; relation to Christianity, 101; sacred alphabet of, 100
Jungianism, 88

Kabbala, 12, 100, 101, 152
Kali Avatāra, 148
Kalidasa, 35
Kali Yuga, 41*n12*
kalpas, 106
Kanlāvalīyam, 100
karma, 37
karma marga, 58
kashf al-mahjūb, 159
Kepler, Johannes, 102, 152
khālid, 39*n2*
khalīfah, al-, 103, 132
khalīfat Allāh, 132, 133
Khayyām, 33
Khun-Lun, 109
Kircher, Athanasius, 101
knowledge: compartmentalization of, 80, 82; ever-changing, 95; of God, 7; harmony in, 82; higher order, 2; incomplete, 82; inward, 101; levels of, 92; of manifestation, 96; metaphysical, 7, 9, 53; positivism in, 4; possibility of, 12; primacy of, 59; principial, 2, 12, 81; relation to the sacred, 1; relation to the whole, 81; in religion, 54; sapiential, 33; scientism in, 4; of truth, 80; unity of, 73; universal, 54
Krishna, 58, 109
Krita Yuga, 41*n12*
Kṛṣṇa, see Krishna
Küng, Hans, 157–166

Lā ilāha illa'Llāh, 133
language; abstract, 98; Arabic, 101; doctrinal, 60; human use of, 13*n3*; of immanence, 22*n1*; nontheistic, 120; of Quran, 48; relation to arithmetic, 114*n21*; sacred, 100, 101, 122; symbolic, 98; of traditional science, 98
laṭā'if, 16
life, eternal, 26
Lings, Martin, 54

Li T'ai Po, 35
logic, 63
Logos, 100, 101, 150
"Love Song of J. Alfred Prufrock"
    (Eliot), 74

ma'ād, al-, 130
mabda', al-, 130
Mach, Ernst, 170
māddah, 153
madīnat, al-, al-fāḍilah, 151
magisterium, 163
maḥabbah, al-, 38, 58
mahāpralaya, 31
Maharshi, Śri Ramana, 21, 22n15
Mahāyāna, 18
Mahdī, 148
makhāfah, al-, 38, 58
malakūt, 9
man. See also Humanity: European,
    154; extraterrestrial origin, 112n9;
    false conceptions of, 49; forgetfulness
    in, 48; glorification of, 134; nature
    of, 49; Neolithic, 102; Primordial,
    99; Promethean, 45, 119, 125, 134;
    relationship to nature, 79, 94n18;
    secularized conception of, 149; self-
    centeredness in, 46; spiritual
    dimension, 48; spiritual traditions of,
    45; supremacy of, 45; as theomorphic
    being, 51n1; Titanic, 134; traditional
    conception of, 46; Universal, 90, 91,
    97, 99; universal, 90, 91, 97;
    Western, 45
Man and Nature (Nasr), 78
maṇḍala, 99, 103
manifestation, 16; cosmic, 34, 100, 104;
    cycles of, 30; Divine, 58, 60; of
    Divine Infinitude, 27; of Divine
    Power, 123; of Divine Principle, 1,
    96; of Divinity, 62; external, 60;
    grades of, 60; hierarchy in, 28;
    knowledge of, 96; relatively absolute,
    62; repetition in, 30

mantra, 100
Manu, 100
Manvantāras, 106
margas, 38
ma'rifah, al-, 38, 58
Marxism, 80, 150, 152, 154
materialism, 82, 147–155
mathematics, 9, 98, 101–102, 102, 120
matter, 26; atomic theory of, 108; in
    constitution of world, 29; domination
    of, 77; relation to time, 31
māyā, 8, 11, 14n10, 16, 32, 38, 56, 96,
    123, 150
Mecca, 109
medicine, 2, 87, 106, 107, 108, 109;
    acupuncture in, 108; divine origin of,
    107; Oriental, 89; psychosomatic,
    109; theory of four elements and
    humors; traditional, 2, 89, 107,
    117n46
Medina, 148
Mencius, 73
Meru, Mount, 109
Messiah, 149
metallurgy, 110
metaphysics, 3, 11, 15, 45, 54, 58, 63,
    85–86, 86, 95, 99, 155, 169; arithmetic
    in, 102; Christian, 12; in Christianity,
    8, 12; of comparative religion, 58;
    and cosmological science, 81; as
    divine science, 54; Eternity in, 26;
    Hindu, 22n1; Islamic, 12, 22n1;
    knowledge of, 7; Oriental, 8;
    philosophia perennis in, 54; reality
    in, 58; as supreme science, 1; time
    in, 26; traditional, 14n12, 18, 21n1,
    54; Western, 9
miracles, 34
mīthāq, al-, 132
modernism, 3; theological, 3, 157–166
monotheism, 72
More, Sir Thomas, 151
motion, 30
Muḥammad, 20, 162

Muḥīṭ, 129
muḥsin, 67*n12*
mu'min, 67*n12*
music, 68*n18*, 102, 109; harmony in, 114*n24*; as sacred art, 35
mysticism, 55, 62, 122, 170

nafas al-raḥmān, 11, 18
nafs, al-, 15, 18
nafs al-ammārah, 18, 19
nafs al-lawwāmah, 19
nafs al-muṭma'innah, 19
nafs al-rāḍiyah, 19
Nāgārjuna, 73
natura, 36
naturalism, 131, 135
nature: alienation from, 140; beauty of, 121, 122; change in, 36; destruction of, 37, 46; Divine, 10, 11; forms in, 124, 129; harmony in, 120; indifference to, 77; inner, 88; laws of, 120; limitations of resources in, 79; of man, 49; manipulation of, 77; man's domination over, 127; man's relationship to, 79, 94*n18*; moral lessons in, 121; philosophy of, 88; of reality, 57, 60; rhythms of, 119, 124, 125; as sacred art, 124; sacred quality of, 129; sacred study of, 3; secularization of, 134; spiritual significance of, 119–125, 135, 142; symbols in, 123; virgin, 36, 38, 93*n15*, 119, 120, 121, 123, 124, 142; worship, 78
Neo-Thomism, 53
Neo-Vedantism, 54–55, 65
Newton, Sir Isaac, 92*n3*, 152
Nichomachus, 114*n23*
nihilism, 11, 76
nirvāṇa, 19, 56, 123
nominalism, 7
Northbourne, Lord, 54
notarikon, 100
numbers, 29, 30, 102, 105

Olearius, John, 101
ontology, 14*n12*
Origen, 159
ousia, 16

Pallis, Marco, 54, 66*n4*
Pañca-tantra, 121
Paracelsus, 109
paradigma, 35
Paradiso (Dante), 32, 41*n16*
paramanu, 108
perfection, 10, 26, 49; of creation, 97; of human soul, 148, 149; models of, 49
Perry, Whitall, 54
Persian Gulf War, 94*n17*
pharmacology, 95, 109
phenomenology, 55
Philopponos, John, 40*n8*
Philosopher's Stone, 106, 107
philosophia perennis, 53–65; branches, 54; meaning of, 53–54; nature of, 64; traditional approach to, 54; truth in, 61
philosophia priscorium, 65
philosophy, 29, 80, 164; Christian, 9; modern, 11; natural, 152, 170; of nature, 88; perennial. *See philosophia perennis*; traditional, 78; Western, 60, 131, 148
physics, 9, 30, 86, 87, 93*n10*, 95, 153, 170
Pico della Mirandola, 101, 152
Planck, Max, 78
Plato, 25, 28, 35, 36, 151
poetry, 35, 137
Polynesians, 99
polytheism, 73
pontifex, 103, 131
positivism, 4, 80, 169, 171
post-Eternity, 38, 39
prakṛti, 153
prayer, 38
pre-Eternity, 38, 39
Primordial Scripture, 128

Primordial Tradition, 57
Primordial Word, 120
Proclus, 114n23
prophecy: cycles of, 30–31, 151; levels
    of, 60
Psalms, 29
pseudo-religion, 61, 66n8, 93n11, 147,
    149, 152, 161
psychoanalysis, 87
psychology, 87, 106, 170; and alchemy,
    116n41
Ptolemaic model, 98
Ptolemy, 104
Purāṇas, 106
Puruṣa, 16, 90, 91, 99

qiyāmat, al-, al-kubrā, 31
Quran, 1, 9, 18, 19, 29, 41n10, 47, 59,
    62, 67n12, 79, 81, 100, 129, 131, 142,
    166; composed, 101, 128; cosmic,
    101, 128; language of, 48; revelation
    in, 12; Spirit in, 47; view of
    environment, 128, 130
Qurān, al-, al-tadwīnī, 128
Qurān, al-, al-takwīnī, 101, 128

raḥmah, al-, 10
Rahner, Karl, 159
Rama, 58
ratio, 65n3
rationalism, 2, 12, 13n2, 51n1, 57, 72,
    129, 134, 135, 166, 170
Rāzī. See Rhazes
Reality: Absolute, 18; angelic, 28;
    cosmic, 36, 104; Divine, 27; Eternity
    as, 32, 33; external, 19, 101; God as,
    7-13; hierarchic nature of, 58, 73;
    Immanent, 15; Infinite, 15; and
    intellection, 13n1; knowledge of,
    80-81; levels of, 11, 15, 28, 72, 92,
    97, 98, 104; metacosmic, 46;
    metaphysics in, 58; of natural
    phenomena, 129; nature of, 18, 57,
    60; primordial, 97; reduction to

abstract, 7; relative, 12; of religion,
    55; spiritual, 110; symbolic
    expressions of, 98; of traditional
    universe, 25; Transcendent, 15;
    Ultimate, 7, 8, 9, 47, 54, 56, 58,
    85–86
reason: distinct from intellect, 65n3;
    principle of, 40n3
relativism, 12; pitfalls of, 3
relativity, 7; in Divine Order, 8;
    meaning of, 11; theory of, 41n16; as
    veil, 8
religion, 54, 55, 56, 57, 58, 59, 61, 64,
    66n7, 149, 157; comparative, 3, 53,
    55, 58, 64; decay of, 62; diversity of,
    59, 60, 92n4; esoteric dimension, 58;
    goals of, 18; hierarchical constitution,
    58; holy family in, 50; knowledge in,
    54; plurality of, 54, 55; reality of,
    55; revival of, 62; role of, 49; social
    aspects of, 56; study of, 53-65;
    temporal existence, 56; transcendent
    origin of, 59; unity of, 60; unity of
    Spirit in, 47
Religionwissenschaft, 55
religio perennis, 60
Renaissance, 45, 49, 51n1, 72, 78, 119,
    134, 148, 149, 152
Republic (Plato), 151
Reuchlin, Johann, 101
revelation, 7, 13, 55, 162; denial of,
    13n2; direct, 57; Divine, 161;
    Eternity in, 26; external, 14n7; grace
    from, 121; inner, 10, 14n7; Islamic,
    139; knowledge from, 12; necessity
    for, 33; Quranic, 12, 101, 128;
    sanctification of symbols by, 123; in
    tradition, 66n4; universal, 17
Revelations of John, 151
Ṛg-Veda, 90
Rhazes (Muḥammad ibn Zakariyyā' al-
    Rāzī), 109
rights: absolute, 20; of God, 135;
    limitations on, 94n18; of nonhumans,

84, 135, 142; of others, 135; precedence of responsibility over, 79, 133

rites, 54; in *philosophia perennis*, 55; religious, 60; sacred, 34

Rockefeller Series Lectures (University of Chicago), 78

Roszak, Theodore, 89

rūḥ, al-, 15, 16

Rūmī, Jalāl al-Dīn, 17, 19, 35, 49, 62, 171

sa'ādah, 80

sacred science. *See* science, sacred

Sa'dī 130

Salafis, 136

ṣamad, al-, 10

samādhi, 36

samsāra, 19, 56, 123

sanātana dharma, 65

Sanclilliensis, Hugo, 117*n52*

Sanskrit, 100, 121, 153

sarmad, 39*n2*

Schrödinger, Erwin, 78

Schuon, Frithjof, 40*n9*, 54, 58, 60, 61, 63, 65, 66*n7*, 68*n24*, 72, 82, 95, 97, 161

science, modern, 3, 9, 71–92, 170; as cause of environmental disaster, 71; criticism of, 136–137, 144*n11*; empiricism in, 2; ethical implications of, 82; evolution in, 3; history of cosmos in, 31; inability to solve problems, 74; loss of confidence in, 76-77; new directions for, 88; rationalism in, 2; relation to Oriental culture, 71-92; time in, 26; totalitarian claims of, 4

science, sacred, 54, 95. *See also* science, traditional; and environmental crisis, 127–143; forgetfullness of, 153; of forms, 50, 51; loss of, 80, 85, 147, 157; meaning of, 1; need for, 88, 169-171; present need for, 2; reformulation of, 53

science, traditional, 2, 95–111, 169, 170; forgetfulness of, 79; goals of, 98; meaning of, 95; metaphysical principles in, 110; spirituality in, 98

science, Western. *See* science, modern

scientia sacra, 164, 169. *See* science, sacred

Scientific Revolution, 72, 81, 152, 153, 171

scientism, 4, 170

Second Vatican Council, 158

Secret Rose Garden (Gulshan-i rāz), 91

secularism, 45, 51*n1*, 74, 82, 98, 125, 140, 149, 151, 153, 160, 166; pitfalls of, 3

Sefer Yeṣira, 100

sefirot, 100

self: awareness, 15–21; centeredness, 46; confrontation with, 84; perfection of, 17, 49; restraint, 48; Supreme, 56; Ultimate, 15-21, 18. *See also* Ultimate Selfhood

septa-dhātu, 108

Seven Sleepers of the Cave, 41*n10*

Shamanism, 123

Shao-Yung, 106

Sharī'ah, al-, 133, 139, 141

Shaya, Leo, 54

Shintoism, 138

Shīrāzī, Quṭb al-Dīn, 96

Simnānī, 'Alā' al-Dawlah, 16

ṣinā'ah, 105, 106

Śiva, 26, 102, 120

skepticism, 11, 12, 66*n7*, 125

Smith, Huston, 54, 66*n8*

Smith, Wilfred Cantwell, 64

social: aspects of religion, 56; disintegration, 47; ethics, 55; structure, 63

sophia, 61

sophia perennis, 12, 53

soul, stages of, 22*n10*

space, 29

Spirit, 16, 19, 45, 47, 48, 50, 88, 123, 124, 125, 130, 131, 141, 142, 143, 155;

Divine, 50; human contact with, 47, 48; multiple reflection of, 65; nature of, 3; unity of, 47, 48

spiritism, 78

spirituality, 88; Oriental, 75

Spiritus, 15

Stonehenge, 102, 114*n*25

subjectivity, 61; hierarchic structure of, 26

Sufism, 8, 11, 16, 17, 19, 33, 49, 60, 63, 66*n*7, 130, 136-137, 162, 171

sunnah, 130

sūnyatā, 47, 60

Supra-Being, 68*n17*

Supreme: Artisan, 36, 143; Essence, 60; Good, 38; Principle, 31, 56; Reality, 33, 56; Science, 169, 171; Selfhood, 62, 162; Substance, 60

symbolism, 2, 104; of animals, 105; geometric, 103; language of, 98; mathematical, 114*n23*; of numbers, 102; of sacred alphabet, 100

symbols, 3, 54; Divine Origin of, 124; in nature, 123; in *philosophia perennis*, 55; religious, 47, 48, 60; revealed, 3, 110; in sacred art, 35; in science, 97; wordless, 103

Taoism, 57, 67*nll*, 95, 120, 127

Tao-Te-Ching, 74

tawḥīd, al-, 10

ta'wīl, 159

technology, 73; alternative forms, 77, 89, 93*n9*; changes in, 90; chemical, 110; ethical implications of, 82, 84; indiscriminate use of, 79; inhuman character of, 83; loss of confidence in, 77; nonmodern forms, 93*n9*; soft, 77, 90; traditional, 110; Western, 77, 83, 128, 137, 139

Teilhardism, 155

temurah, 100

t'hanka, 35

theodicy, 9

theology, 3, 55, 64, 73, 135, 140, 151, 158, 160, 161, 163, 164; Christian, 9, 40*n7*, 63, 140, 150, 154, 155, 157, 164; Islamic, 40*n7*, 166; neo-Scholastic, 158; post-Conciliar, 159; Protestant, 149; scientific, 161; Western, 131

Thomas Aquinas, Saint, 8, 157

Thomism, 158

time, 25-39, 150; abstract, 29, 30; as angel, 150; awareness of limitation of, 27; chronology in, 105; concrete, 29, 30; contraction of, 31; cosmic, 37; distinct from Eternity, 28; divisions of, 105; expansion of, 31; experience of, 25, 27, 31, 41*n10*; levels of, 41*n10*; linear, 31; meaning of, 26; as measure of motion, 30, 97; in metaphysics, 26; as moving image of Eternity, 25-39; objective, 29, 30, 31; origin of, 37; quantitative, 29, 31; reference points, 150-151; relation of man to, 26; relation to eternity, 25; relation to matter and energy, 31; sacred, 34; subjective, 29, 32; tenses of, 32; termination of, 27, 32, 37; transcendence of, 38

totemism, 78

Toute-possibilité, 13*n4*

"Toward a New Consensus in Catholic (and Ecumenical) Theology" (Küng), 157

tradition, 64*n4*; Chinese, 124; Christian, 147; doctrine of, 58; Eastern, 15; Hassidic, 100; historical unfolding of, 55; Islamic, 3, 28, 103, 135, 137, 141; Judaic, 147; Judeo-Christian, 135; meaning of, 66*n4*; mythological, 98; Oriental, 72, 84, 88; Primordial, 57; Pythagorean, 102, 120; spiritual, 45; Western, 15

transcendence, 21*n1*, 27; and contact with Spirit, 47

Tri-dosha, 108

truth, 90; abstract language in, 98; embodied in *philosophia perennis*, 61; and expediency, 158; incarnation of, 150; indifference to, 61; knowledge of, 80; moment of, 32; objective concern for, 63; realization of, 33, 38; religious, 61; as sacred form, 45

Ṭūsī, Naṣīr al-Dīn, 96

'ubūdiyyah, al-, 132
Ultimate: Principle, 73; Reality, 47, 54, 56, 58, 85–86; Selfhood, 15, 16, 17, 18, 19, 21
'ulūm, al-, al-khafiyyah, 111n13
unity: in diversity of religions, 59; of knowledge, 73; multiplicity in, 103, 123; of Spirit, 47, 48; transcendental, 60; veiled, 51
universe: harmony in, 109; hierarchic structure of, 97, 99; inner aspect of, 100; as manifestation of Divine Principle, 96; realities of, 25; religious, 3; sacred quality of, 97; scientific view of, 77; spiritual aspect of, 100; substance of, 11; traditional, 25
Upanishads, 74, 91
urbanism, 89
urbanization, 139
Ushman, 108
utopianism, 151, 152
Uttarakuru, 109

Vedāṅga, 96
Vedanta, 12
veil, 7, 110; cosmic, 16, 27, 32; doctrine of, 8, 11; relativity as, 8; temporal existence, 35

vestigia Dei, 78, 96, 129
Virgin Mary, 32

Wahhābīs, 136
wajh Allāh, 48
war, 46, 93n15; ethical implications of, 82–83, limited, 94n17
Western: anthropocentric culture, 84; civilization, 3, 50, 76, 82, 86, 87, 89, 127, 134; denial of metaphysical teaching, 75; domination, 75, 79, 80, 127, 134, 138, 139; rationalistic thought, 15; technology, 77, 128, 139; thought, 2, 31; tradition, 15; understanding of God, 9
World Soul, 97
worldview: empirically determined, 7; sacred, 2; scientist, 82, 120; total, 88; traditional, 3
World War I, 82–83

Yahweh, 60
yājña, 16
Yāmala Tantra, 100
yantra, 100
Yin and Yang, 108, 117n49
Yoga, 18, 73
Yogācāra school, 18
yugas, 106
Yunus Emre, 130

Zachner, R. C., 66n7
zamān, 28
Zen, 18, 21, 138
Zoroastrianism, 99, 148, 150
zurvān, 28
zurvanism, 150